"Most Christian books on marriage too [ ] saturated with the Word of God. If you [ ] sition of Scripture, this is for you. Scot[ ] using biblical language. *Your Marriage God's Way* will fill your mind with the pure and perfect Word of God. This is what every marriage needs."

Scott T. Brown, pastor, Hope Baptist Church, Wake Forest, NC

"This book is a timely reminder that God is the author of marriage. As a pastor who counsels real couples with real struggles, Scott knows how to deliver practical advice rooted in biblical truth. Get ready for a new appreciation for your marriage and the rewarding gift of love between a husband and wife."

Jay Payleitner, national speaker and bestselling author of *52 Ways to Connect as a Couple*

"*Your Marriage, God's Way* not only tells but shows how to have a strong marriage. Starting with the biblical truth that a fulfilling marriage is possible when each spouse's chief goal is to please the Lord, Scott gently and skillfully guides husbands and wives to life-changing insights that will strengthen relationships young and seasoned."

Steve and Annie Chapman, musical ambassadors to the family, authors

"Scott LaPierre provides an excellent balanced, biblical view of marriage in this practical guide. The need is great. The timeliness of this treatment is critical. It is a word in season to a world of marital disintegration, confusion, and misunderstandings."

Kevin Swanson, pastor, author, host of Generations Radio

"This book is filled with stories, examples, and most importantly, sound biblical guidance for living out a marriage that pleases God. Scott tackles difficult topics head-on with grace and understanding. You'll find guidelines you can apply immediately to reap the benefits of doing marriage God's way."

Melanie Chitwood, author of *What a Husband Needs from His Wife* and *What a Wife Needs from Her Husband*

"Scott LaPierre is like a lifeguard—for marriages. He offers countless insights that serve as life rings of help, teaching couples how to swim together like never before. The book goes deep—but you'll never feel like you're drowning!"

Tim Shoemaker, speaker, author of *The Very Best, Hands-On, Kinda Dangerous Family Devotions*

"When an author combines studiousness, practicality, and inspiration in his written work, you know you hold a good book in your hands. When graciousness, winsomeness, and refreshing humor are added, it goes from good to great. And when the final product is also Christ-centered, gospel-centric, and biblically based, good transforms into excellent. This masterpiece is a must for every couple that seeks to build their marriage God's way."

Emeal ("E.Z.") Zwayne, president, Living Waters

"Your Marriage God's Way is your guide toward the marriage of your dreams. Scott's practically beneficial and doctrinally sound insights will help you build a no-regrets marriage that others will want to emulate."

Rhonda Stoppe, founder of No Regrets Woman,
speaker, author of *The Marriage Mentor*

"*Your Marriage God's Way* clearly and powerfully unpacks God's Word on the most important human relationship most of us will ever have. Scott's willingness to be transparent and to take on unpopular topics like headship and submission are sorely needed in the church today. Help your marriage become all that God intends it to be!"

Bryan Stoudt, pastor, creator of the *How to Prepare for Marriage* course

"In a world where marriage is often considered a hopeless attempt at fleeting happiness, this book will give a Christian couple biblical perspective, good counsel, and hope for their future together. If you are looking for help to restore your struggling marriage, or you just need a good reminder of why godly marriages work, this book provides sound guidance."

David Eddy, senior pastor,
Manchester Community Church, Manchester, WA

"No marriage is perfect, but every marriage can get better as the years go by. This is a great tool for husbands and wives who want a successful and Christ-centered marriage."

Nick Harrison, author of *Magnificent Prayer* and *One-Minute Prayers for Dads*

"*Your Marriage God's Way* not only encourages those whose marriages have grown stale and lifeless, but also provides excellent advice for making marriages that are already healthy and prospering even better."

Wayne Mack, author, founder and professor
of Biblical Counseling of Strengthening
Ministries Training Institute, Pretoria, South Africa

Your Marriage
GOD'S WAY

Scott LaPierre

HARVEST HOUSE PUBLISHERS
EUGENE, OREGON

Cover design by Kyler Dougherty

Cover photo © courtneyk / Gettyimages

Interior design by KUHN Design Group

Italics in quoted Scriptures indicate emphasis added by the author.

For bulk, special sales, or ministry purchases, please call 1-800-547-8979. Email: Customerservice@hhpbooks.com

Your Marriage God's Way
Copyright © 2021 by Scott LaPierre
Published by Harvest House Publishers
Eugene, Oregon 97408
www.harvesthousepublishers.com

ISBN 978-0-7369-8396-9 (pbk.)
ISBN 978-0-7369-8397-6 (eBook)

Library of Congress Control Number: 2021935210

Printed in the United States of America

21 22 23 24 25 26 27 28 29 / BP / 10 9 8 7 6 5 4 3 2 1

Your Marriage God's Way is dedicated to my bride, Katie.

I could not ask for a more wonderful woman to have by my side through this life. Thank you for all the ways you help me, including being a wife who makes it easier to obey God's commands for husbands. You have all my heart, and I am more in love with you now than I was on our wedding day.

Contents

PART SIX: A WIFE'S BEAUTY AND A HUSBAND'S TREATMENT (1 PETER 3:1-7)

PART SEVEN: A BIBLICAL VIEW OF INTIMACY (1 CORINTHIANS 7:1-6)

PART EIGHT: A STRONG FOUNDATION (MATTHEW 7:24-27)

One of the Greatest Gifts
God Has Given Us

Recently something discouraging and painful happened while I was at work. We live only a few hundred feet from my office. When this incident took place, I stood up from behind my desk and decided to walk home. I was hurt, discouraged, and the situation weighed heavily on me. I knew it would take some time before I would be able to resume working as I tried to process what occurred.

I reached our home and Katie welcomed me with a smile, a hug, and a kiss. Immediately I felt better. Some of the burden was lifted. Katie had no idea what had happened, so it wasn't any counsel she gave that improved the situation. Instead, simply being with the bride God gave me made me feel better. In chapter 5 of this book you'll read about wives changing "not good" to "very good" (Genesis 1:31 cf. 2:18), and this was an example in my life.

Unfortunately, Katie and I were not able to be together that night, but knowing what happened earlier in the day, she sent me a text saying, "Praying for you to rest well tonight, and trust that none of this is a surprise to our Lord. I believe He is able to do great things through all of this. You will always have me by your side cheering you on. Love you. Rest well in trusting Him."

This is the wonderful wife God has given me! I was blessed by Katie throughout that painful situation, and this is the kind of blessing God, in His perfect wisdom and love, intends for believers to experience through marriage. Aside from salvation and the Scriptures, the greatest gift God has given us as a husband or wife is our spouse. What is required on our part? For marriage to be all that God intends, we must follow the instructions He's given us, and they are found in His Word.

Katie is not a perfect wife, and I am far from a perfect husband. We could fill the following chapters with mistakes we have made and things we would do differently. I will share some examples! But in this situation Katie followed God's design for marriage, which led her to encourage me as she did. Throughout the book I will repeatedly reference God's design for marriage because following it pleases Him and leads to the greatest blessing for us.

WHY YOUR MARRIAGE GOD'S WAY?

There are thousands of books on enriching your marriage, so why another one? What makes this one different? Is there any reason you should trust me to write it?

First, and of greatest importance, I am not asking you to trust me. Rather, I am inviting you to trust what God says in the Bible. This book is not a collection of my thoughts about marriage. At the church I serve, I set aside a significant amount of time to preach extensively on marriage. Hundreds of hours of studying the Bible were invested in the sermons. I used that material to write this book because God is the author of marriage. He designed the roles and responsibilities for husbands and wives. He knows what couples need so they can experience healthy, joyful, Christ-centered relationships, and He provided the principles in His Word. My desire is to present that guide clearly and biblically in *Your Marriage God's Way*.

Second, I wrote this book because I am passionate about this area of Scripture and life. God designed the family as the primary unit for every aspect of society, including the church. And marriage is the heart of the family. As a marriage disintegrates, the family disintegrates. As families disintegrate, churches disintegrate. As churches disintegrate, society disintegrates.

When marriages are strong, families are strong. When families are strong, churches can be strong because strong churches are made up of strong families.

Third, the marriage relationship is one of the greatest tools believers have for sharing about Christ with others because it is a picture of Jesus and His relationship to the church. Godly marriages can reveal Christ to an unbelieving world. That alone is a key reason I am passionate about seeing marriages strengthened.

Finally, I wrote *Your Marriage God's Way* because of what I have learned as a husband and pastor. As a husband, I have experienced firsthand the blessings that come from obeying God's Word and the negative consequences that come with disobedience. My wife Katie and I grew up together in the same small town (McArthur, California) and went to school together. We both became

Christians in our twenties, and soon after were married. At times the stresses of being a husband, father, and senior pastor (a role that alone could keep me busy from the moment I get up to the moment I go to bed) have put a huge amount of pressure on our marriage. In the following chapters, I will share some of our personal struggles and what we have learned from them.

BUILDING ON GOD'S WORD

As a pastor, I've spent numerous hours performing marriage counseling. The time with husbands and wives has given me familiarity with the most common marriage problems. I have seen people struggle and then find the solutions in God's Word, because it has the power to heal and strengthen any relationship. When I ask you to trust God's Word, I do so because I have seen it work in my relationship with Katie as well as the lives of many couples I've counseled.

This book is designed to encourage practical application and bring real change (because that's what applying scriptural truth does—it brings about change). For this to happen, we must keep God's Word in our heart, as it repeatedly reminds us: "These words which I command you today *shall be in your heart*...lay up His words *in your heart*...the law of his God is *in his heart*...Your law is *within my heart*...Your word I have hidden *in my heart*" (Deuteronomy 6:6; Job 22:22; Psalm 37:31; 40:8; 119:11). While this book is not the Word of God, it is a biblical guide filled with verses. I have written an accompanying workbook that is also available, the *Your Marriage God's Way Workbook*, to help you keep God's Word in your heart and apply the teachings within it.

Scripture allows us to enjoy marriage as God intended it to be—a vibrant, thrilling, fulfilling relationship. Let's journey together, with the Bible as our guide, to experience the blessings of a Christ-centered relationship.

PART ONE

RECOGNIZE THAT...

CHAPTER ONE

Your Marriage Reflects Your Relationship with Christ

A few years ago, Katie and I faced the biggest crisis of our marriage. I started pastoring Woodland Christian Church when it was small, but within three years the congregation tripled in size. I admit that before I became a pastor, I was unaware of how much work is involved in shepherding a church of even a few hundred people. I had been an Army officer, a supervisor at a distribution center for a major retail chain, and an elementary school teacher. But none of those occupations approached the amount of mental and emotional energy and sheer hard work pastoring entails!

Almost all my waking hours were packed with studying, teaching, counseling, making phone calls, sending emails, attending meetings, addressing administrative responsibilities, and tending to benevolence issues. When I was at home, where I should have been an engaged father and husband, I did not have much left for my family mentally, emotionally, or physically.

Although I was failing as a husband and father, I was able to convince myself I was still pleasing the Lord. I compartmentalized my life by saying, "I am a Christian first. I am a spouse second. I am a parent third. I am an employee fourth." Instead, I should have said, "I am a Christian spouse. I am a Christian parent. I am a Christian employee." The danger of seeing ourselves as Christian servants first and spouses second is we can find ourselves believing the lie I bought into at the time: "If I can be a good pastor, I can please God even though I am not the best husband."

The truth is that I was a poor husband, and I should have recognized that meant I was *not* pleasing the Lord.

JESUS DESERVES OUR OBEDIENCE

The reason we cannot please the Lord while failing as a husband or wife is that our Christianity is directly related to the way we treat our spouses. Our marriages are outpourings of our relationships with Christ:

- In Matthew 7:16, Jesus asked, "Do men gather grapes from thornbushes or figs from thistles?"

- In James 3:11-12, the apostle James asked, "Does a spring send forth fresh water and bitter from the same opening? Can a fig tree, my brethren, bear olives, or a grapevine bear figs?"

The point of these verses is that we reveal our Christianity by the way we live. As Jesus clarified: "You will know them by their fruits" (Matthew 7:16). And right living—or right fruit—can only be produced through a strong relationship with Christ.

*Our marriages are outpourings
of our relationships with Christ.*

Because our relationships with our spouses are our most important earthly relationship, what we are as spouses reflects what we are as Christians. Later, we will discuss this in greater depth as we look at the marriage passage in Ephesians 5:21-33, but for now, let's look at the two key commands in Scripture that give us God's own standard for marriage:

- Ephesians 5:25—"Husbands, love your wives, just as Christ also loved the church and gave Himself for her."

- Ephesians 5:22—"Wives, submit to your own husbands, as to the Lord."[1]

Because these commands are from the Lord, our obedience to them affects the kind of relationship we have with Christ. Think of it this way: There is no such thing as a spiritually mature man who does not love his wife. Nor a spiritually mature woman who does not submit to her husband:

- A husband cannot love Christ without loving his wife.

- A wife cannot submit to Christ without submitting to her husband.

A husband loves and cherishes his wife not because she is perfect or because she treats him the way he wants to be treated. He loves and cherishes his wife because he loves Christ. Likewise, a wife submits to her husband not because he is a wonderful spiritual leader or because he loves her the way she wants to be loved. She submits to her husband because she wants to submit to Christ.

A husband's love and a wife's submission are not tests of their obedience to their spouses. They are tests of their obedience to the Lord. This might sound discouraging, but it should be encouraging. When a husband knows his love and a wife knows her submission are acts of obedience to Christ, showing that love and submission can be that much easier.

Yes, there will be times when a husband does not want to love his wife and a wife does not want to submit to her husband. In those moments, husbands and wives can tell themselves, "I am called to do this out of my love for Christ. I want to submit to His commands because of what He has done for me."

I would never try to convince a husband that his wife is worthy of his love, or try to convince a wife that her husband is worthy of her submission. The fact is, no spouse is worthy. But *Christ* is worthy of a husband's love and a wife's submission. He deserves our obedience. It is important to understand this principle before we examine God's instructions for husbands and wives because this gives us the necessary motivation to obey.

The obvious questions, then, are, How can a husband love his wife just as Christ loved the church? And, How can a wife submit to her husband as unto the Lord?

TRUST THE HOLY SPIRIT TO HELP YOU

Unfortunately, when it comes to fulfilling our roles in our marriages, we often feel alone. God's standard for husbands and wives is so high that we ask, "How can I ever obey these commands?"

Two words summarize what goes through people's minds as they consider God's commands to husbands and wives: *intimidating* and *overwhelming*. As a husband, it is intimidating to think of being to your wife what Christ is to the church. As a wife, it is overwhelming to think of submitting to your husband as you should to the Lord. If you are not intimidated or overwhelmed, you do not understand what is expected of you. If you had to obey God's commands in your own strength, you would not only feel overwhelmed or intimidated, but completely hopeless.

But thankfully, because of the power of the gospel at work in our lives and a promise Jesus made to us, we can feel hopeful. Jesus told His disciples, "I will pray the Father, and He will give you another Helper, that He may abide with you forever" (John 14:16). If you have repented of your sins and put your faith in Christ, then you are a Christian and the Holy Spirit lives in you. You are not alone! The Holy Spirit will empower you to do what God has commanded you to do.

The first half of Ephesians 5 is about living in the Spirit, and the second half is about husbands and wives. This is fitting because if there is any area of the Christian life in which the Holy Spirit's help is necessary, it is marriage. In Ephesians 5:18, the apostle Paul states, "Do not be drunk with wine, in which is dissipation; but be filled with the Spirit." It might sound odd to compare drunkenness with being filled with the Spirit, but the parallel that Paul is making has to do with influence. People who drive when they are drunk are "driving under the influence." Just as alcohol has the potential to influence, so does the Holy Spirit.

The New Testament Greek word translated "be filled" is *pleroo,* which means "keep on being filled" or "stay filled" with the Spirit. Paul is talking about a practice that should be ongoing in our lives as believers. We need to allow—and trust—the Holy Spirit to influence us as husbands and wives. The following verses include promises from God's Word—promises that God will enable us to do what He has called us to do. As you read them, consider how they apply to marriage:

- "God is able to make all grace abound toward you, that you, always having all sufficiency in all things, may have an abundance for every good work" (2 Corinthians 9:8).

- "It is God who works in you both to will and to do for His good pleasure" (Philippians 2:13).

- "What is the exceeding greatness of His power toward us who believe, according to the working of His mighty power which He worked in Christ when He raised Him from the dead..." (Ephesians 1:19-20).

- "May the God of peace who brought up our Lord Jesus from the dead…make you complete in every good work to do His will, working in you what is well pleasing in His sight, through Jesus Christ" (Hebrews 13:20-21).

When we become discouraged in our marriages, these are the truths we need to remember. God is the one working in and through us to accomplish every good work. He makes this possible through the incomparably great power that raised Jesus from the dead. God wants us to be equipped to do what He has called us to do, and of all that God wants from us, what could be more important than the way we handle our relationship with our spouse?

Your marriage gives you the opportunity to reflect Christ and the church to others. Does God want Christ and the church to have a great relationship? Absolutely! Does God want the world to witness Christian marriages that wonderfully represent Christ's relationship with the church? Without a doubt! God has given us His indwelling Spirit to help make that happen. It is as if God has said, "The standard I have set for husbands and wives is high, but you do not have to fulfill it alone. I would not command you to do something without also giving you the resources that enable you to obey."

We Cannot Just Sit Back

Let's bring some balance to this discussion by understanding a key distinction: For God to say, "I will help you" is different than Him saying, "I will do everything." The Holy Spirit helps us, but we need to remember that He does not do it all for us. We still have responsibilities. The Holy Spirit is not going to supernaturally take control of a marriage when the individuals involved are not committed to putting forth the necessary effort to do what God has called them to do.

The apostle Paul reveals this fact in Ephesians 2:10: "We are His workmanship, created in Christ Jesus for good works, which God prepared beforehand that we should walk in them." God prepared good works for us, but we must "walk in them." We do not want to miss out on what God desires to do in our marriages because we are being lazy or selfish. Consider the responsibilities placed on our shoulders elsewhere in the New Testament:

- "Let us *walk properly…Put on* the Lord Jesus Christ, and *make no provision* for the flesh, to fulfill its lusts" (Romans 13:13-14).

- "*Put on* tender mercies, kindness, humility, meekness, longsuffering;

[bear] with one another, and *[forgive]* one another...*Put on* love, which is the bond of perfection" (Colossians 3:12-14).

Note the calling we are given: walk, put on, make no provision for, bear with, and forgive. What does this look like in practical terms? How does the Holy Spirit's help work in conjunction with our free will? Here are some examples.

Husband, you plop down on the sofa next to your wife without showing any affection for her, but perhaps the Holy Spirit has been compelling you to be more affectionate. So, the next time you sit next to your wife, put your arm around her.

Maybe the Holy Spirit has also been leading you to be a better listener. Instead of simply hearing your wife speak, pay attention to her and verbally affirm what she says. You may find it helpful to respond by paraphrasing her words back to her and validating her sentiments. If your wife is not used to you doing this, she will notice and appreciate the extra effort.

Wife, you are riding in the car with your husband you notice the light indicating "low fuel" comes on. You may find yourself repeatedly "reminding" him the car needs fuel until he pulls into a gas station. Though he does not like this, you think it beats running out of gas. Lately, however, you've sensed the Holy Spirit leading you to trust your husband, so this time you simply mention it once, and trust your husband to follow through without any further reminders. This may pleasantly surprise him. He might even say, "Thank you for not repeatedly telling me to pull over."

In each case, the spouse would do well to express his or her appreciation for the changed behavior. These are only simple examples of how we might sense the Holy Spirit at work within us. You'll see more examples as you continue your way through this book. Ultimately, we want to be submissive and receptive to the Spirit's guidance.

The Encouraging Balance

Consider this encouraging verse that ties together the truths that (1) God enables us and (2) we are called to carry out our responsibilities: "To this end I also labor, striving according to [God's] working which works in me mightily" (Colossians 1:29). Here, the apostle describes how we are to work side by side with God to accomplish His will. When it comes to our marriages, we should seek to work side by side with God in everything that we do. We are to labor to be the husbands and wives God wants us to be, and we can be encouraged by the truth that while we are laboring, God also works mightily in us.

We are frequently tempted to think the key to a healthier marriage is to work harder in our own wisdom and power. If we roll up our sleeves and give our best effort, surely things will improve, right? No. Many people have experienced ongoing frustration in their marriage after taking this approach. Instead, we must remember that if we're Christians, the power of the gospel is at work in our lives and marriages. With God's help—with the Spirit's enablement—we *can* enjoy the marriage He desires for us!

CHAPTER TWO

Marriage "Problems" Are Really Symptoms

Because our relationships with our spouses reflect our relationships with Christ, our marriage "problems" are merely symptoms. The actual problems are in our relationships with Christ. The horizontal relationship with our spouse is suffering because there's something wrong with the vertical relationship with Christ.

For instance, in my own marriage, the problem looked like I did not have enough time for my wife and children. But that was a symptom. Actually, the problem was that I would not listen to the Holy Spirit's promptings to meet my family's needs, and I was not trusting Christ enough. Instead, I let anxiety consume me.

Thus, the first place to address any symptoms—the things that appear to be problems between the husband and wife—is to look at each person's relationship with the Lord. When I counsel couples and they share a problem they are experiencing, they become confused when I ask, "What does your time in God's Word look like? How is your prayer life? Tell me about your involvement in the church."

A wife might say, "I just told you that my husband yells at me. Why are you asking about his time in the Word?" Because the hope is that as a husband reads God's Word he will be convicted of what he is doing wrong, repent, and become a more patient and loving man. I do not have the power to change a husband's heart, and neither does a wife, or there would be no need for counseling. A husband can only become the man he should be by having a good relationship with Christ.

Likewise, a husband might respond, "I just told you about the ways my wife humiliates me in front of our friends. Why do you ask whether we are part of a small group study?" Because ongoing connections with other believers can provide accountability and require vulnerability and transparency. You can learn from other believers and be challenged by their examples. When you are not actively involved with others who are in the body of Christ, you will not receive the encouragement and exhortation God wants you to have. You will feel alone, as though you are the only people having these problems. You will not have anyone in your life through whom God can regularly speak to you. We are made to have fellowship with other believers. When we do not have it, that lack manifests itself in other areas, including our marriages.

Here are two situations I have witnessed many times. A husband and wife are having marriage problems. They submit to Christ, and soon their marriage improves. Why? Did their difficulties simply disappear? No, those difficulties had been symptoms of the real problem—Christ was not supreme in their lives. When they put Christ first, their marriage improved.

If a couple wants a strong, healthy marriage,
they need a strong, healthy relationship with Christ.

Similarly, I have seen a couple plugged into church. The husband and wife pray and read the Word together. They are doing well spiritually, and their marriage is healthy. Then, for various reasons, they get distracted from the Lord and their priorities shift. They start wavering in church attendance and the spiritual disciplines. They fall out of fellowship. Soon their marriage suffers.

So remember: Marriage "problems" are only symptoms—or negative consequences—of not having Christ as the focal point in the marital relationship. If a couple wants a strong, healthy marriage, they need a strong, healthy relationship with Christ. When a couple's relationships with Christ are weak and unhealthy, the marriage will be weak and unhealthy.

HANDLING FRUSTRATIONS

Your Marriage God's Way is not split into one section for husbands and another for wives. The biblical passages on marriage, such as the New Testament imperatives (commands) in Ephesians 5 and 1 Peter 3, and the Old Testament narratives (accounts) about Abraham and Sarah, Samson and Delilah, and David and Michal contain intertwined exhortations for both spouses. Husbands should read the instructions for wives and wives should read the instructions for husbands so they can understand what is commanded of both of them. If a husband knows what is expected of his wife and a wife knows what is expected of her husband, they can help each other fulfill their biblical responsibilities.

Although there is also a danger you must watch for as you become aware of God's calling for your spouse. Because the standard set by God's Word is so high...

- a husband could easily become frustrated that his wife is not more respectful or submissive, as God's Word commands, and

- a wife could easily become frustrated that her husband does not cherish her or provide the spiritual leadership God's Word commands.

This is illustrated by a situation that took place years ago when I was teaching on marriage. I was discussing the importance of husbands loving their wives when a woman raised her hand. I called on her, expecting that she would ask a question. But she stood up and began criticizing her husband in front of everyone. I could have interrupted and said, "Can we all pray for you two?" or "Let's meet this week at my office," or "Why don't we talk about this after the study?" Instead, I was so caught off guard that I did the worst thing possible—nothing! I simply stood there with a dropped jaw while the angry wife berated her husband.

After that, I decided that whenever I taught on marriage, I would remind couples that the goal in every situation is to improve marriage relationships, not to arm people for World War III. With that in mind, here are three encouraging guidelines I want to give for handling any frustrations that might develop as you read the following chapters:

1. We all have plenty of weaknesses that need to be addressed. Instead of keeping a mental record of all that your spouse does wrong, remind yourself of your own struggles and failures as a spouse.

2. Ask yourself: How can I encourage my spouse to fulfill the role God has given him/her? Is there anything I can do that will make

being married to me easier? If you cannot think of any answers to these questions, you are not thinking hard enough. And if there's a possibility you may be prideful about how "good" of a spouse you are, you'll want to repent of that.

3. Whenever you start to become frustrated toward your spouse, turn your frustrations into prayer. Yield your feelings of hurt, betrayal, or disappointment to God, and pray that He will help your spouse grow in the area that is upsetting you. Pray also for God to help you be as forgiving and gracious as necessary. When it comes to our spouses, most people—myself included—are far more likely to complain, gossip, yell, threaten, pout, or ignore than to pray. If we would spend as much time praying for our spouse as we do getting frustrated with him or her, our marriages would be much better.

EMBRACE THE STRUGGLE

As you work your way through this book, if you find yourself feeling frustration toward your spouse, recognize that God can use this for your good. Romans 8:28 says, "We know that all things work together for good to those who love God, to those who are the called according to His purpose." This can apply to marriage problems too. God is calling your attention to the areas in which you need to improve, and the best way to help each other grow is to be willing to ask each other tough questions.

For example, a husband might say, "Outside of the Lord Himself, do you feel like you are taking second place to anything in my life?" If a wife answers that she does not feel she is the supreme priority in her husband's life, the husband should not try to talk her out of the way she feels or persuade her to see things differently.

Likewise, a wife might ask her husband, "Do you feel like I respect you?" If the husband shares how she makes him feel disrespected, the wife should not argue with her husband and try to convince him he is wrong.

To try to disagree with how your spouse feels could make things worse. Rather, each spouse should listen to the other, acknowledge any weaknesses that are pointed out, and try to make changes that will remedy the situation.

When couples ask each other these kinds of difficult questions, they should expect some painful discussions. That might not seem a positive path to take toward marital growth, but in reality, it's very beneficial. Let me illustrate this using an analogy. A few months ago, I hurt my lower back—again. The injury is a recurring one that reminds me I am getting older. I returned to the chiropractor, and if you have ever been to one, you know they can be forceful as they work on your body—pushing, twisting, snapping, and popping. Frequently you are left feeling sore, but that is supposed to happen. The temporary soreness results from the chiropractor's adjustments to your body, and in time, you'll get better.

But what if you went to the chiropractor and all he did was rub your shoulders, pat your back, and tell you everything looked fine? How would you respond? I know how I would react: "This is not why I came here. I know that if you are going to help me, you have to apply pressure to my body and do some pushing and pulling. I expect tension and discomfort. I realize there will be soreness afterward."

Likewise, if we want to improve our marriages, we need to expect some discomfort, struggles, and tension. We should not be alarmed because it's as we deal with the difficulties that the healing process is able to take place and God is able to work in our hearts.

And what is the alternative? Simple. Close this book. Be lazy. Do not ask each other the difficult questions or have the tough conversations. Do not take your marriage seriously so that you can improve as a husband, a wife, or a Christian.

If you avoid discussing the biblical teachings in this book with your spouse, you will not have any tough issues to wrestle with, but you also won't grow and your marriage won't be strengthened. If you choose to avoid the discomfort now, you will more than likely experience even tougher and more painful situations later.

So I want to encourage you to embrace the struggles because of what they are going to produce. The apostle Paul tells us, "We…glory in tribulations, knowing that tribulation produces perseverance; and perseverance, character; and character, hope" (Romans 5:3-4). Glory in the struggles you are having, knowing that they are producing good results as you, your spouse, and your marriage are refined!

GOD'S CHASTENING IS NOT PUNISHMENT, BUT A FATHER'S LOVING DISCIPLINE

Hebrews 12:5-6 says this about the way God produces good in our lives:

> You have forgotten the exhortation which speaks to you as to sons: "My son, do not despise the chastening of the LORD, nor be

discouraged when you are rebuked by Him; for whom the LORD
loves He chastens, and scourges every son whom He receives."

We often apply these verses to God's punishment of sin, but the context is
God working out certain issues to produce fruit and righteousness in our lives.
Because none of us are perfect, we all have weaknesses in our marriages. We have
certain behaviors and struggles God needs to fix as we grow in our sanctification
and become more like Christ. When necessary, God will chasten us to make that
happen. While that does not always feel good, we should embrace the chastening,
understanding that God is doing something good and worthwhile in our lives.

The author of Hebrews goes on to say this in verses 11-13:

> No chastening seems to be joyful for the present, but painful; nev-
> ertheless, afterward it yields the peaceable fruit of righteousness to
> those who have been trained by it. Therefore strengthen the hands
> which hang down, and the feeble knees, and make straight paths
> for your feet, so that what is lame may not be dislocated, but rather
> be healed.

How true are these verses! Nice, gentle shoulder rubs feel good and are enjoyable, but they don't do much for our back problems. If we want improvement,
we must experience discomfort. Likewise, it is not easy or enjoyable to deal with
our weaknesses. People do not want to talk about their struggles as a husband
or wife, but this is how we grow and allow God to work in us. Indeed, this is
how "the peaceable fruit of righteousness" is produced in our lives and marriages.

Interestingly, the above verses suggest that this does not happen for everyone. Only certain people receive the "peaceable fruit of righteousness." According to verse 11, it is those who "have been trained by [the chastening]." The New
Testament Greek word translated "trained" is *gymnazo*, which is related to our
English word *gymnasium*. It means "to exercise vigorously." Improving our marriages is hard work. As we embrace the struggles in our relationships, talking
about them and working through them, we need to give ourselves the exhortation the author of Hebrews gives to his readers. Let's strengthen our weak hands
and feet, trusting God to make straight paths for our marriages to be healed.

LEARNING FROM PAINFUL SEASONS

At the opening of chapter 1, I shared about the painful season Katie and I
endured in our marriage when I hadn't prioritized our relationship as I should

have. I am thankful for having gone through and learned from that. As awful as that season was, God used it for our benefit as He does all our trials. James 1:2-4 says:

> My brethren, count it all joy when you fall into various trials, knowing that the testing of your faith produces patience. But let patience have its perfect work, that you may be perfect and complete, lacking nothing.

We don't like trials, but there's nothing else in life that can perfect us and complete us like they can. What does this have to do with marriage? You've experienced trials in your relationship with your spouse, and you can be encouraged by the great blessings that come from them—the powerful lessons God teaches you through them. It is not easy to understand the importance of obeying Scripture until you have disobeyed it and experienced the negative consequences. It is not easy to understand how God's Word works when you have not applied it. But after you have, you gain firsthand experience in its power, which gives you greater confidence in how it can help you. That difficult time in my marriage taught me the importance of doing what God's Word says and leaning on the Holy Spirit for help. That season taught me several of the principles I will share with you in this book.

I also had to embrace our marriage problems so our relationship could improve. I had to ask Katie tough questions, such as, "What do we need to do to make this work? In what ways have I sinned against you? How do you want me to change?" I had to ask her to forgive me for the ways I had failed her.

Are you willing to do the same? If so, then you can be confident the trials you experience won't be wasted. You can look forward to the wonderful ways God will use them to strengthen your marriage. My prayer is that the following chapters do just that, and help you enjoy the blessings God desires for your relationship. I've seen the biblical principles that I'll outline work in my marriage, the church, and the lives of people I've counseled. They can work for you too! Be encouraged that we'll go through this together. Each step of the way I will be with you, and most importantly, so will God!

PART TWO

CREATION OF MARRIAGE AND THE FALL (GENESIS 1–3)

CHAPTER THREE

God's Establishment
of Adam's Headship

S oon after I became a Christian in my early twenties, a pastor's daughter told me what she wanted in a husband: a man who would be a spiritual leader and the head of their home. I hardly knew anything about the Bible at this point, so everything she said sounded odd to me. I didn't object until she started talking about wives submitting to their husbands. That's when I thought she had gone too far. Sadly, I vividly remember saying, "That is ridiculous! Men and women are equal. How could a husband have authority over his wife?"

I was in for a shock as I started reading the Bible and learning what it says about husbands and wives. Verses kept jumping out at me that supported what the pastor's daughter said. If you're unfamiliar with the Bible's teaching on marriage, or you believe like I did that husbands and wives have identical roles and responsibilities, you might be in for a shock too.

God has a master design for marriage relationships that has very definite purposes and benefits. We live in a culture that is far removed from the beauty and brilliance of God's plan. While we as fallen people might initially chaff at the ideas of headship and submission (as I did), and believe it means men and women aren't equal (as I did), because we live in a society that insists everyone should be viewed identically, it's important to recognize that in God's eyes and according to His design, yes, husbands and wives have equal value (more on this later in the chapter), but they have different roles and responsibilities.

Let's ease into the delicate subjects of headship and submission by considering that twice in the New Testament the apostle Paul stated the headship of a husband:

- "I want you to know that the head of every man is Christ, the head of woman is man, and the head of Christ is God" (1 Corinthians 11:3).

- "The husband is head of the wife, as also Christ is head of the church; and He is the Savior of the body" (Ephesians 5:23).

While these verses are found in the New Testament, that doesn't mean a husband's headship had its beginning under the new covenant. Neither did his headship have its beginning in the Old Testament under the old covenant. Nor did it begin at the fall.

The husband's headship has its beginning at creation itself. This is important for us to know, because if we think headship began after the fall, then this leadership becomes part of sin's curse. But if we understand that the husband's headship began at creation, we will see it as part of God's natural, healthy, divine plan for husbands and wives.

Genesis 1:1 proclaims the incredible truth that "in the beginning God created the heavens and the earth," and the rest of the chapter gives a grand overview of all six days of creation. God created man and woman on the sixth day. Then, in Genesis 2:7-25, God zooms in on the creation of Adam and Eve because mankind is the pinnacle of God's creation. We are so familiar with the account that it is easy to miss the significance of some of the details. Therefore, let's approach this passage as though we are reading it for the first time. It is in this account that God established the husband's headship.

Because God created the animals in pairs, male and female, what would we expect Him to do with the creation of humankind? We would expect Him to create the first man and woman at the same time—as a pair, male and female. But that is not what He did, and in creating man first and woman second, God revealed several important details about His design for the marriage relationship.

GOD'S FIRST COMMAND

After God created Adam, He placed him in the Garden of Eden to work (Genesis 2:15). Creating Adam before Eve meant that God's first command would be given to Adam alone. Genesis 2:16-17 says,

> The LORD God *commanded the man*, saying, "Of every tree of the garden you may freely eat; but of the tree of the knowledge of good

and evil you shall not eat, for in the day that you eat of it you shall surely die."

Managing the garden was Adam's duty, but when Eve was fashioned from him, he had the responsibility of passing along to her what he had heard from God. Then Eve had the responsibility of trusting her husband's account. God did not have to do it this way. He could have given the command to both of them after Eve was created, but in giving the command to Adam alone, God established Adam's headship in the relationship.

ADAM NAMES THE ANIMALS AND EVE

In Genesis 2:19-20, we read that God had Adam name the animals:

> Out of the ground the LORD God formed every beast of the field and every bird of the air, and brought them to Adam to see what *he would call them*. And whatever *Adam called each living creature*, that was its name. So *Adam gave names to all cattle*, to the birds of the air, and to every beast of the field. But for Adam there was not found a helper comparable to him.

Again, we see God do something with Adam that He could have had Adam and Eve do together. There are two reasons God had Adam name the animals without Eve. First, God wanted man to have authority over creation. In Genesis 1:26, God said,

> Let Us make man in Our image, according to Our likeness; let them have dominion over the fish of the sea, over the birds of the air, and over the cattle, over all the earth and over every creeping thing that creeps on the earth.

God established Adam's authority by directing him to name the animals.

Second, instead of simply giving Adam a helper or telling him he should desire one, God chose to reveal this lack to him by bringing the animals to him in pairs. This disclosed Adam's lack of a companion. Adam quickly noticed that the animals were in pairs, but he himself was not part of any pair. As Genesis 2:20 describes, he observed there was no "helper comparable to him."

With Adam now longing for a mate, God was ready to fashion Eve. Here again, familiarity with the creation account may cause us to miss the significance of certain details. Up to this point, one recurring theme has been God's creation of living things from ordinary dirt:

- "The LORD God formed man *of the dust of the ground*, and breathed into his nostrils the breath of life; and man became a living being" (Genesis 2:7).

- "*Out of the ground* the LORD God made every tree grow" (Genesis 2:9).

- "*Out of the ground* the LORD God formed every beast of the field and every bird of the air" (Genesis 2:19).

With this pattern in place, we would expect to read, "The LORD God formed woman *of the dust of the ground*, and breathed into her nostrils the breath of life; and woman became a living being." Instead, Genesis 2:21-23 says:

> The LORD God caused a deep sleep to fall on Adam, and he slept; and He took one of his ribs, and closed up the flesh in its place. Then the rib which the LORD God had taken from man He made into a woman, and He brought her to the man. And Adam said: "This is now bone of my bones and flesh of my flesh; she shall be called Woman, because she was taken out of Man."

Earlier, God brought the animals to Adam to be named, demonstrating Adam's authority over them. Adam then named his wife, demonstrating his authority over her: "She shall be called Woman." This is one more indication of God establishing Adam's headship within the marriage relationship.

HISTORY'S FIRST SURGERY

God performed history's first surgery by using Adam's body to fashion Eve, and what modern science reveals about this is fascinating. Every cell in our bodies contains our entire genetic blueprint or DNA. Therefore, God could take some of Adam's cells and use their DNA to create Eve. The reverse, however, would not work, because men's DNA contains both X and Y chromosomes (XY), while women's DNA contains only X chromosomes (XX). If God had created woman first, it would have been impossible to fashion man from woman because there would be no Y chromosomes, which is the chromosome that determines male gender. Adam had the genetic material—both X and Y chromosomes—for a woman to be created from his DNA, allowing for the reproduction of men and women.

Because Eve was fashioned from Adam, she has the unique distinction of being the only part of creation not formed out of the ground. And because Adam was created in the image and likeness of God, Eve was just as wonderfully created in the image and likeness of God. We should also consider that while God created woman from man, He brought forth every other human being since Eve from woman. The apostle Paul explained it like this:

> For man is not from woman, but woman from man. Nor was man created for the woman, but woman for the man…Nevertheless, neither is man independent of woman, nor woman independent of man, in the Lord. For as woman came from man, even so man also comes through woman (1 Corinthians 11:8-9, 11-12).

A final detail of significance is that God's creation of woman from man involved far more than Adam's rib. The Hebrew word translated "rib" is *tsela*. The word occurs 41 times in the Old Testament, but only here in Genesis 2:21-22 is it translated "rib." Nineteen times *tsela* is translated as "side," and 11 times as "chamber." Here are a few examples:

- Exodus 25:12—"You shall cast four rings of gold for [the ark], and put them in its four corners; two rings shall be on one side [*tsela*], and two rings on the other side [*tsela*]."

- 2 Samuel 16:13—"As David and his men went along the road, Shimei went along the hillside [*tsela*] opposite him and cursed as he went."

- 1 Kings 6:8—"The doorway for the middle story was on the right side [*tsela*] of the temple."

Eve came from Adam's side, not just his rib—a fact that is also made clear when Adam, in Genesis 2:23, calls Eve "bone of my bones and flesh of my flesh."

Why did God choose to create Eve from Adam's side instead of creating her from the dust of the ground like everything else? God wanted Adam and Eve to understand the unity between them. We see that in the next verse, Genesis 2:24, which says, "Therefore a man shall leave his father and mother and be joined to his wife, and they shall become one flesh." At first glance this seems like an odd statement because Adam and Eve are the only two people in history with no "father and mother." Therefore, this verse is not primarily about them, but is instructive about the nature of the marriage relationship itself.

Genesis 2:24 further supports the husband's headship. Why does the command mention a man leaving his father and mother but not a woman leaving her father and mother? It is because the man is moving out from under his parents' authority and establishing his own headship—or authority—over his family. But the woman is not doing the same. She is simply moving from being under her father to being under her husband.

This is why 1 Corinthians 11:3 does not say, "The head of every man and woman is Christ." Instead, it states, "The head of every man is Christ, [and] the head of woman is man." A wife remains under a man's authority—first her father's, and then her husband's. And these men are under Christ's authority. This biblical principle is played out at weddings symbolically when the father walks his daughter down the aisle and gives her to the man who is about to become her husband. The imagery is that of a transfer of authority from father to husband.

EGALITARIANISM VERSUS COMPLEMENTARIANISM

Complementarianism is the term used to describe the belief that God has designed distinct roles and responsibilities for men and women that allow them to balance and support each other. *Egalitarianism* is the view that God does not have distinct plans for men and women, but that they are equal and interchangeable in terms of their roles and responsibilities. Egalitarians reject the concept of the husband's headship in the marriage relationship.[1]

To hold to egalitarianism, people must reject the plain teaching of Scripture that describes the differences between men and women, including the affirmation of the husband's headship. The Scripture most cited by egalitarians is Galatians 3:28: "There is neither Jew nor Greek, there is neither slave nor free, *there is neither male nor female*; for you are all one in Christ Jesus." But using that verse to support egalitarianism requires taking the passage out of context—all the preceding verses clearly deal with salvation. Everyone, whether Jew, Gentile, slave, free, male, or female is saved in the same manner—by grace through faith apart from the law and works (Galatians 3:1-25). What's more, if Paul were saying men and women are identical in terms of roles and responsibilities, he would be contradicting numerous other scriptures he wrote outlining the differences between the genders.

Bible scholar James Fowler explains:

Egalitarian assertions are based on false premises. [Identical] responsibilities and authority produces the chaos of no one having ultimate authority or responsibility. The egalitarian premises of socialistic communism are unworkable. Identity, value and worth are not found in gender function, but in a personal Being beyond ourselves.[2]

Complementarianism, on the other hand, recognizes the gender roles in Scripture are meaningful and, when embraced, promote spiritual and emotional health that allows people to reach their God-given potential. Scripture says, "God created man in His own image; in the image of God He created him; male and female He created them" (Genesis 1:27; see also Genesis 5:2; Mark 10:6). The emphasis is not on God's creating people but on His creating two different types of humans: one male and one female. Other Scripture passages reveal to us the distinct plans God has for each, and we will look at all of them in this book. While men and women equally share God's image and together have dominion over creation, God designed them differently to accomplish certain purposes that He intends for them to fulfill.

A common criticism of complementarianism is that it is chauvinistic—it identifies one gender as superior to the other. Egalitarians insist that a difference in roles and responsibilities implies a difference in equality. But it *is* possible for two people to be different and equal. Men and women do in fact have the same value and significance before God, even though they are not identical in their roles or responsibilities. This is clearly evident to us in the Trinity—God the Father, God the Son, and God the Spirit. The three persons have distinct roles to fulfill, but they are all equal.[3]

Pastor David Guzik states:

> In our day, many say there is no real difference between men and women. This makes sense if we are the result of mindless evolution, but the Bible says "male and female He created them." To God, the differences between men and women are not accidents. Since He created them, the differences are good and meaningful. One of the saddest signs of our culture's depravity is the amount and the degree of gender confusion today. It is vain to wonder if men or women are superior to the other. A man is absolutely superior at being a man. A woman is absolutely superior at being a woman. But when a man tries to be a woman or a woman tries to be a man, you have something inferior.[4]

We cannot expect the secular world to agree with God's Word and embrace complementarianism. The real tragedy, however, is when Christians hold to an egalitarian view, seeing no differences between men and women's roles in the home and the church. Such individuals may not condone unbiblical forms of sexuality such as homosexuality and transgenderism, but because egalitarianism blurs the lines between men and women, it makes it easier for the world to further blur the lines and do away with gender distinctives and undermine God's Word.

Just as men are needed in the home and the church in crucial ways, so women are needed in the home and the church in crucial ways. But the way each gender is needed is different, and we must maintain the distinctions if we are to obey God's Word and experience the best of marital bliss the way God intended.

BETTER TOGETHER

In chapter 5, we will take a closer look at Genesis 2:18. For now, let's appreciate how God called Eve "a helper comparable to [Adam]." This affirms that God's calling for Eve—and all wives—is a truly noble calling. The Hebrew word translated "comparable" is *neged*. Other Bible translations say "suitable for him" (NASB, NIV) and "fit for him" (ESV). The literal translation of the Hebrew text means "opposite" or "contrasting."

God is all-perfect, all-loving, and all-wise. As the Author of marriage, we can trust His plan.

Men and women were designed to fit together perfectly in all ways—physically, emotionally, mentally, and spiritually. When a husband and wife become one flesh on their wedding day, they are two people who complement and complete each other. As Genesis 2:24 says, "A man shall…be joined to his wife, and *they shall become one flesh.*" Together, they become something stronger and more magnificent than they could ever be alone. The strengths of each compensate for the weaknesses of the other:

- When a husband thinks about his wife, he should see her as God's suitable companion for him.

- When a wife thinks about her husband, she should see herself as God's perfect fit for him.

We should give thanks to God for His wonderful design and do everything we can to fulfill the roles He has given us. Only then can we truly experience healthy, joyful marriages.

The world wants to throw counterfeits at us, so we must keep in mind that the blueprint is in the Bible. God is all-perfect, all-loving, and all-wise. As the Author of marriage, we can trust His plan. His way allows husbands and wives to experience all the blessings He desires for us.

CHAPTER FOUR

Male Leadership Is God's Pattern

—————

was not raised in a Christian home. While my parents were moral, hardworking, and I learned much from them, they didn't model gender roles for me as they're presented in Scripture. This led me to believe men and women are identical regarding their roles and responsibilities. Aside from the obvious, such as not going into the bathroom of the wrong gender or playing on the opposite gender's sports team—things that tragically our world is even starting to get wrong—I didn't think of men and women acting much differently from each other.

This was even the case when I went through ROTC and then became an Army officer. Except for a few differences, such as lower requirements on the physical fitness tests, I didn't see men and women facing different expectations or being treated differently. Although I wasn't a Christian at the time, and even though I couldn't put my finger on it, there was a nagging suspicion that men, versus women, should lead. You probably have this thought in the back of your mind too. Why is that? Because, as Scripture reveals, God created men to lead. We see that throughout the history of God's people. The pattern of male leadership began at creation and is maintained throughout Scripture:

- There were patriarchs instead of matriarchs.

- The tribes of Israel were named after men.

- The only legitimate mediators between God and people were men (i.e., priests instead of priestesses).

- God appointed kings instead of queens.

- God called men to serve as the focal points of His covenants with mankind (for example, Adam, Noah, Abraham, Moses, David, and Jesus).

FEMALE LEADERS IN THE BIBLE

So why do we see examples of female leadership in Scripture? What about queens, prophetesses, and at least one female judge—Deborah? Were these women anomalies? Are they examples of rebellion against God's design, or is there another explanation? To answer these questions, let's look at them individually.

Queens

Scripture mentions three prominent queens, and they fall into two categories: evil and good. Jezebel (1 Kings 16-22; 2 Kings 9) and Athaliah (2 Kings 8, 11) were evil women who seized control and became tyrannical leaders. Jezebel instituted the worship of the false god Baal across Israel and persecuted followers of Yahweh. Athaliah murdered her grandchildren upon the death of her son and then seized the throne of Judah. Clearly, neither woman serves as a good example.

On the other hand, Esther stands in contrast as a godly queen. We see through the account of her life that she supported male leadership through her submission first to her adopted father, Mordecai, and then to her husband, King Xerxes of Persia. This wasn't the only factor that allowed her to save her people from annihilation. There was also her courage in going before the king knowing "that any man or woman who goes into the inner court to the king, who has not been called, he has but one law: put all to death, except the one to whom the king holds out the golden scepter, that he may live" (Esther 4:11). All of this reveals a heart that's yielded to God. The whole of her life contributed to her submissive attitude and made her useful to God.

Priestesses

Under the Mosaic covenant, only men could be priests because they were the teachers: "[The priests] may teach the children of Israel all the statutes which the Lord has spoken" (Leviticus 10:11). When priestesses are mentioned, they are associated with pagan religions such as the worship of Astarte or Baal. Wayne Grudem, professor of theology and cofounder of the Council on Biblical Manhood and Womanhood, explains: "Think of the Bible as a whole, from Genesis to Revelation. Where is there one example in the entire Bible of a woman publicly teaching an assembled group of God's people? There is none."[1]

Prophetesses

While we find no scriptural examples of women publicly teaching an assembly, it's worth noting that no negative association is attached in Scripture to women being prophetesses. They could occupy this office because it was not a leadership position, and it did not cause them to teach men. Authors John Piper and Wayne Grudem explain:

> It is instructive to note in the Old Testament that some women were prophets, but never priests. It is the priests who had the more settled and established positions of leadership in Israel. Prophecy is a different kind of gift from teaching, and when women functioned as prophets they did so with a demeanor and attitude that supported male leadership. Women who had the gift of prophecy did not exercise it in a public forum as male prophets did. The reason for this is that such a public exercise of authority would contradict male headship.[2]

If we briefly consider two examples of the most prominent prophetesses in the Old Testament, we see how their ministries not only didn't conflict with male headship but actually supported it. The first is Moses's sister Miriam. After the people of Israel crossed the Red Sea, Moses led the nation in a song of praise (Exodus 15:1-19). Then Miriam did something similar in Exodus 15:20-21, but with an important difference: "Miriam the prophetess, the sister of Aaron, took the timbrel in her hand; and *all the women went out after her* with timbrels and with dances. And Miriam answered them: 'Sing to the LORD...'" Note that Miriam led only the women in singing, as opposed to leading both women and men as her brother Moses had done.

Conversely, consider what happened when Miriam joined Aaron in challenging Moses's leadership. In Numbers 12:2, Miriam and Aaron asked, "Has the LORD indeed spoken only through [you]? Has He not spoken through us also?" Apparently, they thought they should have some of Moses's authority. In response, God quickly called the people of Israel to the tabernacle of meeting, appeared in the pillar of cloud, rebuked Aaron and Miriam, defended Moses, and gave Miriam leprosy for rebelling against God's appointed leader (Numbers 12:4-10).

After Moses interceded for Miriam, her leprosy was removed, but God still commanded that she be put outside the camp for seven days (Numbers 12:13-15). What's puzzling here is that Aaron engaged in the same sin as Miriam, yet only she was punished in this way. Why the difference? Scripture gives no indication that Miriam did anything worse, or even different than Aaron: "Then Miriam and Aaron spoke against Moses...So *they* said, 'Has the Lord indeed spoken only through Moses? Has He not spoken through us also?'" (Numbers 12:1-2). While it was bad for Aaron to try to usurp his brother's authority, it was worse for Miriam because she was the initiator.

We fast-forward almost one millennium to another prominent prophetess: Huldah. While Miriam lived during the wilderness wanderings, Huldah lived during the reign of one of Judah's greatest kings: Josiah. During his restoration of the temple, the Book of the Law (Pentateuch) was discovered. When it was read before Josiah, he was grieved to discover how far his nation had strayed from following God. Tearing his clothes, Josiah sent messengers to "inquire of the LORD" (2 Kings 22:13). Those messengers went to Huldah the prophetess. The significance of Huldah's response is that she did not publicly proclaim God's Word. Rather, she explained it privately to the messengers (2 Kings 22:15-20). She exercised her prophetic ministry in a way that did not obstruct, but instead, supported male headship.

Numerous other prophetesses are listed throughout Scripture, making clear this role was not an anomaly:

- Deborah, who also served as a judge (Judges 4:4)
- The wife of Isaiah the prophet (Isaiah 8:3)
- Anna, who spoke about Jesus's birth in the temple (Luke 2:36-38)
- The four daughters of Philip the evangelist (Acts 21:9)

In each case, however, like Huldah, there is no record of these women having the public teaching ministries of their male counterparts.

Other women in the Bible are not called prophetesses but are recorded as prophesying:

- Hannah, mother of Samuel the prophet (1 Samuel 2:1-10)
- Elizabeth, mother of John the Baptist (Luke 1:39-45)
- Mary, the mother of Jesus (Luke 1:46-55)

In every instance, the women prophesied under the headship of a husband or father or, in the case of the widow Anna, the temple's male leadership.

DEBORAH THE RELUCTANT JUDGE

Judges were Israel's primary rulers for almost three-and-a-half centuries. They also commanded armies, making these some of the strongest leaders in Scripture. So why did Deborah serve as judge? In discussions about the role of women in church leadership, Deborah is often the first example brought up to support the idea of female leaders. For this reason, Deborah's example is worth looking at more closely. We'll see she also supports the principle of male leadership.

Throughout the book of Judges, as men rise to leadership, we read verses that confirm they were chosen or empowered by God:

- "The LORD raised up a deliverer…Othniel" (Judges 3:9).

- "The LORD raised up a deliverer…Ehud" (Judges 3:15).

- "The LORD [said to Gideon], 'Go in this might of yours, and you shall save Israel…Have I not sent you?'" (Judges 6:14).

- "The Spirit of the LORD came upon Jephthah" (Judges 11:29).

- "Samson…grew and the LORD blessed him. And the Spirit of the LORD began to move upon him" (Judges 13:24-25).

But with Deborah, there is no indication God specifically appointed her to that role. Judges 4:4 simply says, "Now Deborah, a prophetess, the wife of Lapidoth, was judging Israel at that time." When we are introduced to her, we read that she is female, and what is missed in the English translations of the Bible is a negative emphasis that appears in the original Hebrew text of this passage. Wayne Grudem writes:

> Judges 4:4 suggests some amazement at the unusual nature of the situation in which a woman actually has to judge Israel, because it piles up a string of redundant words to emphasize that Deborah is a woman. Translating the Hebrew text literally, the verse says, "And Deborah, a woman, a prophetess, the wife of Lapidoth, she was judging Israel at the time." Something is abnormal, something is wrong—there are no men to function as judge! This impression

is confirmed when we read of Barak's timidity and the rebuke he receives as well as the loss of glory he could have received.[3]

Judges 4:5 says Deborah "would sit under the palm tree...and the children of Israel came up to her for judgment." The people approached her privately. She did not publicly teach the Word of God, as was the case with Huldah and other prophetesses. Rather, Deborah is another example of a woman limited to private and individual instruction. Even when Deborah called for Barak, Judges 4:6-7 shows her speaking to him privately:

> She sent and called for Barak the son of Abinoam from Kedesh in Naphtali, and said to him, "Has not the LORD God of Israel commanded, 'Go and deploy troops at Mount Tabor; take with you ten thousand men of the sons of Naphtali and of the sons of Zebulun; and against you I will deploy Sisera, the commander of Jabin's army, with his chariots and his multitude at the River Kishon; and I will deliver him into your hand'?"

Let's note some key phrases in these verses:

- The statement "Has not the LORD God of Israel commanded?" should not be understood as Deborah giving orders to Barak. As a prophetess, Deborah received a word from God and passed it along to Barak, confirming what he already should have known—that God had commanded him to lead the army.

- The directive "Go and deploy troops" is particularly significant because Deborah was judge at the time. She was in the position typically occupied by Israel's commander. But rather than summon or command troops herself, she let Barak know that God had called him to lead.

- The phrase "against you I will deploy Sisera" clarifies God's plan for Sisera to attack Barak, not Deborah.

- "I will deliver him into your hand" indicates God wanted Barak, and not Deborah, to receive the victory over Sisera.

These are confirmations that even while serving as judge, Deborah affirmed the rightness of male leadership when it came to leading God's people, not only looking to Barak to lead but letting him know this was what God wanted. Sadly, Barak did not step up and assume the role God wanted him to fulfill. Instead, Barak told Deborah, "If you will go with me, then I will go; but if you will not go with me, I will not go!" (Judges 4:8). We recognize here that something is not right about a man telling a woman, "I will not go to battle unless you go with me."

Not surprisingly, Deborah rebuked Barak's reluctance: "I will surely go with you; nevertheless there will be no glory for you in the journey you are taking, for the LORD will sell Sisera into the hand of a woman" (Judges 4:9). Deborah's prophecy came true. God routed Sisera's army before Barak, but it was a woman, Jael, who ended up defeating the enemy commander (Judges 4:17-22). Barak should not have insisted Deborah accompany him into battle. Instead, he should have taken leadership of the army himself.

This entire account is not advocating for female leadership; instead, it is presented as a criticism of Barak. The book of Judges records some of Israel's worst days, and the absence of male leadership is a strong reflection of the time. One of the most common mistakes people make when they approach Scripture is to take a descriptive passage (or one that merely describes) and turn it into a prescriptive passage (or one that prescribes). In other words, they treat a descriptive historical account as though it is prescriptive instruction that should be followed. This is the danger of citing Deborah's judgeship as evidence for female leadership over God's people. Her example actually serves as a rebuke to the nation of Israel regarding the absence of male leadership.

Later, during another dark period in Israel's history, the prophet Isaiah asserted that when women ruled over the people, that was a sign of God's judgment: "As for My people, children are their oppressors, *and women rule over them*. O My people! Those who lead you cause you to err, and destroy the way of your paths" (Isaiah 3:12).

Neither the book of Judges nor the account of Deborah and Barak are presented as examples to follow. The book of Judges is largely an example *not* to follow, as it recounts the serious breakdown of leadership among God's people. Judges 17:6 and 21:25 offer valuable perspective to us about that time period: "In those days there was no king in Israel; everyone did what was right in his own eyes." The nation had abandoned God—that is the context in which Deborah ended up becoming a judge. And as we saw, she served that role privately and reluctantly.

Although Deborah's judgeship is not prescriptive of female leadership, is there application here for marriages? Absolutely:

- When men expect their wives to assume responsibility for taking the family to church or praying and reading the Word together as a family, they are acting like Barak. They are abandoning the role God has given them.

- When a wife is urging her husband to lead and a husband resists or prefers that his wife take charge instead, he is acting like Barak.

If Deborah is prescriptive of anything, it's that of encouraging Barak to lead and do what God desired of him. She rebuked him when he would not take charge. Note especially that when Barak refused to lead, Deborah did not take control of the situation herself. Rather, she let God direct Barak's steps and victory. Her story should motivate women to do what she did—encourage a man to lead. And Barak is prescriptive in that his example should motivate men to avoid the mistake he made—failing to lead.

THE PATTERN CONTINUES TODAY

The pattern of male leadership established at creation is maintained throughout the Old Testament and carried into the New Testament. The 12 disciples were men. Jesus could have chosen six men and six women, but He chose all men for these leadership positions. The 70 evangelists who were sent out after the 12 were all men (Luke 10:1). Again, though Jesus could have chosen 35 men and 35 women, we see that He chose all men.

In the New Testament, church elders are identified as men. Consider the qualifications for elders as stated in 1 Timothy 3:1-5: "If a *man* desires the position of a bishop, *he* desires a good work…the *husband* of one wife…one who rules *his* own house well, having *his* children in submission." We see the same when Paul discusses elders in Titus 1:6, 9: "If a *man* is blameless, the *husband* of one wife…holding fast the faithful word as *he* has been taught." When churches appoint female pastors or elders, they have rejected the teaching of God's Word. God does not recognize women in those positions because according to the scriptural pattern, only men can occupy those offices.

In 1 Timothy 2:12-14, the apostle Paul instructs: "I do not permit a woman to teach or to have authority over a man, but to be in silence. For Adam was formed first, then Eve. And Adam was not deceived, but the woman being deceived, fell into transgression." Elsewhere Paul wrote about women praying and prophesying (1 Corinthians 11:5) and teaching younger women (Titus 2:3-5); therefore, it is clear he didn't expect them to "be in silence" all the time.

Instead, when the church has both men and women present, women should take on the role of silent learner (versus teacher). Again, this has to do with authority—a woman is not to usurp the role of a male leader and put herself in a position over a man. The foundation of these verses comes from two truths we already discussed:

1. Adam was created first.

2. Eve was deceived. While it sounds as though Adam is commended for not being deceived and Eve is condemned for being deceived, the opposite is true. Eve was not as much at fault because she was deceived, while Adam was more at fault because he sinned knowingly.

You might be wondering if there are some exceptions to the principle of male leadership. Yes, there are. When I was an elementary school teacher, most of the principals I worked for were women. I submitted to their authority and did my best to serve them, the school, and my students in ways that glorified Christ. Even in the family and the church, where these verses have the clearest application, exceptions occur. In our home, when we show the children how to cook or paint, I'm happy to defer to Katie and follow her lead. One morning as we prepared to return from a family vacation, as we got ready to leave, I asked Katie how she wanted us to pack up and unload when we arrived home.

Twice a year at Woodland Christian Church the ladies' planning meeting takes place to iron out the details for the next six months' worth of events. This is a stressful and difficult job for the woman in charge. For the weeks leading up to the meeting, and during the meeting itself, I do my best to support the ladies' planning coordinator. Many of the events planned at this meeting end up being overseen by women, such as our Family Camp and Beach Camp. I try to serve the women in charge, asking them if there are any ways I can serve them, such as announcing information from the pulpit or putting signup forms in the foyer. Many of our plays have female directors. When I've been in the plays, I take my orders from women. Our vacation Bible school has often been led by a woman because most of the men are working during the day when the preparations and the event itself are taking place. I do my best to support the women in these various roles.

THE REAL QUESTION

In our gender-confused world there is objection to male headship. There is a clash in our culture with resurgent feminism creeping into the church and family, but we must hold to the clear teaching of the Bible. Sometimes people ask, "Why can't women be in leadership over men?" Let me affirm that in no way do the Bible's teachings on this matter mean that women are less worthy, less useful, or less valuable—not at all! We will see in the upcoming chapters that although women are not identical to men, they are equal to men and they have strengths that men do not have. The Bible's teachings also have nothing to do with talent. Some women are fantastic teachers and leaders, and they should use their gifts accordingly, except for in those areas where Scripture has specifically stated otherwise, as seen earlier in this chapter.

What it does have to do with is the order of creation—Adam was created first—and Eve's being deceived. Beyond that, I cannot say because those are the only two reasons Paul gives in 1 Timothy 2:13-14. The real question we should be asking is not, Why can't women lead? The real question—and it is the same question we often face in our marriages—is, What does God's Word say?

God knows what's best for all areas of life, including the family and the church. His design for marriage is the ideal.

I understand this is not an easy teaching to absorb in today's cultural climate. Habakkuk 2:4 says, "The just shall live by...faith" and Hebrews 11:6 says, "Without faith it is impossible to please [God]." When we think about walking by faith, we might imagine missionaries going overseas to dangerous parts of the world or taking on a ministry that terrifies us. But in our daily lives, walking by faith means trusting God when we don't understand His Word, or perhaps even disagree with it. Walking by faith means being willing to say, "This doesn't make sense, but I'm going to trust and obey."

This might need to be the case for you with the Bible's teaching on male leadership. As we move into the following chapters and look at what the Bible says about headship and submission in more detail, let me remind you that God knows what's best for all areas of life, including the family and the church. His design for marriage is the ideal. He wants us to have strong, healthy, joyful relationships. When we follow God's Word, we can fully enjoy the benefits and beauty that give us marriages God's way.

I want to invite you to remember this now, because in the following chapters we're going to start digging into what it looks like being a Christian husband and wife. Some of what the Bible says might be unfamiliar territory to you, contrary to what you expect, or even conflict with what you've believed up till now. Should that be the case, remind yourself that God knows best, and He wants what's best for you—especially in your marriage, because it's a picture of His Son's loving relationship to the church.

CHAPTER FIVE

The Help a Man Needs

For six straight days, God created dry land, sun, moon, stars, sea creatures, birds, and animals. At the end of each day God saw what He created and saw that it was good (Genesis 1:4, 10, 12, 18, 21, 25). But after God created Adam, for the first time in the creation account He saw something that was not good—man being alone: "The LORD God said, 'It is not good that man should be alone; I will make him a helper comparable to him'" (Genesis 2:18).

God's statement is even more interesting when we consider that Adam and Eve had not yet disobeyed Him. We do not typically think of anything being "not good" until after the fall. Because Adam had not sinned yet, it was not Adam himself who was not good. Neither was it anything he had or had not done that was not good. It was simply Adam being alone that was not good. Although there are some exceptions, such as those Paul discussed in 1 Corinthians 7,[1] let's understand why it was not—and still is not—good for man to be alone.

If man is alone, he does not have the help he needs. Leading and providing for a family is a lot of work. There is a significant load on men's shoulders, and a wife can help lighten it. This is why the apostle Paul states, "Nor was man created for woman, but woman for the man" (1 Corinthians 11:9). A lot of discouragement can come a man's way, and if he does not receive encouragement from his wife, where will he get it? Yes, there are other resources such as Scripture and relying on the Lord, but if those were all God wanted men to have, He would not have said, "I will make him a helper."

If man is alone, he cannot fulfill the second command God gave: "Be fruitful and multiply; fill the earth and subdue it" (Genesis 1:28). Children are one of God's greatest blessings.

If man is alone, he cannot enjoy the healthy desires God has given men and women to enjoy within marriage (Hebrews 13:4).[2] Some of these desires go beyond physical intimacy. God creates people as relational beings with emotional, mental, and social longings that are best fulfilled in marriage. People can serve as great friends, but they do not take the place of a spouse. For those who choose to get married, God wants them to have a steadfast companion all through life, and part of the reason He created the marriage relationship is to make that possible.

If a man is alone, he does not have the benefit of a woman's positive influence. While it is not always the case, it is common for married men to become gentler and more sensitive. After Katie and I were married, my parents frequently told me how much she influenced me for the better.

If a man is alone, he will not experience the sanctifying effects of marriage itself. God accomplishes much of the work He wants to do in our lives through marriage. After Scripture and the Holy Spirit, marriage is the greatest way God teaches us forgiveness, sacrifice, patience, dying to self, and more. When people remain single, they are more vulnerable to selfishness as they get used to living only for themselves. A married person has the obligation to care for their spouse, and this is wonderfully sanctifying.

A nice companion verse to Genesis 2:18 is Proverbs 18:22: "He who finds a wife finds a good thing, and obtains favor from the Lord." When a man receives a wife, he should understand he is not receiving a gift that is neutral or amoral. Instead, he is receiving a gift that is positive and moral. To illustrate how much of a good thing a wife is, consider God's observation when He finished creating the heavens and the earth: "God saw everything that He had made, and indeed *it was very good*. So the evening and the morning were the sixth day" (Genesis 1:31). This is the end of the sixth day, but earlier in the day, in Genesis 2:18, God observed, "[This] is not good." What had changed in between "not good" and "good"? God had created a woman. That is how much of "a good thing" a wife is. The addition of a woman can transform a situation from "not good" to "very good."

A husband should see his wife as someone who takes him from "not good" to "very good." When a wife thinks about her husband, she should see her role as helping him move from "not good" to "very good," and treat him in such a way that he can see her as "a good thing" and as "favor from the Lord." She should gladly strive to give him the help he needs and, most importantly, the help God wants him to have.

A HELPER COMPARABLE TO HIM

Some women might find it offensive to be identified as their husband's "helper," but the title does not imply that Eve was insufficient in some way. Instead, the term "helper" identifies Adam's inadequacy! In the Amplified Bible, Genesis 2:18 reads, "The Lord God said, 'It is not good (sufficient, satisfactory) that the man should be alone.'" Woman is the helper man needs because he is lacking without her. God created woman to remove man's deficiency. Marriage experts and authors Richard and Sharon Phillips explain it this way:

> To call a woman a helper is not to emphasize her weakness, but her strength. Not to label her as superfluous but as essential to Adam's condition and to God's purpose in the world. Helper is a position of dignity given to the woman by God Himself.[3]

The Hebrew word translated "helper" is *ezer*, and it means "help" or "one who helps." The word occurs 21 times in the Old Testament, including twice in Genesis 2—first in verse 18, then again in verse 20 when Adam named the animals and could not find "a helper comparable to him." In the other 19 appearances, *ezer* is never used in a negative sense. The term isn't used to speak of a sycophant, minion, or slave. Instead, it is used to describe great strength and support. Consider these verses:

- "Happy are you, O Israel! Who is like you, a people saved by the Lord, the shield of your help [*ezer*] and the sword of your majesty!" (Deuteronomy 33:29).

- "I will scatter to every wind all who are around him to help [*ezer*] him, and all his troops" (Ezekiel 12:14).

Considering these contexts, identifying a woman as her husband's *ezer* reveals her as a powerful and influential companion.

God as Our *Ezer*

We see the word *ezer* used 11 times in the Psalms. Every time, it describes God as our helper. Some examples include:

- "Our soul waits for the Lord; He is our help [*ezer*] and our shield" (Psalm 33:20).

- "Make haste to me, O God! You are my help [*ezer*] and my deliverer" (Psalm 70:5).

- "O Israel, trust in the LORD; He is their help [*ezer*] and their shield" (Psalm 115:9).

The very word used to describe a woman's role is a title that describes God Himself! Because the identification of God as our helper does not make us think less of God, we should not let it think it diminishes a woman's role as her husband's helper.

The Holy Spirit as Our Helper

In the New Testament, Jesus used the title of "Helper" in reference to the Holy Spirit when He promised not to abandon the disciples after His departure:

- "I will pray the Father, and He will give you another *Helper*" (John 14:16).

- "The *Helper*, the Holy Spirit, whom the Father will send in My name..." (John 14:26).

- "It is to your advantage that I go away; for if I do not go away, the *Helper* will not come to you" (John 16:7).

What a privilege for women to carry the same title Jesus gave to the Holy Spirit! The title of *ezer* or helper is not one of inferiority but of honor.

The Commendable Nature of Helping

Biblically speaking, helping and serving are two of the most admirable actions we can engage in as Christians. Jesus modeled such behavior and called His followers to do the same:

> Whoever desires to become great among you, let him be your servant. And whoever desires to be first among you, let him be your slave—just as the Son of Man did not come to be served, but to serve, and to give His life a ransom for many (Matthew 20:26-28).

Few actions are commanded as often in Scripture or look more like Christ than helping and serving. As a result, wives should find it encouraging to be called their husbands' helpers. They should not let society's stereotypes influence their thinking. Instead, they should joyfully embrace the role God has given them. Well-known author and speaker on marriage Nancy Campbell says,

> [Ladies] are you feeling base and discouraged? Don't listen to these lies any longer. Lift up your head and embrace your mandate from God. You are not working for any earthly employer, but for the King of kings and Lord of lords, the Sovereign God of the universe. When He calls you a helper you can hold your head high.[4]

HELP SUITED TO THE HUSBAND

You would think that if God called wives to be helpers, He would have provided specific instructions on how to help! But interestingly, there is no list in Scripture telling wives how to fulfill this role. I suspect this is because every man is unique. Every husband has different strengths and weaknesses, which makes it impossible to absolutely say how a wife should help because men will want—and need—help in different ways.

Some men love to cook and enjoy taking on that responsibility. For men who struggle just making toast, they will find it helpful if their wives do the cooking. Some men could not balance a checkbook if their lives depended on it, and for those men, it will be helpful if their wives handled the finances. For other couples, the wives feel better about letting their husbands oversee the budget. The important point about being a helper is that wives have the opportunity to learn what their husbands need, then strive to help in those ways.

Let me share an example from my own life. Much of my ministry revolves around preaching, and Sunday's sermon receives significant attention. I go over the message twice each week with Katie, and her feedback greatly improves it. She is a godly woman who knows the Word well, so she makes wonderful contributions. A weakness I had when I started pastoring was sharing a lot of technical information in my sermons, but little in the way of application. My wife has helped me in this area by regularly asking, "What does this have to do with our lives? How is this going to challenge us in the different roles we find ourselves?"

Katie has also helped me to speak more clearly, letting me know when something I say is confusing. I might respond, "This is what I was trying to say," and she will say, "That's not how it sounded before. What you just said makes more sense." Because of this feedback, I often say from the pulpit, "When I was going over the sermon with Katie…" The congregation knows how much Katie helps me, so I often hear people say, "You two make a great team." And they're right! I am a better preacher because of the time and effort Katie has committed to going over my sermons with me.

While your husband probably isn't a preacher, the principle is still the same. As a wife, you want to look for the unique areas in which your strengths can complement your husband's needs and weaknesses.

Hopefully, a wife will be committed to helping her husband even if the way she helps is not something she enjoys doing. Consider what happens when children say they want to help. When we give them suggestions for what they can do, they sometimes respond, "I would rather do this instead." As a result, the children end up not being much help at all. Unfortunately, some wives have a similar attitude. They say they want to help their husbands, but only if they can do something they enjoy doing. Wives who have this attitude can end up not being much help to their husbands.

HELPING IS A TWO-WAY STREET

One of the most common complaints I hear from wives is "My husband doesn't communicate with me!" Wives are not mind readers, and husbands are notorious for giving short and sometimes ambiguous answers. Plenty of wives who desire to be good helpers cannot do so because they don't know what their husbands want. Husbands can help their wives tremendously by communicating with them clearly and more frequently. I will say it like this: Husband, help your wife be your helper by letting her know how she can help you.

Also, just because God graciously gave Adam a wife to complement him and help meet his needs does not mean that a wife should endlessly serve her husband while he does not lift a finger. Though Scripture identifies wives as helpers, husbands are also to help their wives. There may even be times when a husband is called to take over some of his wife's responsibilities.

Katie has a condition called *hyperemesis gravidarum*, which means she gets extremely sick during pregnancy. During this season, Katie can barely get out of bed some mornings, much less care for five other children eight and under. We homeschool, so they need their work supervised. Our youngest child needs to be watched so she does not fall down the stairs, put something in her mouth that she should not, or find herself crushed when her older brothers wrestle with each other.

By God's grace, my job has a flexible schedule. On those days (or weeks) when Katie's sickness is worst, I stay home in the morning and work later in the evenings. I also take over several of Katie's everyday responsibilities. Every time I "play mom," I am reminded of how hard my wife works, and this causes me to be very thankful for her.

WHAT DOES A WIFE'S HELP LOOK LIKE PRACTICALLY?

Just as the curse was pronounced on Adam's work, it also was pronounced on Eve's labors. God's Word reveals the two areas in which He primarily wants women invested. In Genesis 3:16, He said to Eve, "I will greatly multiply your sorrow and your conception; in pain you shall bring forth children; your desire shall be for your husband, and he shall rule over you." In this passage, God mentioned a woman's children and husband because this is where most of her time and energy are committed and needed. This pattern continues all through Scripture: When God speaks about a wife's calling in life, her husband, children, and home are emphasized. For example, 1 Timothy 2:15 says women "will be saved in childbearing if they continue in faith, love, and holiness, with self-control." We know from other passages in Scripture that this doesn't mean women are *spiritually* saved by having children. So what does it mean that women "will be saved in childbearing"?

First, raising children is the primary sphere of ministry in which married women serve the Lord and work out their salvation. Second, in this verse, "saved" is used synonymously with sanctified. Any mother can tell you raising children is sanctifying! Is there any other occupation that teaches patience, gentleness, self-denial, and self-sacrifice more than mothering? My wife says nothing in her life causes her to cling to the Lord and trust Him more than caring for our children. This is one of the reasons children are a blessing (Psalm 127:3).

Several verses in Scripture encourage married women to focus on the care of their homes:

- "The wise woman *builds her house*" (Proverbs 14:1).

- "I desire that the younger widows marry, bear children, *manage the house*" (1 Timothy 5:14).

- "Older women…admonish the young women to love their husbands, to love their children, to be discreet, chaste, *homemakers*" (Titus 2:3-5).

Our culture diminishes the value of a woman caring for her home, but because Scripture emphasizes it so much, we can tell it's important to God. Keeping this in mind helps us appreciate the value of homemaking because value is determined by God. Even if homemaking is despised in the world's eyes, if it's important to God, then it is important regardless of what anyone else says. The woman who cares for her home is doing something that pleases God and has spiritual and eternal value.

This isn't to say a woman can *only* care for her home, family, and children. While these are a woman's primary sphere of influence, this doesn't mean they are her only realms of influence, as we'll see later in the chapter.

Important Considerations

Life does not always go the way we expect. I have known couples who would like the wife to be able to stay home, but economic realities, an injured husband, or a financial emergency required the wife to bring in some income. Some women don't have husbands because they never married or they are widowed. Their greatest desire might be staying home, but they find it necessary to work so they can provide for themselves and their children.

A young wife might long to have children, but perhaps she's been unable to get pregnant. She takes good care of her home and husband, but she still has enough time to do some work outside the home. She is willing to do so and is able to contribute to the income without neglecting her other responsibilities.

Then there is the very difficult dilemma faced by a single mother. She might want more than anything to have a husband who provides for her and her child so she can stay home. But the most responsible thing for her to do is work to care for herself and her child.

Women who find themselves in these and other situations should never be made to feel condemned because, given their circumstances, the best way for them to honor God and care for their families (or themselves) is by working outside the home.

Don't Despise the Day of Small Things

Let me share an account from the Old Testament that I hope will encourage wives. When the Babylonians conquered the southern kingdom of Judah in 586 BC, they destroyed the temple in Jerusalem. They then took most of the Jews into exile in Babylon.

Decades later, King Cyrus of Persia permitted the Jews to return to their land and rebuild the temple. Keep in mind that some of these exiles had seen Solomon's temple before it was destroyed. When the people laid the foundation for the new temple, "many of the priests and Levites and heads of the fathers' houses, old men who had seen the first temple, wept with a loud voice when the foundation of this temple was laid before their eyes" (Ezra 3:12). They wept because they thought the new temple wouldn't compare with the previous one. God rebuked them with two questions He asked through the prophets:

- Haggai asked, "Who is left among you who saw this temple in its former glory? And how do you see it now? In comparison with it, is this not in your eyes as nothing?... The glory of this latter temple shall be greater than the former" (Haggai 2:3, 9). In man's eyes, the new temple was inferior to Solomon's temple, but in God's eyes, it would be greater.

- Zechariah asked, "Who has despised the day of small things? For these seven rejoice to see the plumb line in the hand of Zerubbabel. They are the eyes of the LORD, which scan to and fro throughout the whole earth" (Zechariah 4:10).

When the prophet wrote, "These seven...are the eyes of the Lord," he wasn't saying God has seven eyes. Rather, in Scripture, seven is the number of completion, and here, the prophet refers to God's omniscience or complete knowledge, which allows Him to see "throughout the whole earth." A "plumb line" is a builder's tool, and God "rejoiced" to see it in the hand of Zerubbabel, the Jews' leader. As the Jews rebuilt the temple, they "despised" it as a "day of small things," but in God's eyes, the work was great enough to cause Him to "rejoice."

This applies to all of us. We may find ourselves despising what God wants us to do by viewing our work as small things. When that happens, we should encourage ourselves with Zechariah's words to the Jews. God rejoices in the seemingly small. We shouldn't despise the things that cause God to rejoice, for that means they aren't small! They're great because they please Him and bring Him joy. A calling or task is great when it brings God pleasure.

We find similar examples of this in the New Testament. In the parable of the talents, the master commended the first two workers, saying to them, "Well done, good and faithful servant; you were faithful over *a few things*, I will make you ruler over many things. Enter into the joy of your lord" (Matthew 25:21;

see also verse 23). Similarly, in the parable of the minas, the master said, "Well done, good servant; because you were faithful in *a very little*, have authority over ten cities" (Luke 19:17). Note that in both parables, the master didn't commend faithfulness over great things. Instead, he rewarded faithfulness over "very little" and "few things." These small areas of faithfulness might seem insignificant from an earthly perspective, but because the workers pleased the master, they brought him joy, and earned wonderful rewards.

God rejoices in the seemingly small...
A calling or task is great when it brings God pleasure.

What does this have to do with wives helping? When wives focus on caring for their homes and families, their lives might seem to be filled with small, despised things such as laundry, meals, and cleaning. If God has called women to do these things, then they aren't small to Him, which means they shouldn't be considered small to us. Women will find themselves tempted to pursue the things that seem great from an earthly perspective, but they're doing great things when they do what is great in God's eyes: care for their husbands and homes. J.R. Miller said, "The woman who makes a sweet, beautiful home, filling it with love and prayer and purity, is doing something better than anything else her hands could find to do beneath the skies."[5]

THE VIRTUOUS WIFE

A well-known passage reveals what it means—and does not mean—biblically for a wife to be her husband's helper. Proverbs 31 includes a portrait of what is commonly known as the virtuous wife. One might say this is a description of the ideal woman. Interestingly, these verses were written in a cultural context when women were not only legal possessions of men, but their sphere of influence traditionally did not extend beyond the home and raising children. As a result, this passage's description of the attributes of a virtuous woman can help us to break out of stereotypes that are often perpetuated about women's roles.

Verses 11-12 say, "The heart of her husband safely trusts her; so he will have no lack of gain. She does him good and not evil all the days of her life." This husband trusts her in more ways than one. He knows she works hard and does not need someone looking over her shoulder to ensure she is making good use of her time or the family's finances. He also trusts her faithfulness to him, knowing she is the opposite of the adulterous wife in Proverbs 7:10-23, who entices the foolish young man with the temptation, "My husband is not at home." The husband of a virtuous woman has "no lack of gain" because, as his helper, she works hard to "[do] him good."

The rest of the passage elaborates on the ways a virtuous wife does good for (or helps) not only her husband, but also her family and others. Proverbs 31:13-16 describes her activities:

> She seeks wool and flax, and willingly works with her hands. She is like the merchant ships, she brings her food from afar. She also rises while it is yet night, and provides food for her household, and a portion for her maidservants. She considers a field and buys it; from her profits she plants a vineyard.

She gathers materials to help her family. She is diligent with her hands and journeys to secure the best food for her loved ones. Her hardworking nature is shown in the way she gets up before dawn to have food prepared not just for her family, but also for the servants. She is industrious and resourceful; she buys a field and then reinvests the profits to make more money. This is important because it shows that women can engage in work that provides for their families financially. Simply put, men are not the only ones who can earn money.

The passage then elaborates on other ways this woman helps her family, the poor, and herself. Proverbs 31:17-22 states:

> She girds herself with strength, and strengthens her arms. She perceives that her merchandise is good, and her lamp does not go out by night…She extends her hand to the poor, yes, she reaches out her hands to the needy. She is not afraid of snow for her household, for all her household is clothed with scarlet. She makes tapestry for herself; her clothing is fine linen and purple.

This virtuous woman's hardworking nature enabled her to be strong and healthy. Everything she made for her family, such as food and clothing, was of high quality, and she was willing to work late into the night to make these provisions. Her inventory was large enough to help those in poverty. She anticipated her family's needs and made sure they were met. While providing for others, she did not neglect to provide high-quality possessions for herself.

Verse 24 continues, "She makes linen garments and sells them, and supplies sashes for the merchants." That is, her efforts bless many. Note especially that while she was working for the benefit of others, she was careful to keep her home a priority: "She watches over the ways of her household, and does not eat the bread of idleness" (verse 27).

The virtuous wife is a skilled homemaker, yet at the same time is able to be engaged in industrious activities outside the home. In the New Testament, we find two examples of godly women working:

- Lydia "was a seller of purple...who worshiped God" (Acts 16:14).

- Priscilla and her husband Aquila "were tentmakers" (Acts 18:3).

How do we reconcile these two investments of time and energy for women—working and homemaking—that seem to be at odds with each other? The simple answer is women worked without neglecting the care of their families. They probably performed many of these activities from their homes. Whatever work a wife does should still allow her to care for her home and help her husband. These are her most important ministries; therefore, they should never suffer from anything she engages in.

THREE THREATS TO A WIFE AS A HELPER

There are three major threats that can prevent a wife from being the helper God desires for her to be.

Threat One: Pursuit of Wealth

The wealth a wife accumulates while caring for herself and her family is not a threat. Instead, the threat is the *pursuit* of wealth that comes from keeping up with neighbors or pursuing a more upscale lifestyle than necessary or can be afforded. While it's reasonable for women to work for the reasons previously mentioned, it's unreasonable for them to work for selfish pursuits that cause them to neglect their home and husband. No godly woman will look back and say,

- "I'm so glad we got this bigger house, even though it meant hardly seeing my children."

- "This extra income has been such a blessing, even though it meant late nights away from my husband."

- "I'm so thankful for that promotion, even though it meant rarely being home."

Threat Two: Idleness

First Timothy 5:13 warns women against being "idle, wandering about from house to house, and not only idle but also gossips and busybodies, saying things which they ought not." The Proverbs 31 woman is the opposite of what Paul described—she's busy with her own house and her own family's affairs rather than the houses or affairs of others.

Even when women are at home, idleness can still cause them to neglect their husband, children, or home. They must be intentional to ensure they aren't overly invested in frivolous activities. There are plenty of ways women can waste their time, and you'll know best where your time wasters are if you ask God to reveal them to you.

There are many activities Scripture doesn't forbid, yet engaging in them prohibits women from paying sufficient attention to the priorities God has given them. Though the Proverbs 31 woman engaged in several activities that could be called hobbies, we can see that those pursuits benefited her family.

Threat Three: Misplaced Self-Worth

Some women don't find the same satisfaction caring for their homes, husbands, and children that they find in the workplace. Money, promotions, praise, and the opportunity to compete with men can appeal to their sense of self-worth. While on the surface these might seem good things, we need to remember where Scripture places its emphasis with regard to a married woman's calling. What seems to us to be small things are great in God's eyes, which also means that what seems great in our eyes can be small in God's eyes. What does God value most?

Romans 12:2 says, "Do not be conformed to this world, but be transformed by the renewing of your mind, that you may prove what is that good and acceptable and perfect will of God." God has informed us, in Scripture, about His "good and acceptable and perfect will." We've seen passages that affirm the greatness of a woman as a helper who cares for her home and children as well as affirm that a virtuous woman can pursue business interests outside the home. Because both are possible, it's vital for us to remember what is of greatest value to God so a woman's self-worth isn't misplaced.

Biblically speaking, women have allowed themselves to become conformed to this world when they work outside the home for these reasons:

- They believe focusing on home and family gives them less value.

- They assume their self-worth is based on work pursuits and not caring for their home and family.

- They feel that caring for their home and family doesn't allow them to experience the fulfillment they crave.

When any of these perspectives affect a woman's thinking, she has been influenced more by the world than by Scripture. When that happens, she will want to renew her mind by reading God's Word and letting it shape her thinking, as urged in Romans 12:2.

When a married woman fulfills God's priorities for her, she will receive her greatest sense of value. When she focuses on being a helper, she will experience her greatest sense of self-worth. The married woman who is humbly fulfilling the role and responsibilities God has called her to should feel more valuable than if she were a company's CEO.

Although our culture is quick to put a positive light on women climbing the corporate ladder, research suggests there are many women working outside the home who are finding less satisfaction in their jobs and are longing to return to their families.

Researcher Daniele Lup, a senior lecturer in quantitative sociology at Middlesex University, studied ten years of data from thousands of male and female employees who were promoted to upper- and lower-management roles. She concluded that men reported an increase in job satisfaction after being promoted, but women experienced significantly less satisfaction when they were promoted.[6] This was true even in corporate America.

In 2009, the IZA Institute of Labor Economics published "The Paradox of Declining Female Happiness."[7] The study found that in the 1970s, women rated their overall life satisfaction higher than men. Since then, with more women working outside the home, the women's scores have continually decreased while men's scores stayed around the same. By the 1990s, women were unhappier than men even though their salaries went from earning less than 60 percent of a man's median salary to earning more 75 percent of it. In other words, even while women continued to seek satisfaction in the business world and experienced greater success, their happiness headed in the other direction.

This serves as confirmation that true fulfillment is found not in following culture's expectations, but God's design.

PRAISE FOR SUCH A HELPER

How does the virtuous wife's family react to her? Proverbs 31:28-29 says, "Her children rise up and call her blessed; her husband also, and he praises her: 'Many daughters have done well, but you excel them all.'" There are not many satisfactions a woman can enjoy more than receiving her husband and children's praise for her diligence in caring for them!

Verse 30 goes on to say, "Charm is deceitful and beauty is passing, but a woman who fears the LORD, she shall be praised." Of all that can be said about the virtuous wife, this is the highest compliment, indicating she is as strong and impressive spiritually as she is in all the other areas of life. Her character outweighs her industriousness or business expertise. Holiness and godliness are of greater importance—and deserve more respect—than any amount of charisma, natural talent, or physical beauty.

Proverbs 31 concludes with verse 31: "Give her of the fruit of her hands, and let her own works praise her in the gates." While this passage is instructive for women, it is a strong admonition to husbands to praise their wives when they pursue excellence in their labors. Women who have done so much for others should, in turn, be thanked and rewarded for what they have done.

In our day, the reference to "praise her in the gates" might be like putting a notice in a public place, such as the local newspaper, a community bulletin board, or social media. In Bible days, the gates were where the leaders of the city sat in session and where the news and commerce were distributed. Earlier in the passage, we were told that the virtuous wife's husband "is known in the gates, when he sits among the elders of the land" (verse 23). He is a well-known leader in the community and, by implication, part of his good reputation results from his wife's good reputation. But a loving husband does not merely bask in his wife's good reputation. The implication here is that he openly brags about her to others because of the wonderful helper she is. We husbands should never complain about our wives, but rather, make a point to praise them to others.

Despite what the world preaches and promotes, let's keep in mind that in God's eyes, women who care for their homes and families serve an incredibly valuable role. What seems small in the world's eyes is often great in God's eyes. Women can have a very powerful influence on their husband, children, and many others beyond their immediate family. Every work that they do that pleases the Lord will bless the people in her life and will have eternal consequences.

CHAPTER SIX

Consequences of the Fall for Husbands and Wives

During college I participated in Army ROTC, which means I was just like other students on the university campus except that I also received leadership training and took military science classes. Upon graduating, I was commissioned as an armor (tank) officer. Because I was in a combat arms branch, which is one of the most likely to engage in battle, I was trained to look for an enemy's weaknesses. After the military, I taught elementary school and coached wrestling and football teams. During this time, I did my best to train my athletes to determine their opponent's weaknesses.

I mention all this because the devil used this same approach when he successfully convinced Adam and Eve to sin! Mankind's first temptation involved the serpent attacking Adam's recently established headship in his relationship with Eve. Genesis 3:1-4 says:

> Now the serpent was more cunning than any beast of the field which the LORD God had made. And he *said to the woman*, "Has God indeed said, 'You shall not eat of every tree of the garden'?"
>
> And the woman said to the serpent, "We may eat the fruit of the trees of the garden; but of the fruit of the tree which is in the midst of the garden, God has said, 'You shall not eat it, nor shall you touch it, lest you die.'"
>
> Then the serpent *said to the woman*, "You will not surely die."

Note an important contrast here between the creation account in Genesis 2 and the fall in Genesis 3:

- In Genesis 2:16, "the LORD God *commanded the man.*"

- In Genesis 3:1 and 4, "[the serpent] *said to the woman.*"

God spoke to Adam, but the devil spoke to Eve. Why? The devil saw a weakness. He knew Adam had received the command from God, but Eve had received it from Adam. Part of the reason God placed Eve under Adam's headship was for her own protection.

When the devil tempted Eve, she had two choices:

- She could trust her husband, who had given her God's command, and submit to him.

- She could trust the devil, which meant submitting to him.

Genesis 3:6 reveals her choice, which, as we now know, had severe consequences: "When the woman saw that the tree was good for food, that it was pleasant to the eyes, and a tree desirable to make one wise, she took of its fruit and ate. She also gave to her husband with her, and he ate."

At this point, Adam also had two choices:

- He could obey God, who gave him the command, and submit to Him.

- He could obey his wife, which meant submitting to her instead.

We all know what happened, and Genesis 3:9-12 details for us the devastating outcome of that decision:

> The LORD God *called to Adam* and said to him, "Where are you?"
>
> So he said, "I heard Your voice in the garden, and I was afraid because I was naked; and I hid myself."
>
> And He said, "Who told you that you were naked? Have you eaten from the tree of which I commanded you that you should not eat?"
>
> Then the man said, "The woman whom You gave to be with me, she gave me of the tree, and I ate."

It is significant that this conversation about the fall took place between God and Adam. God did not address Eve until Genesis 3:16, where He explained how sin's curse would affect women. God went to Adam because he was the head of the relationship; therefore, as the New Testament reveals, God held him more responsible for the fall:

- Romans 5:12-19—"Through *one man* sin entered the world…death reigned *from Adam*…the transgression of *Adam*…by the *one man's offense* many died…by *one man's offense* death reigned…through *one man's offense* judgment came…by *one man's disobedience*."
- 1 Corinthians 15:21-22—"By *man* came death…In *Adam* all die."

Because Eve sinned first, we would expect to read that sin and death entered the world through her, but God placed the blame squarely on Adam's shoulders. Why? As the recipient of God's command and the head of the relationship, Adam had higher accountability. So how does all this apply to husbands and wives?

- Wives should consider how poorly it went for Eve when she stepped out from under Adam's headship. While staying under a husband's headship is no guarantee everything will go perfectly, wives can be encouraged that this is God's design for their own best interests and safety. This places wives in positions for God to work through and bless their obedience.

- Husbands should consider that even though Eve made the initial wrong choice, the sobering fact is that God still held Adam responsible! This is a warning to all husbands regarding the accountability God has placed on their shoulders. When God confronted Adam, Adam tried to blame Eve (Genesis 3:12). But that did not work for Adam, and it does not work today for husbands to blame their wives when things go wrong. As the God-appointed head of the relationship, the husband is responsible for what takes place in his marriage and home.

THE RESULTS OF ADAM AND EVE'S DISOBEDIENCE

Prior to the fall, Adam and Eve lived in perfect harmony with each other. But when sin entered the world, conflict came as well. The fall affected both sides of the marriage relationship. Before banishing Adam and Eve from the Garden of Eden, God revealed what their relationship would be like in a fallen world. Genesis 3:16-17 records what would happen:

> To the woman He said: "I will greatly multiply your sorrow and your conception; in pain you shall bring forth children; *your desire shall be for your husband, and he shall rule over you.*"

> Then to Adam He said, "*Because you have heeded the voice of your wife,* and have eaten from the tree of which I commanded you, saying, 'You shall not eat of it…'"

The italicized words identify the three specific struggles—or temptations—husbands and wives would face as a result of their fallenness. Let's look at each of them.

A Wife's Temptation to Control Her Husband

The phrase "your desire shall be for your husband" refers to a wife's desire to control her husband. Before the fall, Eve would have willingly and eagerly submitted to Adam, but in her fallen state, she would find herself wanting to resist his headship and control him instead.

How do we know this is what is the verse is saying? First, this is a curse and not a blessing. Thus it cannot mean wives are going to love their husbands or desire them in any positive way. Second, a basic rule of Bible interpretation is to determine the meaning of words by looking at their use elsewhere in Scripture. Whenever possible, an example from the same book of the Bible is preferred, because often the author and time of writing will be the same for both uses of a word. The Hebrew word translated "desire" is *teshuwqah,* and it occurs only three times in Scripture—twice in Genesis and once in Song of Solomon 7:10: "I am my beloved's, and his desire [*teshuwqah*] is toward me."

For our purposes, let us consider the second usage of *teshuwqah* in Genesis, just one chapter later. The word is used shortly before Adam and Eve's firstborn son, Cain, murdered his brother, Abel:

> Abel also brought of the firstborn of his flock and of their fat. And the LORD respected Abel and his offering, but He did not respect Cain and his offering. And Cain was very angry, and his countenance fell.

> So the LORD said to Cain, "Why are you angry? And why has your countenance fallen? If you do well, will you not be accepted? And if you do not do well, sin lies at the door. And *its desire* [*teshuwqah*] *is for you,* but you should rule over it."

Now Cain talked with Abel his brother; and it came to pass, when they were in the field, that Cain rose up against Abel his brother and killed him (Genesis 4:4-8).

When God rejected Cain's offering, Cain faced the two choices we all face when rebuked: (1) be humble, repent, and do what is right, or (2) be prideful, angry, and pout. The latter allows sin to remain in our lives. As God graciously warns Cain about what sin wants to do to him, the parallelism with Genesis 3:16 is obvious:

- Genesis 3:16—"Your desire [*teshuwqah*] shall be for your husband, and he shall rule [*mashal*] over you."

- Genesis 4:7—"[Sin's] desire [*teshuwqah*] is for you, but you should rule [*mashal*] over it."

What kind of "desire" did sin have for Cain? Was it gentle, supportive, and affectionate? No, it was the desire sin has for everyone—to control mind and actions. God told Cain he needed to rule over sin, but Cain failed to obey God, and instead, he let sin control him so much that he murdered his brother. The application is this: Just as sin had a desire to control Cain, God warned Eve in Genesis 3:16 that wives will have a desire to control their husbands.

A Husband's Temptation to Dominate His Wife

In Genesis 3:16, we are also introduced to a struggle husbands face: "And he shall rule over you." This may sound as though God is establishing authority in the marriage relationship, but we have already seen that headship was established before the fall. So what is God communicating with these words? He is describing what women would have to endure because of the curse. Just as God pointed out the "desire" women would have to control their husbands, so He also pointed out the temptation men would have to dominate their wives.

As a result of the fall, the Battle of the Sexes will forever plague the marriage relationship. On one side, the conflict has led women to desire to control their husbands and reject their headship. On the other side is men being harsh, cruel, and dictatorial. Genesis 3:16 could be understood as a prophecy that wives will have to resist wanting to control their husbands, and husbands will have to resist being tyrants to their wives.

A Husband's Temptation to Fail to Lead

Another temptation husbands face is mentioned in Genesis 3:17: "Because you have heeded the voice of your wife…" When Adam and Eve sinned, they both violated God's divine pattern for marriage by reversing their roles:

- Eve usurped her husband's authority by acting independently of him and ignoring the command God had communicated to him.

- Adam abandoned his appointed role as leader by submitting to Eve instead of to God.

While it's true that many husbands struggle with the temptation to be domineering, at the same time, they can also be too passive—that is, not lead at all. Both temptations have serious consequences. It is terrible for men to mistreat their wives by being pushy and cruel, but it is also terrible for men to mistreat their wives by failing to lead.

So which temptation do men surrender to most commonly? That varies widely according to culture. In parts of the world where women still rank as little more than a possession, cruelty is a more common sin. While there are many abusive men in Western nations where both men and women can claim legal protections, the more common temptation seems to be passivity and spiritual laziness.

Why is this the case? A likely answer is this: In our Western culture, both secular society and the church rightly consider it unacceptable for men to be cruel to women. But it is generally considered acceptable, even within Christian circles, for men to be passive when it comes to leading in the home and the church.

I witnessed a particularly unhappy illustration of this some years back when a married man began attending our church without his wife. I learned that she attended a different church, where she occupied a position of leadership and teaching over men and women. He shared, "I would like her to go to church with me, but she won't. Will you speak with her and convince her to embrace a biblical view of marriage?"

We began counseling sessions, but when I shared the Bible passages that instruct wives to submit to their husbands, she would argue and justify not having to obey Scripture. During that time, the wife's authoritarian personality put her at odds with the church she was attending, so she began accompanying her husband to our church. When I began preaching the same series on marriage that I am presenting in this book, she grew so frustrated that her husband told me, "My wife wants to leave the church."

I encouraged him to lead in his marriage, but they left a few months later. The situation could have been avoided if either of them had chosen to obey Scripture. Instead, a passive man would not lead, and a rebellious woman would not submit.

Sadly, their situation parallels what happened in the Garden of Eden. Adam abdicated his leadership role, and Eve usurped his authority. The couple's dilemma also illustrates what can happen to a marriage when the husband and wife fail in their roles. Frustration and regret will inevitably result.

The Need for Leadership

Ultimately, it is impossible for someone *not* to lead. The only way for nobody to lead is for both spouses to make no decisions and to do nothing. Yet if a couple wants to do something, no matter how small or insignificant, *someone* must take the initiative and get things moving in a certain direction. If a man prefers to be passive and lazy, someone will step into the leadership role, and that usually ends up being the wife.

Because the concept of male headship receives so much criticism from society, and sometimes even from within the church, you would expect the most common complaint from women to be "My husband wants to lead and I hate it. It is so barbaric and chauvinistic. He acts like such a dictator." In reality, the frustration I hear more often is just the opposite: "My husband won't lead. I wish he wasn't so passive!"

God originally created women to desire a strong leader. Because of the fall, women struggle against male headship. Yet a Christian woman—as she seeks to follow God—possesses deep within a longing that craves a spiritual man she can follow.

The Consequences of a Lack of Leadership

One of the purposes of the Old Testament is that it provides examples for us to learn from—it serves as a backdrop for New Testament instructions. Consider these verses:

- Romans 15:4—"Whatever things were written before [that is, the Old Testament] were written for our learning, that we through the patience and comfort of the Scriptures might have hope."

- 1 Corinthians 10:11—"All these things happened to them as examples, and they were written for our admonition, upon whom the ends of the ages have come."

This includes guidance on the topic of marriage. As we continue our way through this book, we will look at individuals in the Old Testament who can help us discover practical applications for New Testament commands. Some of these people will serve as positive examples through their obedience, while others will serve as negative examples through their disobedience.

Abraham's Failure

Along with Adam, Scripture provides two other instructive examples of men who gave in to the temptation to succumb to their wives' control.

The first is Abraham, whom God promised would be the father of a nation (Genesis 12:2). When God promises you a child, how long do you expect to wait? About nine months. So Abraham and Sarah could hardly have expected decades to pass before God fulfilled His promise. Because so much time was passing, Sarah became doubtful and succumbed to unbelief. This, in turn, led her to a desire to control her husband:

> Now Sarai, Abram's wife, had borne him no children. And she had an Egyptian maidservant whose name was Hagar. So Sarai said to Abram, "See now, the LORD has restrained me from bearing children. Please, go in to my maid; perhaps I shall obtain children by her." And *Abram heeded the voice of Sarai* (Genesis 16:1-2).

Do these words sound familiar?

- Genesis 3:17—"Then to Adam He said, "Because you heeded [*shama*] the voice [*qowl*] of your wife."

- Genesis 16:2—"Abram heeded [*shama*] the voice [*qowl*] of Sarai."

Abraham faced the same two choices Adam faced: obey God, or obey his wife. Instead of leading as God commanded, Abraham submitted to Sarah—just as Adam had done to Eve. The consequence was conflict between Hagar's son Ishmael and Abraham's God-designated heir, Isaac—a conflict that has continued for thousands of years between their descendants and plagues our planet to this very day.

Ahab's Failure

The second example is Ahab, a king of Israel, and his wife, Jezebel, a wicked and tyrannical queen who imposed Baal worship on the Israelite people. Ahab was just as wicked as her, but he was also spineless. He wanted a vineyard that belonged to a godly man named Naboth. Even though Ahab offered Naboth a substantial amount of money and a better vineyard, Naboth declined (1 Kings 21:3).

This sent Ahab home pouting. When he told Jezebel what was wrong, she had an immediate solution: "You now exercise authority over Israel! Arise, eat food, and let your heart be cheerful; I will give you the vineyard of Naboth the Jezreelite" (verse 7). Tragically, Jezebel had Naboth murdered. When Jezebel informed Ahab of her success, he jumped into his chariot and gleefully rushed to take possession of the property (verses 8-15).

Because Jezebel had Naboth murdered, would God hold Ahab responsible? The prophet Elijah gave the answer when he caught up to Ahab at Naboth's vineyard: "Thus says the LORD: '*Have you murdered* and also taken possession?...In the place where dogs licked the blood of Naboth, dogs shall lick your blood, even yours'" (verse 19). Yes, God held Ahab responsible for Naboth's murder—even though Jezebel was the one who gave the command. This is consistent with the way God held Adam responsible for eating the forbidden fruit—even though Eve ate first and seemed more responsible because she ate first and gave the fruit to Adam.

Ahab and Jezebel's marriage is summarized in 1 Kings 21:25: "There was no one like Ahab who sold himself to do wickedness in the sight of the LORD, *because Jezebel his wife stirred him up*." This summary should serve as a sobering reminder to husbands and wives:

- Jezebel shows wives the great influence they can have on their husbands. Women can stir up their husbands for evil (as Jezebel did) or for good.

- Husbands should notice that even though Jezebel influenced Ahab to wickedness, God still held Ahab responsible for the results. Whether it is Adam, Abraham, or Ahab, God appointed men to lead, and they cannot turn around and say, "My wife made me do it." God holds a man responsible for how he responds to his wife's influence.

EMPOWERED BY GOD'S GRACE

Before the fall, God called man to lead. If the fall had never taken place, Eve would have been able to submit to Adam's leadership with joy and humility, and

Adam would have been able to lead with perfect love, compassion, and kindness. After the fall, a husband is still expected to lead, and a wife is still expected to submit, but now there is conflict instead of peace. Husbands and wives were designed to be lifelong companions living in perfect harmony, but the sinful desires at work in us try to destroy what God has "joined" (Genesis 2:24). The curse has turned God's ordained roles into struggles that are spurred by pride, selfishness, and self-will. How can a marriage survive this kind of conflict?

---

*God doesn't command us without giving us
the necessary grace to fulfill His calling.*

There is good news! The gospel works in our hearts, transforming us into the husbands and wives God desires us to be. We have been given a guide in the Word that reveals God's design apart from the effects of the fall. His power enables…

- harsh and passive men to become loving, godly leaders.

- controlling, manipulative women to become gentle and respectful.

If we had to obey God's commands in our own effort, we would be discouraged and defeated because it's not possible. But if we remember that God's grace enables us to obey, we can be encouraged: "God is able to make all grace abound toward you, that you, always having all sufficiency in all things, may have an abundance for every good work" (2 Corinthians 9:8). God doesn't command us without giving us the necessary grace to fulfill His calling. As has been said before, "God does not call the equipped. He equips the called." He is with us, providing for us and enabling us. His grace has the glorious effect of producing obedience.

In the chapters that follow, we will look in detail at God's commands for husbands and wives and see how we can apply them to experience marriages such as God intended for Adam and Eve—and all their descendants, including us—before the fall. While you read, keep in mind that God's grace empowers you to obey: "It is God who works in you both to will and to do for His good pleasure" (Philippians 2:13).

PART THREE

UNDERSTANDING LOVE

CHAPTER SEVEN

What Is Love?

---

hat are a few things I love? I love my kids, eating popcorn, and teaching the Bible. Another man might say, "I love my wife, football, and working on my car." For this man's wife's sake, let's hope he loves his wife differently than he loves football and automobiles. For my kids' sake, let's hope I love them differently than I love eating popcorn.

Have you ever noticed that the English word *love* can be used in a wide variety of ways that fail to distinguish between different shades of meaning? Obviously, the love we have for things we enjoy is different than the love we experience in relationships. Even within our relationships, the kinds of love we experience will vary significantly. We love our parents differently than we love our spouse, and we love our children differently than we love our pastor, fellow church members, or coworkers.

Within a marriage relationship, what kind of love should a husband have for his wife? Or a wife for her husband? What does such love look like? If we are to obey God's command to love our spouse, we must be able to answer these questions. The New Testament was originally written almost entirely in Greek, a language that contains four different words for love: *eros, phileo, storge*, and *agape*. Let's define and examine a biblical picture of each. With a clearer understanding of three of those words for love—*eros, storge*, and *phileo*—we will be better prepared to understand the superior form of love: *agape*.

Why is it so important for us to understand *agape*? This word appears twice in Ephesians 5:25: "Husbands, love [*agape*] your wives, just as Christ also loved [*agape*] the church and gave Himself for her." *Agape* is the love husbands are commanded to have for their wives, and it is the love Christ has for His bride, the church. It is also the love God has for each of us: "God so loved [*agape*] the world that He gave His only begotten Son, that whoever believes in Him should not perish but have everlasting life" (John 3:16). We must understand *agape* so husbands will know how to love their wives, so wives will know how they should be loved by their husbands, and so we can all realize the greatness of God's love for us.

DEFINING THE DIFFERENT KINDS OF LOVE

Eros—Physical Attraction

Eros is the only Greek term for love that is not used directly in Scripture. The word refers specifically to physical attraction or romantic love. We will examine it fully in chapter 19 when we discuss physical intimacy.

Storge—Natural Affection

Storge refers to natural affection, or familial love, such as the love a parent feels toward a child, or the love siblings feel toward each other. The word *storge* is not used in Scripture in its simple form; it appears twice as *astorgos*, which is *storge* with an *a* in front of it, making it mean the opposite—without love or without natural affection. The apostle Paul uses this term when he states that people will not "retain God in their knowledge [therefore He] gave them over to a debased mind, to do those things which are not fitting; being filled with all unrighteousness…[including being] unloving [*astorgos*]" (Romans 1:28, 31). Paul uses the word again when he writes to Timothy: "In the last days perilous times will come: for men will be…unloving" (2 Timothy 3:1, 3).

In both instances, Paul wasn't simply saying that people are unloving. Rather, he was saying people will lack the natural love or affection that family members should have for each other. A biblical example of *astorgos* (the absence of *storge*) is Cain murdering Abel. A present-day example is mothers who consent to murdering their babies in the womb. An abortion is the height of *astorgos*, or a lack of natural love, because even in nature, mothers have a built-in predisposition to fiercely protect their offspring.

Storge is also used once in Scripture in combination with a third form of love, *phileo*: "Be kindly affectionate to one another with brotherly love" (Romans 12:10). The words "kindly affectionate" are a translation of *philostorgus*, which is a Greek word that combines *phileo* and *storge*. Within the context of Romans 12, the term refers to the family affection brothers and sisters in Christ should have for each other.

Phileo—Strong Affection

Phileo can be defined as strong affection. Most commonly, this applies to kindness between friends. When Jesus wept at Lazarus's gravesite in John 11:36, the eyewitnesses said, "See how He loved [*phileo*] him!" *Phileo* forms part of the words *philosophy*, an affection for wisdom, and *philanthropy*, an affection for fellow man. The name for the church at Philadelphia, which is mentioned in Revelation 3:7-13, literally means "the church of brotherly love." When people consider themselves close friends, *phileo* is the affection they have for each other.

Phileo does not always have a positive connotation. In Matthew 6:5, Jesus makes this accusation: "[The religious leaders] love [*phileo*] to pray standing in the synagogues and on the corners of the streets." Their strong affection was directed at receiving the adoration of men.

When it comes to the marriage relationship, it is natural to think in terms of romantic love, or *eros*. But in doing so, we forget that marriage is the union of two best friends. In many ways, *phileo* is a great description of what marriage is meant to be: a deep and close friendship. Your spouse should be your best friend. That's why it's sad when people are closer to their friends than they are to their spouse. It is tragic when people say, "Oh, my spouse is leaving for a week. I can't wait—what a wonderful break!" If a husband or wife feel this way toward their spouse, he or she should pray that God increases the *phileo* in their relationship.

Agape—A Superior Love

The fourth form of love—and the one most mentioned in the New Testament—is *agape*. A conversation between Jesus and Peter reveals its superior nature. The background to this encounter was Peter's earlier pledge to lay down his life for Jesus (John 13:36-38). Even when Jesus warned Peter that he would deny Jesus three times, Peter vowed his unswerving love. In fact, he boasted, "Even if all the other disciples deny You, I will not!"

But sure enough, when Jesus was arrested, Peter ran to save his own skin and denied—three times—ever knowing Jesus. During Peter's third denial, Scripture tells us Peter made eye contact with Jesus (Luke 22:59-62). We are not told what Peter saw during that brief look from Jesus, but Peter became convicted to the point of stumbling away and weeping bitterly. I doubt there was a lower point in Peter's life.

By John 21, Peter has learned of Jesus's resurrection and at least twice had been with the other disciples when Jesus appeared to them (John 20:19-31). But the shame and anguish of his betrayal must have remained a heavy burden. We see confirmation of this in John 21. While the disciples were out fishing, Jesus called to them from the shore. Notice Peter's response: He immediately dove into the water and swam to shore. Then while the disciples are eating with Jesus, we see reconciliation and forgiveness take place.

> So when they had eaten breakfast, Jesus said to Simon Peter, "Simon, son of Jonah, do you love [*agape*] Me more than these?"
>
> [Peter] said to Him, "Yes, Lord; You know that I love [*phileo*] You."
>
> [Jesus] said to him, "Feed My lambs" (John 21:15).

In asking if Peter loves Him more than *these*, Jesus could be referencing the fish, which would be akin to saying, "Do you love Me more than fishing?" Or He might have the other disciples in mind, in which case Jesus would be asking, "Do you love Me more than you love these other disciples?" But based on Peter's earlier prideful declaration that he loved Jesus more than anyone else, Jesus was probably asking Peter if he still believed that to be true: "Do you love Me more than these other disciples love Me?" Regardless of intent, Jesus was inquiring about Peter's love for Him, and the word He used was *agape*.

Peter was aware of how he had failed his Master and was humbled by this realization that he had responded to Jesus with the word *phileo* instead of *agape*. He knew that his earlier actions prevented him from being able to claim the superior form of love Jesus asked about.

> [Jesus] said to [Peter] again a second time, "Simon, son of Jonah, do you love [*agape*] Me?"
>
> [Peter] said to [Jesus], "Yes, Lord; You know that I love [*phileo*] You."
>
> [Jesus] said to [Peter], "Tend My sheep" (John 21:16).

As though to make His question easier, this time Jesus dropped the phrase "more than these." But He still used the word *agape*, and again Peter responded with the word *phileo*.

> [Jesus] said to him the third time, "Simon, son of Jonah, do you love [*phileo*] Me?" Peter was grieved because He said to him the third time, "Do you love [*phileo*] Me?"

And [Peter] said to [Jesus], "Lord, You know all things; You know that I love [*phileo*] You."

Jesus said to [Peter], "Feed My sheep" (John 21:17).

This time Jesus also used the word *phileo*. He had stopped asking if Peter had *agape* for Him. The passage reveals that this grieved Peter. In fact, the whole conversation would have been painful to him. First, Jesus asked Peter three times, "Do you love Me?" The three questions would remind Peter of his three denials. Being asked the same question three times would make Peter think Jesus did not believe his professions of love. Then in the third question, Jesus shifted to the word *phileo* as though calling into question even this inferior love Peter professed for Him. The possibility that Peter did not even possess *phileo* for Jesus broke the disciple's heart.

What may have added to Peter's pain is that throughout this conversation, Jesus did not use the new name He had given Peter (Matthew 16:18). *Peter* means "rock," signifying strength and a firm foundation. Jesus reverted to calling Peter by his original name, Simon, which implied that Jesus was not seeing Peter at this moment as a rock. Considering Peter's arrogance when he boasted of his love for Jesus, he undoubtedly needed this reminder of his own weakness and humanity so as not to place so much trust in himself again.

The point to notice in this account is that Peter recognized the higher calling associated with *agape*. As a result of his earlier denials, he did not feel comfortable telling the Lord he had this superior love for Him.

Jesus's words to Peter should move us to carefully evaluate our own love for the Lord. I cannot help but picture Jesus asking, "Scott, do you love Me?" When Jesus looks at my life, what kind of love does He see for Him? Is it simply an affectionate *phileo*, or does He see all-encompassing *agape*? Would Jesus have to ask me three times whether I love Him, and humble me as He did Peter?

A WIFE'S *PHILEO*

Phileo is the love wives are instructed to have for their husbands. Titus 2:3-4 commands "older women [to]…admonish the young women to love their husbands." The Greek word for "love their husbands" is *philandros*, a combination of *phileo* and *aner* (the Greek word translated "husband"). So while husbands are commanded to have *agape* for their wives (which we will discuss in detail later), wives are commanded to have *phileo* for their husbands.

Why the difference? What is the implication of this in a marriage relationship? Is it that husbands do not want or need *agape*?

The reason for the difference is that the needs of husbands and wives are different. Most men—myself included—would say it can be very discouraging and trying at times being a husband, father, provider, spiritual leader, and all the other roles and responsibilities that fall on men's shoulders. What could be more encouraging for a husband than a wife who is also a best friend, regularly lavishing *phileo* on him? Conversely, what could be more discouraging for a husband than a wife who acts more like a mother reprimanding him?

Our ability to love others doesn't rest entirely on us...
we can do so because of the initiating love of God.

On the other hand, a wife needs the *agape* of her husband because she lives under his authority. She needs him to treat her with the tender, sacrificial *agape* Christ showed His bride, the church. We have already spoken of the temptation for husbands to be harsh and domineering. How much more so was this needed in the day when Paul wrote these words, for ancient cultures viewed a woman as being literally owned by her husband. In those days, a husband could demand his wife serve him and meet his every need, but a wife could not in turn demand kindness, concern for her needs, or even basic necessities. For a husband to show his wife such love as Christ pours out on the church was a choice that had to be made of his own free will. And that is still true today, no matter what culture says. Such love is not easy or natural for a husband to show, which is why we husbands need the command to demonstrate this kind of love toward our wives.

Perhaps there are other reasons God commands *phileo* of a wife and *agape* of a husband that we will not know this side of heaven. But we can know for certain that a husband needs his wife's *phileo*; he needs her to be his best friend. A wife needs her husband's *agape*; she needs him to care for her as his most cherished treasure, and not as an object or employee who satisfies his needs. She needs him to love her sacrificially, as Christ loved the church.

What does *agape* look like? We'll spend the next few chapters answering this question! For now, let me leave you with some wonderful encouragement. Why are we able to love others? We are clearly told, "We love because he first loved us" (1 John 4:19 ESV). This is so reassuring because it means our ability to love others doesn't rest entirely on us. Whether loving our spouse, parents, children, coworkers, or even our enemies as Jesus commands in Matthew 5:44, we can do so because of the initiating love of God. Yes, we play a part, but let's keep in mind that our ability to love is rooted not in ourselves, but in the enabling grace of God—the power of the gospel at work in our relationships.

CHAPTER EIGHT

Characteristics of *Agape*

How does the world think about love? Cupid comes to mind. As popular culture states, he shoots people with his arrows and they fall in love. Society has also made it "normal" for people to fall out of love because supposedly love is an emotion over which we have no control. It's as though people are walking along, they trip, and the next thing they know, they've developed feelings for someone.

According to this understanding of love, a man could tell his wife that he was at work and he didn't mean to develop feelings for his coworker. They just kept running into each other in the hallway and the break room, and before he knew it, he "fell" in love with her. A man could also tell his wife, "I'm sorry, but I no longer love you. I don't know how or when it happened, but I just fell out of love with you." Feelings come and go, and because so many people today define love as a feeling, they assume that love comes and goes.

The biggest problem with this incorrect understanding is that it completely contradicts the way Scripture presents love (*agape*). It's not a feeling or emotion. *Agape* is a choice, an act of the will. We choose whether we do or don't love. God can command us to show this kind of love because we do, in fact, have control over it. Two of *agape*'s characteristics make this clear.

AGAPE IS UNCONDITIONAL

Phileo is conditional. Two friends might have *phileo* for each other because of qualities they share or circumstances that bring them together, but if those qualities or circumstances change, their *phileo* for each other might also change.

In contrast, *agape* is unconditional. It is not affected by a person's actions, looks, or possessions. People might successfully create *phileo* for someone else by being a better friend, but *agape* cannot be earned or merited. Nothing can be done to increase or decrease *agape*. It can only be given. *Agape* does not demand reciprocation and it is independent of how it is treated in return. *Agape* loves even when rejected, mistreated, or scorned. That is what makes this form of love so unique and distinguishable.

The Old Testament provides a beautiful picture of *agape's* unconditional nature. In fact, if a husband asked me, "Pastor, how far should I be willing to go in my love for my wife?," I would tell him to read the book of Hosea (chapters 1 and 3 specifically). The prophet Hosea's story began when God told him to marry a woman named Gomer as an object lesson about God's relationship with Israel: "The LORD said to Hosea: 'Go, take yourself a wife of harlotry and children of harlotry, for the land has committed great harlotry by departing from the LORD'" (Hosea 1:2).

We don't know whether Gomer was already a harlot when Hosea married her or she became one later, but at some point, Gomer left Hosea—either to resume her career as a harlot or to pursue adulterous relationships. Eventually she found herself destitute and she either sold herself or someone else sold her into slavery. We know this was a sexual slavery, akin to human trafficking today, because God commanded Hosea, "Go again, love a woman *who is loved by a lover and is committing adultery*" (Hosea 3:1). Notice the present—versus past—tense of the verse. Hosea was to love Gomer even while she was in an adulterous relationship.

In obedience to God, Hosea purchased Gomer back from slavery and restored her to her position as his wife. It is significant that God not only instructed Hosea to *return* to Gomer. He commanded him to *love* her: "Go again, love a woman." Going back to Gomer after her unfaithfulness would have required an unimaginable amount of forgiveness and grace, but Hosea had to go above and beyond and love her as well. This is unconditional love. This is *agape*.

Did Hosea obey? Did Gomer respond? The context would indicate that they did because the account is presented as a parallel to the love story between God and His people. Let's see how the story ends: "Afterward the children of Israel [represented by Gomer] shall return and seek the LORD their God...I [God] will heal their backsliding, I will love them freely" (Hosea 3:5; 14:4). The parallel shows a repentant bride and a husband who liberally loves and forgives. It is a wonderful picture of what can take place in even the most broken marriages when a husband will *agape* his wife. Let me give you an example of such a situation.

Katie and I have some dear friends I'll call Brian and Jennifer, and they gave me permission to share their Hosea and Gomer story. Much of their testimony revolves around Jennifer's unfaithfulness to Brian early in their marriage before they were Christians. Jennifer was running around on Brian, even living with other men for stretches of time. Days went by when Brian didn't know where Jennifer was or how she was doing.

As Brian and Jennifer share their testimony, there is one point at which Jennifer always becomes emotional. She shares how she had been with a man for a period of time and came home hoping to have pushed Brian far enough that he would divorce her. Jennifer didn't know that while she was gone, Brian had become a Christian. Though Brian recognized the sin in Jennifer's life, he also recognized the sin in his own life. He knew he needed a Savior just as much as Jennifer. As a result, he was willing to forgive her. When Jennifer walked in, Brian was sitting in a chair reading his Bible. Looking up at her, he said, "I'm so glad you're home, because I was so worried about you."

Just as Hosea's unconditional love for Gomer finally won her back, Brian's unconditional love for Jennifer won her back. She became a Christian and is one of the godliest women we know. Over the decades of their marriage, this couple has faithfully served Christ and furthered His kingdom. God used Brian's *agape* to redeem Jennifer and make her an instrument for His glory.

AGAPE IS SACRIFICIAL

Agape is an action. It's about what we are willing to do. First Corinthians 13 is known as the Bible's love chapter, and in verses 4-7 we read,

> Love suffers long and is kind; love does not envy; love does not parade itself, is not puffed up; does not behave rudely, does not seek its own, is not provoked, thinks no evil; does not rejoice in iniquity, but rejoices in the truth; bears all things, believes all things, hopes all things, endures all things.

How many words here describe feelings and emotions? None! How many words are verbs or action words describing what love is willing to do? All of them. Love is what love does.

Jesus told a parable in Luke 10:25-37 that perfectly illustrates the active and sacrificial nature of *agape*. The prelude to this story is that a lawyer sought to test Jesus when he inquired, "Teacher, what shall I do to inherit eternal life?"

"What is written in the law?" Jesus asked.

In response, the lawyer loosely quoted two well-known Old Testament passages: "You shall love [*agape*] the LORD your God with all your heart, with all your soul, with all your strength, and with all your mind" (Deuteronomy 6:5), and "love [*agape*] your neighbor as yourself" (Leviticus 19:18).

"You have answered rightly," Jesus assured the lawyer. "Do this and you will live."

The lawyer understood that to receive eternal life, he needed to have *agape* for God and his neighbors. But nobody can exercise *agape* perfectly, which may explain why the lawyer tried to justify himself by asking another question: "And who is my neighbor?"

Jesus never specifically answered the question. Instead, He told the parable of the good Samaritan to illustrate what *agape* looks like. A Jewish man traveling from Jerusalem to Jericho was attacked by thieves who robbed him of his clothes and left him half-dead. A Jewish priest and Levite passed by but did not bother to help. Then a Samaritan, both a foreigner and historic enemy to the Jewish people, saw the man. With compassion, he tended to the man's wounds, set the man on his donkey, and took him to a nearby inn, where he left funds to help provide for the man's care.

Jesus then asked the lawyer, "Which of these three do you think was neighbor to him who fell among the thieves?" His question could as easily be phrased, "Which of these three do you think showed *agape*?" Let's consider how this parable depicts *agape*.

The Samaritan's love was not conditional on anything the wounded man had done for him. In the story, the two were clearly strangers. So why did the Samaritan help him? Was it all the good times they had shared together? All the wonderful things the injured man had done in the past for the Samaritan? Some expectation the man would pay back the Samaritan in the future? No. The man had done absolutely nothing for the Samaritan, and the Samaritan did not expect anything in return. That is the unconditional nature of *agape*.

The Samaritan's *agape* is shown in that he loved a man who despised him. The Jewish people of that day refused to interact with Samaritans, but the Samaritan was willing to help the man anyway. *Agape* loves even when it is rejected.

The Samaritan's actions reveal the sacrificial nature of *agape*. He bandaged the man's wounds. There were no first-aid kits in those days, so he must have made the bandages from his clothes. He used oil and wine to clean the wounds. He put the man on his animal and took him to an inn, where he paid the man's bill and promised to pay even more in the future if needed. All this took time, effort, and money. *Agape* is demonstrated not by words but by actions and sacrifice.

AGAPE IS MAN'S LOVE FOR SIN

Up to this point we have discussed the positive elements of *agape*, but for a full understanding of this term, we must be aware of the fact it is used one other way in Scripture. Interestingly, *agape* also describes man's love for sin. This usage occurs in the same passage that mentions God's *agape* in John 3:16. The setting is a late-night meeting between Jesus and a Pharisee, Nicodemus. After explaining God's *agape* for the world in John 3:16, Jesus says just three verses later, "This is the condemnation, that the light has come into the world, and men loved [*agape*] darkness rather than light, because their deeds were evil" (verse 19).

Considering what we have learned so far, this usage for *agape* should make perfect sense:

- *Agape* loves even when the love is not reciprocated. Man loves sin even though sin does not love in return. In fact, sin does the opposite: "The wages of sin is death" (Romans 6:23). Sin's response to those who love it is death.

- *Agape* loves unconditionally. It is a love that is completely independent of how the object of the love acts toward or treats the one loving it. Thus, man continues to love sin regardless of the guilt, punishment, suffering, or discipline he experiences as a consequence of engaging in it.

- *Agape* loves sacrificially. Think of everything people are willing to give up for sin: health, dignity, jobs, finances, children, parents, marriages, friendships, churches, and even relationships with the Lord. The tragedy is that there is little man will not sacrifice for sin.

First John 2:15-16 instructs us, "Do not love [*agape*] the world or the things in the world. If anyone loves [*agape*] the world, the love [*agape*] of the Father is not in him. For all that is in the world—the lust of the flesh, the lust of the eyes, and the pride of life—is not of the Father but is of the world." When we give in to these lusts, we choose sin over our spouses. What does this look like? Let's consider some examples.

A husband gives in to

- the lust of the flesh when he gets drunk

- the lust of the eyes when he looks at pornography

- the pride of life when he does his work with the motive of receiving praise

A wife gives in to

- the lust of the flesh when she makes purchases behind her husband's back

- the lust of the eyes when she covets her friend's home

- the pride of life when she embraces the flirtations of a man who is not her husband

When we satisfy these and other lusts, we demonstrate a greater love for sin than for our spouse. The motivation behind sin is always selfish, whereas the motivation behind loving one's husband or wife is always the best interests of the spouse. Sinning is an act of the will, but so is *agape* love. We choose to *agape* love our spouse when we choose not to *agape* love sin.

AGAPE IS GOD'S LOVE FOR MAN

First John 4:8 and 16 tell us, "God is love [*agape*]." He is the embodiment of *agape*. As we saw earlier, one of Scripture's most famous verses describes God's *agape* for us: "God so loved [*agape*] the world that He gave His only begotten Son, that whoever believes in Him should not perish but have everlasting life" (John 3:16).

Think of the other ways this verse could be worded: God so loved the world that He…created a beautiful planet for people to enjoy. Or He…gave us the wonderful gift of marriage. Or He…blesses us with children. Or He…established the church so His people could be part of a spiritual family. All these are true statements, but they are not examples of God's *agape* because they lack one of *agape*'s required characteristics: sacrifice. The sacrificial nature of God's *agape* is made evident in "that He gave His only begotten Son."

Likewise, 1 John 4:10 says, "This is love, not that we loved [*agape*] God, but that He loved [*agape*] us and sent His Son to be the propitiation for our sins." This communicates the unconditional nature of *agape* in that God loved us even when we did not love Him. The words "sent His Son to be the propitiation for our sins" communicate the sacrificial nature of God's *agape*.

---

*The words "Christ died for us"
reveal the depth of the sacrificial
nature of God's agape.*

Romans 5:8 reveals the same two characteristics of God's *agape* toward us: "God demonstrates His own love [*agape*] toward us, in that while we were still sinners, Christ died for us." The unconditional nature of God's *agape* is revealed in the words "while we were still sinners." God loved us even when we were in rebellion against Him. Just as God sent Hosea back to Gomer to love her when she was committing physical adultery, so God loved us even when we were in rebellion against Him and committing spiritual adultery. The words "Christ died for us" reveal the depth of the sacrificial nature of God's *agape*.

I never understood the extent of God's unconditional, sacrificial *agape* until I became a father. Children can be cruel. When they rebel against their parents, how do most parents respond? Do they stop loving their children? No. I remember a conversation with our oldest child, Rhea, who was seven at the time. She asked me if I would still love her even if she did certain things she considered to be terrible. Each time she asked a question, she started out, "Would you still love me if I...?" Finally, I told her, "Yes, I love you so much that there is nothing you could ever do that would make me love you any less. Truthfully, I love you so much I don't know how I could even love you more."

When I said this to Rhea I meant it, and I know other parents would say the same to their children. That is *agape*. And the depth of God's *agape* becomes more vivid to us when we contrast our *agape* with God's. If I, a fallen, sinful, selfish man with imperfect love, can demonstrate this kind of love toward my children, how much greater must God's *agape* be for us, considering His perfection? Considering He is love?

I love Rhea because she is my daughter, but the far greater unconditional and sacrificial nature of God's *agape* was demonstrated when He was willing to sacrifice His Son for unloving sinners who lived in active rebellion against Him and adopt them so they could be His sons and daughters. That is *agape*; that is the kind of love God has for us.

PART FOUR

A HUSBAND'S CALL TO AGAPE AND A WIFE'S CALL TO RESPECT (EPHESIANS 5:25-33)

CHAPTER NINE

A Husband Should *Agape* His Wife

A
s we begin this chapter, here is a question that deserves serious thought: What does it look like for a husband to love his wife? As we discussed earlier, love is not feelings and emotions—rather, it is actions. So another way to ask that question is this: What do good husbands *do*? If we were to pose that question to different people, we might get answers like these:

- Buy their wife expensive jewelry
- Take her to fancy restaurants
- Whisk her away on exotic vacations
- Provide an impressive home for her to live in

In the world's way of thinking, a husband's love for his wife is demonstrated through material goods. This is why a husband can be a failure in the world's eyes while being a great husband in God's eyes, or a great husband in the world's eyes while failing in God's eyes. The good news—at least for husbands—is that we don't have to buy our wives anything expensive or glamorous to be pleasing to God. The bad news is that spending money on our wives is much easier than doing what God requires of us as husbands.

With Christ as the standard for husbands, every man
must recognize that he always has more room to grow.

With a good understanding of *agape*, we are now prepared to see just how high the standard is for husbands. The primary passage about husbands loving their wives begins, "Husbands, love [*agape*] your wives, just as Christ also loved [*agape*] the church and gave Himself for her" (Ephesians 5:25). *Agape* is used twice to describe two different relationships:

- A husband's relationship with his bride
- Christ's relationship with His bride, the church

The two words "just as" reveal that the way Christ loves the church and gave Himself for her is the way a husband is commanded to love his wife and give himself for her. A man should model his relationship with his bride after Christ's relationship with His bride. With Christ as the standard for husbands, every man must recognize that he always has more room to grow. No husband can ever sit back, relax, and feel as though he has arrived.

Ephesians 5:25 reveals for us the characteristics of *agape*:

- The words "gave Himself for her" reveal the sacrificial nature of Christ's *agape*. In John 3:16, if God the Father's *agape* for the world is shown in being willing to sacrifice His Son, then in Ephesians 5:25, the Son's *agape* for His bride, the church, is shown in being willing to be sacrificed. Christ gave everything He had, including His own life. That is the standard for husbands—they are commanded to show an unreserved, selfless, sacrificial love for their wives.

- The absence of the word *if* reveals the unconditional nature of Christ's *agape*. The verse does not say, "Husbands, love your wives *if…*" Just as Christ loves the church unconditionally, a husband is to love his wife unconditionally. Christ loves the church even when it does not submit, does not love Him in return, or disrespects Him. Simply put, Christ loves the church even when she's unlovable. A husband should love his wife even when she's unlovable and does not submit, does not love him in return, or disrespects him. When a husband is upset with his bride, he needs to remind himself of the love Christ has for His bride—a love that is steadfast regardless of what the bride has or hasn't done.

Pastor and theologian John MacArthur writes:

What higher motive could there be for the husband to love his wife? By loving her as Christ loved the church, he honors Christ in the most direct and graphic way. He becomes the embodiment of Christ's love to his own wife, a living example to the rest of his family, a channel of blessing to his entire household, and a powerful testimony to a watching world.[1]

So, back to the question asked at the beginning of this chapter: What does it look like for husbands to love their wives? Ephesians 5:25 gives the command that husbands are to follow, and the subsequent verses describe what it looks like to obey the command.

AGAPE INCLUDES SANCTIFYING AND CLEANSING

Ephesians 5:26 says this about Christ's love for His bride: He gave Himself for her "that He might sanctify and cleanse her with the washing of water by the word." Through Christ, the church is sanctified and cleansed. Because the relationship between Christ and the church is meant to serve as an example for husbands with their wives, this obligates husbands to sanctify and cleanse their wives. A husband is at least partially responsible for his wife's sanctification or spiritual growth. As Christ prepares His bride to be pure, so must husbands contribute to their wives' purity.

This sanctifying and cleansing takes place through washing by the Word of God:

- In John 15:3, Jesus speaks to the church, setting the example for husbands with their brides: "You are already clean because of the word which I have spoken to you."

- In John 17:17, Jesus prayed, "Sanctify them by Your truth. Your word is truth."

Husband, let me address you directly. There are several ways you can "wash" your wife with the Word:

- Through consistent attendance at a Bible-teaching church. It is tragic when husbands, who are called to be the spiritual leaders in their marriages, do not take the initiative to carry out one of the most basic and foundational practices of the Christian life—corporate worship on the Lord's day—a priority.

- Through participation in Bible studies, Sunday school classes, or home fellowships that place both of you in a position to have God's Word wash over you.

- Listen together to Christian radio programs or to an audio Bible in the home or while driving.

- Read God's Word with your wife. I have had men tell me, "I don't know how to read the Bible with my wife." If you can read, you can read the Scriptures with your wife. Choose a book and start at chapter 1, verse 1. Whatever verse you stop at is where you will pick up next time.

- Make God's Word a priority in your marriage. While I would never say Christians cannot have televisions, I would encourage them to think about what brings a couple together most often. Is it the television, watching movies, doing some other activity, or is it spending time in the Word of God?

A Husband Sets the Standard for Holiness

A husband living an unholy life cannot help his wife with her holiness. Because husbands are commanded to have a sanctifying influence on their wives, it only makes sense that a husband must maintain a high standard of holiness in his own life. It is not the wife's responsibility to establish the spiritual atmosphere of the home. That responsibility belongs to the husband. He is responsible for

- what comes into the home and influences the family
- what the family watches
- what the family listens to
- how the family talks or jokes
- what company the family keeps
- how the family presents itself to others by their words, dress, and actions
- how the family spends their time
- what the family does recreationally
- how involved the family is in the church

Without getting specific, I will say there are some movies, music, clothing, jokes, language, and activities that should not enter our homes. As the head of the family, husbands are the ones who need to make sure negative or inappropriate influences are not present in the home. If they have entered, husbands have the responsibility to make sure they are removed. A man who *agapes* his wife keeps out anything that would be detrimental to her and the family. When we as husbands compromise on the kinds of influences that enter our homes, we're making our wives and children spiritually vulnerable.

As a pastor and a speaker at marriage conferences I've gotten to know many couples. I would like to share about a pattern I've noticed through the years. Let me be clear that this is my own observation rather than a truth from Scripture. The pattern is this: I rarely encounter a husband who complains about his wife's lack of holiness, but I have encountered plenty of wives who complain about their husband's lack of holiness. These wives express concern about what their husbands watch, listen to, or say, but rarely is it the other way around.

Similarly, I don't often hear men say, "My wife won't go to church with me…join a home fellowship with me…pray or read the Bible with me." But I do hear wives say these things about their husbands. This is tragic because God has called husbands to set the standard for holiness in the home. It is terrible when wives feel like they must be the spiritual leaders in the relationship because their husbands aren't taking on that responsibility. Unfortunately, this is a common problem.

A Husband Gets the Wife He Prepares for Himself

Ephesians 5:27 continues the description of Christ sanctifying and cleansing the church: He does this so "that He might present her to Himself a glorious church, not having spot or wrinkle or any such thing, but that she should be holy and without blemish." There is a tremendous truth contained in these words. Christ does what He does in verse 26—sanctifying and cleansing the church—so that He can obtain for Himself the glorious church (or bride) described in verse 27: one that has no spot or wrinkle, but is holy and without blemish. The ESV Bible puts it this way: "So that He might present the church to Himself in splendor." Here is the simplest way to sum it all up: *Christ gets the church He prepares for Himself.*

Again, this is a picture for husbands and wives. What is the apostle Paul implying by this truth? Just as Jesus gets the church He prepares for Himself, a husband generally gets the wife he prepares for himself. Wives respond well to love, holiness, and obedience to God's Word. When a husband treats his wife forgivingly, lovingly, and tenderly, he will generally receive a more forgiving, loving, and tender wife. When a husband treats his wife unforgivingly, unlovingly, and harshly, he will generally find himself with a wife who is less forgiving, loving, and tender.

Rather than be cruel or harsh toward their wives, some husbands tend to be apathetic or indifferent. They take no interest in their wives. They do not invest in them or even become annoyed with them. We will discuss this more when we look at 1 Peter 3 in chapters 16 through 19 in this book, but for now, we should note that 1 Peter 3:7 commands husbands to "dwell with [their wives] with understanding." Husbands must try to know and understand their wives. This is what enables wives to blossom and grow. When husbands fail to show interest in their wives, they end up with cold, bitter, frustrated wives.

Earlier we learned about a husband's responsibility regarding his wife's sanctification. Another way to look at this is that husbands are responsible for the wives *they get* for themselves! It is a simple equation. If a husband is helping his wife with her sanctification and spiritual cleansing, he is going to get a sanctified and spiritually cleansed wife.

So aside from the fact that God commands a husband to take his wife to church, read the Word with her, pray with her, and help her grow spiritually, another great reason for him to do so is that he will receive a more spiritually mature wife. What kind of qualities will be produced as a result? Galatians 5:22-23 gives the answer: "The fruit of the Spirit is love, joy, peace, longsuffering, kindness, goodness, faithfulness, gentleness, self-control."

Conversely, husbands who do not lead their wives spiritually are likely to receive wives who are less spiritual. What is the opposite of that which is spiritual? The flesh: "Walk in the Spirit, and you shall not fulfill the lust of the flesh. For the flesh lusts against the Spirit, and the Spirit against the flesh; and these are contrary to one another" (Galatians 5:16-17). Verses 19-22 go on to list the "works of the flesh" that are manifest in a person who is not walking in the Spirit: hatred, contentions, jealousies, outbursts of wrath, selfish ambitions, dissensions, envy, even adultery.

How many husbands see these behaviors in their wives because they have been poor spiritual leaders? How many wives might be more spiritually mature if their husbands were nurturing them spiritually, praying for them, and reading the Bible with them? Tragically, I have heard some husbands talk terribly about their wives without considering the fact they may have received the wives they have prepared for themselves. Men have come into my office and told me how badly their wives act, only to make themselves look bad. I'm listening and thinking, *Would your wife be acting this way if you had been sanctifying and cleansing her as God's Word commands? It sounds like you may have gotten the wife you prepared for yourself.*

Galatians 6:7 tells us, "Do not be deceived, God is not mocked; for whatever a man sows, that he will also reap." While it's true that the context of this verse has to do with giving to the church, the principle also applies to a husband's relationship with his wife. Husbands generally reap what they sow in a marriage. When husbands invest in their wives by sowing seeds of love and interest—when they plant spiritual seeds of sanctification—they are more likely to reap what they've sown.

Let's summarize what we've learned up to this point by keeping these two truths in mind:

- Husbands should contribute to sanctifying and cleansing their wives. God has commanded this and will hold husbands accountable for whether they fulfill this calling.

- Husbands are to love their wives and lead them well so that they receive loving, sanctified wives. The good news is that God's command to husbands benefits them as much as it benefits their wives. A husband who loves his wife as God commands will bring great blessings to himself.

A HUSBAND'S CONCERN FOR HIS WIFE

Do you remember Adam's response upon seeing Eve for the first time? "This is now bone of my bones and flesh of my flesh; she shall be called Woman, because she was taken out of Man" (Genesis 2:23). Just as in English, the Hebrew words for man (*iysh*) and woman (*ishshah*) are closely related, revealing that Adam recognized his closeness with his wife. Adam knew that Eve had come from him; that's why looking at her was like looking at himself. Loving Eve was like loving himself. When Adam cared for Eve's body and physical needs, he was caring for his own body—literally, because her body had earlier been his body and physical needs. Her flesh was his flesh.

There can be little doubt that Paul had Adam and Eve in mind when he wrote Ephesians 5:28-29: "Husbands ought to love their own wives as their own bodies; he who loves his wife loves himself. For no one ever hated his own flesh, but nourishes and cherishes it, just as the Lord does the church." The connection Paul makes to Adam and Eve becomes even clearer when he finishes his instruction to husbands by quoting Genesis 2:24 in Ephesians 5:31: "For this reason a man shall leave his father and mother and be joined to his wife, and the two shall become one flesh."

Just as Adam saw Eve as an extension of his own bone and flesh, so God wants husbands to see their wives as extensions of themselves. A husband should care for his wife as well as he cares for himself. When he views her body as part of his body, the result is that when he loves her, he is loving himself. Because no husband hates his own flesh, but rather, nourishes and cherishes it, husbands should offer their wives the same concern and devotion they lavish on themselves.

Nourishing and Cherishing

In Ephesians 5:29, we read about the twin responsibilities God has given to husbands: nourish and cherish. "Nourishes" refers to taking care of our wives spiritually. The New Testament Greek word here is *ektrepho,* which means "to nourish up to maturity." The word occurs only two times in Scripture, both in Paul's letter to the Ephesians. The other occurrence is in Ephesians 6:4: "Fathers, do not provoke your children to wrath, but bring them up [*ektrepho*] in the training and admonition of the Lord." Fittingly, because men should be spiritual leaders in their home, each usage of *ektrepho* references how a man should nourish up to spiritual maturity the most important people in his life: his wife and children.

The second word, "cherishes," denotes caring for our wives physically, mentally, and emotionally. It refers to being tenderly affectionate, warm, and comforting.

Husband, let me ask you some questions that convict me when I ask them of myself:

- Are you as concerned about how your wife is doing as you are about how you are doing?

- Are you as concerned about how much sleep your wife is getting as about how much you are getting?

- Are you as concerned about how your wife is doing when she is sick as you are about yourself when you are sick?

- Are you as concerned about your wife's overworking herself as you are about overworking yourself?

If you love your wife as your own body, the answer to these questions will be yes!

The Sacrifice Needed to *Agape*

What does a husband's love look like in practical terms? Fittingly, because *agape* involves sacrifice, it looks like sacrificing for a wife. When it comes to daily living, a husband should be willing to lay aside his own agenda for the sake of his wife. He must be willing to give up things he would not have to give up if he wasn't married. That could be time. Sleep. Sports. Video games. Television. Socializing with friends.

This kind of sacrifice means putting aside anything that prevents you from loving and caring for your wife the way you love and care for yourself. I'm not saying you need to give up all your sleep, friendships, and so on. Rather, you need to make sure you are loving and caring for your wife in the way God commanded. Do you love her as you love yourself? Do you love her as Christ loves the church? Do you love her in a sanctifying and spiritually cleansing way?

Showing such love means applying the words of 1 Corinthians 13:11: "When I was a child, I spoke as a child, I understood as a child, I thought as a child; but when I became a man, I put away childish things." Loving one's wife as God commands means putting away childish things—the things we tend to be selfish about and that hinder us from loving our wives as we should. Here's another way of saying that: "I need to stop being a child. That is what boys do. I need to give this up and start being a man so I can love my wife as much as I love myself. It is time for me to man up."

CHRIST'S SACRIFICIAL LOVE FOR HIS BRIDE

The marriage passage concludes with these words: "We are members of His body, of His flesh and of His bones...This is a great mystery, but I speak concerning Christ and the church" (Ephesians 5:30, 32). In Scripture, the word "mystery" refers to something previously concealed and then later revealed. The "great mystery" Paul spoke of began at the creation of Adam and Eve, was concealed throughout the Old Testament, and was then revealed in the New Testament: Marriage is a picture of Christ's relationship to the church. It is the mystery we are exploring throughout this book.

Just as Adam was Eve's head, so too is Christ our head (Ephesians 5:23; Colossians 1:18). Just as Eve served as Adam's helper, the church serves as Christ's helper—as the body of Christ, we carry on Christ's work on the earth in His physical absence (1 Corinthians 12:12-27).

While Christ had followers who worked alongside Him during His earthly ministry, He did not have a bride until He laid down His life on the cross. Prior to His death the Twelve were called *disciples, apostles,* or even *friends* (John 15:15), but it wasn't until after the resurrection that Jesus called them *brothers* (Matthew 28:10; John 20:17). This new relationship, which includes believers becoming Jesus's bride, was made possible because He pledged Himself to us through His sacrifice. An analogy would be a young man deeply loves a young lady, but until he pledges himself to her, she does not become his bride.

Consider this: If Adam cared for Eve because she was part of his flesh and bones, how much better will Christ care for us who are His body, flesh, and bones? If you can imagine the love Adam had for Eve, imagine the much greater love that Christ has for us. As husbands, we are commanded to sacrifice for our wife, and in doing so, we can be blessed as we think upon the even greater sacrifice Jesus made for us.

CHAPTER TEN

Spiritually Strong Husbands

started lifting weights in college, and for years, I worked out four or five days per week, month after month, year after year. Sadly, looking back, I think I cared more about my physical strength than my spiritual strength. The constant goal was growing more muscle and lifting more weight. I wish I would have had an even stronger desire to grow in my sanctification and become more like Christ, because little did I know that only a few years later, physical strength would take a backseat to the mental, emotional, and—most importantly—spiritual strength needed to be a Christian husband and father.

When your family is experiencing a trial and they look to you for strength, the number of pounds you can lift in the gym could not be more irrelevant. At that moment, what is needed is mental, emotional, and spiritual strength the family can draw on—especially a spiritual strength that can help lift the family the way physical strength can lift a barbell.

Likewise, when a wife is discouraged, defeated, or depressed, she doesn't need a man with big muscles. She needs a husband who says, "Would you like me to read a few psalms to you? This is a difficult time, but with the Lord's help, I know we can make it through this. Can I tell you about these verses I read that I think will be very encouraging?"

By way of example, at the time of this writing, our youngest, Lydia, who is less than a year old, has been sick the last few days. She hasn't been sleeping well, which means we—and especially Katie, who's been getting up trying to nurse her—haven't been sleeping well. When we were up in the middle of the night recently and Katie was in tears because she didn't know what to do, physical strength couldn't have meant less to her. What did matter to her was when I asked, "Can I pray?"

When a young man asks me whether I think he is ready to get married, I ask him, "When things are difficult and your family suffers, can you hold them up in prayer and point them to Christ as the answer to their needs? Are you ready to gather your wife and children regularly around the Word of God? As the head of the home, will you take responsibility when things don't go well? If your answer is no, then you don't yet have the spiritual strength necessary to get married."

In the previous chapter, we looked at what it means for a husband to care for his wife physically, mentally, and emotionally. A man doing so may appear to be a loving husband. Similarly, many husbands work hard to care for their wives financially—and they should. There are physical, mental, emotional, and financial aspects of loving well, but if a husband doesn't care for his wife spiritually, his love is incomplete. He's not fulfilling the most important responsibility God has given him. Sadly, during my years as a pastor, I have seen more husbands fail with regard to the spiritual leadership and protection of their homes than any other provision.

STRONG HUSBANDS PROTECT THEIR HOUSE SPIRITUALLY

Imagine asking a godly woman, "Would you rather have a man who's physically strong or spiritually strong?" A godly woman will take a spiritually strong man over a physically strong man any day; she knows if her husband is spiritually weak, their home will be vulnerable. A Christian woman should want a spiritually strong husband who will lead and protect the family.

When it comes to becoming physically strong, we must exercise and nourish ourselves well with the right foods. Likewise, if we want to become spiritually strong, we must nourish ourselves well with the right spiritual food, which is God's Word, and live out the spiritual disciplines, which strengthen us—disciplines such as meditating on God's Word, praying, serving, and being involved in the body of Christ.

We are certain to have our own ideas of what a husband should be willing to do for his wife, but God's ideas are quite different from ours. Most husbands are instinctively ready to protect their family physically. They'll tell you, "If someone broke into my house, I would tell my family to hide and I would put myself in harm's way so they could be safe." Or, "If a car were heading toward my wife or children, I would throw myself in front of it to save them." But let's be honest: How likely is it that intruders will ever break into our homes, or that we'll ever have to throw ourselves in front of a vehicle to save our children? These scenarios are unlikely to occur.

But there are certain types of enemies that can break into our homes and attack our families quite frequently—not physical ones, but spiritual ones: the devil and the world. How often can this occur? Every day.

What does it take for a husband to be spiritually strong so he is able to protect his family?

Because the devil is a much greater threat to our family than any physical intruder, spiritual protection is needed constantly. Husbands may invest in locks, alarms, guns, and other protective devices to shield their family from physical enemies, but how much do they invest in spiritual means of protection? God warns us that the spiritual battles are ongoing and dangerous:

- "We do not wrestle against flesh and blood, but against principalities, against powers, against the rulers of the darkness of this age, against spiritual hosts of wickedness in the heavenly places" (Ephesians 6:12).

- "The weapons of our warfare are not carnal but mighty in God for pulling down strongholds" (2 Corinthians 10:4).

Spiritual battles require spiritual weapons; therefore, the best protection for families is a spiritually strong man. In Matthew 12:29, Jesus told a short but profound parable that illustrates this: "How can one enter a strong man's house and plunder his goods, unless he first binds the strong man? And then he will plunder his house." Once we understand the point of the parable, we can consider the application.

The strong man is Satan, the strong man's house is Satan's kingdom, and the strong man's goods are people who belong to Satan. Physically there are many different kingdoms on earth, but spiritually there are only two, and everyone is part of one or the other. There's the kingdom of God, which every believer is part of, and there's the kingdom of Satan, which every unbeliever is part of. The phrase "plunder his goods" describes what happens when people are saved. Jesus takes them from Satan's kingdom and makes them part of His kingdom. Nobody can enter the strong man's house and plunder his goods unless he first binds the strong man—otherwise, the strong man would stop him.

Spiritual battles require spiritual weapons; therefore, the best protection for families is a spiritually strong man.

The only way someone could plunder the strong man's goods is if he's stronger than the strong man. Every time Jesus saves someone, He demonstrates how much stronger He is than Satan.

Let's consider the application by taking a closer look at the parable.

STRONG HUSBANDS PREVENT THEIR FAMILIES FROM BEING PLUNDERED

First, consider the words "How can one enter a strong man's house…?" Note that the whole house is protected by one man. The house rises or falls on his shoulders. Do you see the application? Husbands are the protectors. Our families rise or fall on our shoulders. This is why it's so important for husbands to be spiritually strong.

Consider the words "plunder his goods." Husband, let me ask you a question: Are there goods in your home that you need to protect? Yes—your wife and children! You need to make sure they aren't plundered. Strong husbands protect their family so they aren't plundered by sin, compromise, the world, and ungodliness.

STRONG HUSBANDS ARE NOT BOUND, BLIND, OR MUTE

Consider the part of the passage that reads "unless he first binds the strong man? And then he will plunder his house." The word "he" reveals we're talking about an individual. Every man needs to know there's an enemy who wants to enter his house, bind him, and plunder his goods, and that enemy is the devil. Jesus said, "The thief does not come except to steal, and to kill, and to destroy" (John 10:10). Satan wants to enter our homes and steal, kill, and destroy our marriages, wives, and children. First Peter 5:8 says, "Be sober, be vigilant; because your adversary the devil walks about like a roaring lion, seeking whom he may devour." We must recognize there's an adversary, or enemy, who wants to devour our families. Strong husbands fight to prevent this from happening.

Going back to Matthew 12:29, notice the words "first" and "then." There's a progression. The enemy can't plunder the house unless he first binds the strong man. He wants to bind husbands so he can plunder their families. If a husband is bound, the family is vulnerable. Think about the word "bound," or "tied up" as it's translated in the NIV. What imagery does this convey? A person who is helpless, unable to do anything. This is what Satan wants to do to fathers and husbands.

A few verses earlier, in Matthew 12:22, we read about "a demon-oppressed man who was *blind and mute* [and] was brought to [Jesus], and he healed him, so that the man *spoke and saw*" (ESV). The devil made the man blind and mute, but Jesus enabled him to speak and see.[1]

From a spiritual standpoint, that's what Satan wants to do to every Christian man. He wants to take away our voice and leadership:

- He wants to make us as husbands spiritually blind so we can't understand spiritual truths or see what's happening in our homes.

- He wants to make us spiritually mute so we won't teach our family or address the issues faced by our wife and children.

Jesus healed the man so that he both "spoke and saw." This is what Jesus wants to do for husbands:

- He wants to help us speak spiritually so we can lead in our homes and preach the gospel and teach the Word.

- He wants to open our eyes spiritually so we can learn the Word and see what's happening in our families.

What does this look like practically? A man comes home from work and he's tired. Satan tempts him to sit on the couch, ignore his wife, and neglect his children. Satan tempts him to avoid dealing with the problems around him and hope they go away on their own. The devil fills his mind with thoughts unrelated to his family and tempts him to find anything to do other than lead his family spiritually, including through prayer and reading the Word. In these ways, husbands become spiritually blind and mute and allow Satan to bind them and plunder their family.

An even worse situation occurs when a husband binds himself. He does this when he develops addictions to sins, such as pornography, alcohol, lying, or anger. A man in this condition is in no place to provide spiritual protection for his family because he is defenseless: "A man without self-control is like a city broken into and left without walls" (Proverbs 25:28).

CHRIST PROVIDES THE VICTORY OVER SATAN

While it is true that husbands should protect their family from Satan, we must understand Scripture never calls us to fight Satan. You would think that if

Satan is trying to destroy our homes and husbands are the protectors, we would see verses commanding husbands to defeat Satan. But none of the New Testament epistles contain any instructions along those lines.

Why aren't husbands called to defeat Satan? Jesus already defeated him:

- "[Christ] disarmed principalities and powers, He made a public spectacle of them, triumphing over them" (Colossians 2:15).

- "[Jesus will] destroy him who had the power of death, that is, the devil" (Hebrews 2:14).

- "The Son of God was manifested, that He might destroy the works of the devil" (1 John 3:8).

When people cast out demons in the Gospels and Acts, how did they do it? They didn't roll up their sleeves, summon all their strength, and defeat him in their own effort. They called on Christ:

- "John said, 'Master, we saw someone casting out demons in Your name'" (Luke 9:49).

- "The seventy returned with joy, saying, 'Lord, even the demons are subject to us in Your name'" (Luke 10:17).

Even Michael the all-powerful archangel didn't attempt to fight Satan in his own power: "Yet Michael…in contending with the devil, when he disputed about the body of Moses, dared not bring against him a reviling accusation, but said, 'The Lord rebuke you!'" (Jude 9).

In Scripture, people experienced victory over Satan's kingdom by relying on Christ: "Thanks be to God, who gives us the victory through our Lord Jesus Christ" (1 Corinthians 15:57). Only Jesus can achieve victory over Satan, which is why we must put Christ first in our lives if we want to experience victory in our marriage.

STRONG HUSBANDS PUT CHRIST FIRST

Now, even though I drew an application from the parable of the strong man in Matthew 12:29, the parable is not primarily about husbands protecting their homes. Rather, it is about Jesus being stronger than the devil. To be clear, I'm not suggesting husbands attempt to take on Satan or protect their families by fighting the demonic realm in their own strength. Rather, I'm encouraging husbands to protect their family by pointing them to Christ and speaking God's truths to them. After all, Christ is the true leader of our homes. Ultimately, we who are husbands need to be abiding in Him so that we can protect our families.

What does it look like for a husband to do this practically? Simply put, he strives to have a Christ-centered home seven days of the week. Some couples spend Sunday morning in church, but the other six days of the week their marriage looks little different than the marriages of unbelievers. As the head of the relationship, it is the husband's responsibility to make sure he is praying and reading the Word with his wife (and children if they have any) throughout the week.

Earlier I talked about the days when I was actively involved in developing my physical fitness. If I can go back to that season for a moment, there was a big debate at the time about cardio: Should people do cardio first thing in the morning on an empty stomach, or later in the day after a meal? Should people do high-intensity cardio for a short period of time, or low-intensity cardio for a long period of time? Finally, I read an article that resolved the dilemmas: "Regardless of the time of day or length of time, the most important issue is simply that people perform cardio."

Similarly, I have had many people ask me, "When is the best time to pray and read the Bible together? And how long should it last?" I respond, "The most important issue is simply that it takes place." This is what spiritually strong husbands do. They put Christ first by praying and reading the Word with their family. Spiritually strong husbands who do this will be protecting their home from the greatest threats they face.

Husband, may I speak to you directly? Brother in Christ to brother in Christ? Let me encourage you to be that spiritually strong man who puts Christ first. I know from experience that it is not easy because I have failed more times than I would like to acknowledge. But let's keep in mind that we don't need to rely on our own strength as we do this. We can rely on Christ's strength. It is the power of the gospel at work in our hearts that gives us the strength we need and enables us to put Christ first. We can do it, with Christ's enablement—and our families will be blessed because of it!

Protecting Your Marriage

A newly married young woman had an argument with her husband. Because she had a good relationship with her father, in the midst of her hurt and anger, she went to see him. She knew her father would affirm how wonderful she was, and how wrong her husband had been.

When she arrived, the father opened the door, looked at his daughter, knew she was upset, invited her in immediately, and asked her what was wrong. After a few pleasantries, the daughter began divulging details about the argument she just had with her husband. The father gently rebuked her and suggested she return home. He explained, "Your husband is now the most important man in your life. You two will have problems, and you can't come back to me when that happens. You must learn to work things out together. I love you and I'm all for the best for your marriage, which is why I'm giving you this counsel."

Scripture agrees with the father's response. Genesis 2:24 says, "A man shall leave his father and mother and be joined to his wife, and they shall become one flesh." The term *leaving and cleaving* comes from this verse. We know it portrays God's divine plan for marriage because it was instituted at creation and brought forward into the New Testament by Jesus and Paul (Matthew 19:5; Mark 10:7; Ephesians 5:31).

KEEP THE MARRIAGE IN THE MARRIAGE

When Paul commanded "a man [to] leave his father and mother and be joined to his wife" (Ephesians 5:31), he was, in effect, encouraging couples to keep the marriage between the husband and wife. Married individuals should cling to their spouses instead of anyone else, including their parents. When couples experience conflict, as all couples will, they should work things out together instead of running to others. The father in the story above understood an important truth about marriage: under most circumstances, problems should remain between the husband and wife.

In fact, in-laws can end up contributing to marriage problems, especially with newlyweds who aren't used to being separated from their parents. But this scenario isn't limited to parents. When couples experience conflict, frequently they are tempted to go to friends or coworkers to criticize their spouse and talk about how badly they have been treated. The reason they want to do this is that they expect those close to them to take their side in the dispute. Some wives turn to their girlfriends. Some husbands talk to their guy friends. While parents are the only ones mentioned in Ephesians 5:31, we can extend this principle to say that if we shouldn't complain to our parents about our spouse, we shouldn't complain to anyone else either.

The dangers here should be obvious. Pouring out our anger merely stokes it. This will make us feel justified in responding poorly to our spouse, feed our belief that we deserve better treatment than we are receiving, and discourage us from seeking forgiveness for our fault in the conflict. We'll be filled with pride instead of humility, which will make an already-strained relationship worse.

An even worse scenario is when the offended party shares the grievances with someone of the opposite sex. The result will be:

- A married woman thinking, *I wish my husband listened to me the way he listens to me. I bet he would never treat me the way my husband treats me.*

- A married man thinking, *I bet she would show me more respect than my wife shows me. She would appreciate me and all my hard work.*

Complaining about your spouse to someone of the opposite sex is detrimental to your marriage and can easily become the first step toward gossip and—even worse—a sinful relationship.

SEEKING GODLY COUNSEL IS THE EXCEPTION

Before I go any further, I want to bring up this important point: In cases of abuse, I am not suggesting that people cannot go to their parents or others for help. We'll discuss abuse in more detail in chapter 13. For now, let's discuss the other major exception to the rule of not going outside the marriage, and that's when husbands and wives need godly counsel. Couples who are having problems commonly make one of two mistakes:

1. They do not want to admit they are having problems and thus pretend everything is okay. They want to believe the problems will go away on their own. Pride causes them to keep their struggles a secret. As a result, they do not get help, and their marriage worsens. This is one time the marriage should not stay in the marriage. When a couple is truly unable to resolve their marital problems, they should seek spiritually mature help outside the relationship. They must put their relationship ahead of their pride.

2. They act as though they are seeking godly counsel when, in fact, they are only looking for the opportunity to disparage or gossip about their spouse. People who do this say, "I'm having problems in my marriage and would like some advice." They then proceed to list everything bad their spouse has ever done without any intent of receiving counsel. Nor do they take any responsibility for their part in the dispute. They do not acknowledge any of their own weaknesses or failures. They never say, "I know I shouldn't have done this. It was sinful. What do you think I should have done differently? How could I be a better spouse?" These people are not looking for godly advice. They are just looking for an opportunity to complain or slander.

Unfortunately, those who want to bad-mouth their spouses will not have much trouble finding someone who will listen. Some people are all too eager to hear the denigrating information that should remain private.

If you want good and helpful counsel, do not seek out friends who are more concerned about maintaining your friendship than helping your marriage. Many of these "friends"—who usually end up hearing only half of the story—will poison a husband or wife against the spouse. In doing so, they will worsen the situation or even encourage sin against God. Typical responses from such people sound like:

- "I can't believe your wife did that. She's gone way too far. You should be mad!"

- "Your husband doesn't know what he has in you. You don't have to put up with that. You deserve so much better than him."

Instead of speaking to people who will provide biased or faulty counsel, go to spiritually mature individuals and be willing to receive criticism and hear what you need to do to bring about change. Seek out trustworthy, godly friends who love you and care about your marriage. Pursue counsel that sounds like this:

- "You shouldn't have responded that way. You need to go back and ask for forgiveness."

- "Scripture commands you to love your wife. I'm sorry she did that to you, but you need to think about what Christ wants you to do."

- "God says you should respect your husband. He shouldn't have done that, but you need to stop talking to him like he's a child."

If you take the marriage outside the marriage, look for people who have the wisdom and willingness to offer hard truths such as these. These are the ones who will give you the counsel necessary to help strengthen your marriage, and most importantly, your relationship with the Lord.

LET NOT MAN SEPARATE

Genesis 2:24 is instructive about the permanence of marriage. Again, Jesus remains the standard for husbands. In John 10:28, He said this regarding His bride, the church: "I give them eternal life, and they shall never perish; neither shall anyone snatch them out of My hand." In the same way that Jesus is committed to preventing His bride from being taken away from Him, husbands should be committed to preventing their bride from being taken away from them.

Weddings are wonderful events where God divinely joins two separate individuals into one flesh. The Greek term translated "joined" is *proskollao*, and it means "to glue upon." When a husband and wife are married, two people are glued together to create one whole, hence the words "they shall become one flesh."

A marriage should never come apart. The fact God designed for husband and wife to have a one-flesh relationship reveals why divorce is so terrible. When asked about divorce, Jesus quoted God's original command in Genesis 2:24, adding an even stronger injunction: "Therefore what God has joined together, *let not man separate*" (Matthew 19:6). Divorce tears apart what God Himself created.

For a married couple to divorce is like ripping apart two pieces of metal that have been welded—or joined—together. The result will never be a nice split. Both pieces of metal will be damaged and take some of the other piece with them. When I say this, I am not trying to condemn those who have already gone through a divorce (and the vast majority of people who have experienced the tragedy of divorce would confirm what I am saying here about the damage divorce causes). Rather, I want to urge married couples never to consider divorce as an option. My hope is to spare families, especially those with children, the deep heartache divorce brings. My experience has been that most people who have been through a divorce are among the first to encourage pastors to preach strongly against it. They want to see others avoid the grief they have suffered.

More importantly, how does God feel about people destroying what He has joined together? He hates it: "Let none deal treacherously with the wife of his youth. For the LORD God of Israel says that He hates divorce, for it covers one's garment with violence" (Malachi 2:15-16). These strong words equate divorce with violence. Why is that? Because divorce is the tearing apart of one flesh into two. God's hatred of divorce conveys two responsibilities to professing Christians:

1. No matter how difficult it might be—and it *is* tough when we see people struggling in their marriage—believers have a responsibility to encourage others to stay married. While separation should be supported under certain circumstances, including abuse, divorce should always be discouraged. When God says that He hates something, how can we as believers think of supporting it? Christians have the responsibility to help "what God has joined together" to stay together.

2. Christians should not use the word *divorce* in relation to their own marriages. Once this word is spoken, even if it is forgiven, it is often not forgotten. My wife and I counseled a couple who could not trust each other because both had used the *d* word. Each was convinced the other said it first, but that didn't matter because both had said it. Neither could forget what the other had threatened, leaving husband and wife with little confidence in the other's commitment to their union.

THE BRIDE'S SUPREMACY

When Scripture says, "A man shall leave his father and mother and be joined to his wife" (Ephesians 5:31), it isn't encouraging husbands to cut their mother and father out of the couple's lives. But it *is* a profound command that should challenge husbands to examine their priorities. A man's wife should be more important to him than his parents. To appreciate the significance of the command, we need some familiarity with the marriage customs of Jesus's and Paul's day.

A Jewish betrothal (or engagement period) typically lasted one full year. During that time, the groom's main responsibility was preparing a place for himself and his bride. He would then return at an unexpected day and hour for his bride and take her to be with him at the place he prepared. For those acquainted with Jesus's own promise to His future bride in John 14:1-3, this should sound familiar:

> Let not your heart be troubled; you believe in God, believe also in Me. In My Father's house are many mansions; if it were not so, I would have told you. I go to prepare a place for you. And if I go and prepare a place for you, I will come again and receive you to Myself; that where I am, there you may be also.

Where is the place Jesus is preparing for His bride, the church? His Father's house. Similarly, a Jewish groom would prepare a place for himself and his bride on his father's property. The newly established residence might even be an addition to his father's residence. This kept the newly married couple under the groom's parents' authority.

With this custom in mind, when Jesus and Paul quoted Genesis 2:24 that "a man should *leave his father and mother*," their words could not have sounded more radical to the culture of the day. Even though a man's father and mother have been the most important earthly figures in his life up until his wedding day, he is commanded to leave them to be joined to his new bride. Because a husband is to leave his parents for the sake of his wife, he should be willing to forsake anything (except for Christ) for her. Second to a husband's relationship with Christ, his wife must be the supreme person in his life. A wife should never feel threatened by anyone or anything. A husband should have no earthly relationship that competes with his union with his bride.

Perception Is Reality

When wives feel like they are in second place, it's not usually because of another woman. More often, women feel like their husbands have put an activity or hobby first. It could be sports, television, cars, poker night, alcohol, friends, work, video games, education, and even children. Yes, a husband's relationship with his wife should be supreme even above his relationships with his children. I love my children more than I can express in words, but I still let them know—and more importantly, let Katie know—that I love Katie the most. The kids have asked me, "Who do you love the most?" I tell them, "That's easy. Mommy!"

Second to a husband's relationship with Christ,
his wife must be the supreme person in his life.

Note the emphasis here is on how a wife *feels*. A husband might insist, "My wife is the supreme priority in my life. She is more important to me than anything else." But the wife might not feel that way. A wife's perception is her reality. It's not about what the husband thinks, but about how the wife feels.

A few years ago I attended a friend's softball game and watched him make the game-winning hit. As we talked after the game, I could tell something was bothering him. He began to criticize his wife: "She doesn't support me. I hate that she never comes to my games. I won the game, but when I go home to tell her about it, she won't even care."

At first I thought he was right: *Why wasn't she there cheering for him? As his wife, she should be his biggest supporter!* Then it occurred to me that while he's playing, she's at home taking care of their children. If she's anything like Katie (and most other wives), after her husband is gone at work all day, she probably wants him to spend time with his family and help her with the kids. She may even hope that he will give her a break because she's been so busy with the children. This same friend also played basketball regularly on other evenings during the year. I began to wonder if his wife was having trouble respecting a man in his forties spending more time with his teammates than he does with her.

Am I saying there's anything wrong with a grown man playing in a local sports league? No, but I am saying there's something wrong with him making his wife feel like she's second place to a sports league.

Are Hobbies Okay?

I will be quick to admit that I have not always been successful in this area.

Let me share a personal story from early in my marriage that still embarrasses me, and I would much rather not write about this in a book. The experience is humbling, but through it I learned a lot, and I hope it might be instructive for you too.

Back when I was an elementary school teacher, I tried to teach summer school as often as possible for the extra income. One summer the opportunity was not available, and I came up with the terrible idea to play World of Warcraft, an online video game. I quickly found myself addicted.

At one point, I remember Katie expressing surprise at what I was doing. She was not angry or threatening, but I could tell she was disappointed and losing respect for me.

Then something life-changing happened. Our first child, Rhea, was born in July. About one week later, Katie had a breakdown. It was difficult for her to see me like this as her husband, but it was even worse for her because I was now a father. She said she was afraid for our future and how my gaming addiction would affect our kids.

I repented, and by God's grace, I immediately stopped playing. I thought it would be difficult to quit, but it was actually easy. I felt like a huge weight had been lifted off my shoulders. I no longer felt like a slave, and the condemnation and shame I had felt were gone. There was peace in my relationship with the Lord, and I could pray and read the Word again without terrible conviction about my misplaced priorities. Katie told me she was proud of me and that she was now able to respect me again.

Husband, let me address you directly. I share this in the hope that if you have something in your life that has become a misplaced priority that you cannot imagine getting rid of, you, too, might be given confidence to humble yourself before the Lord. Repent this very minute. Do not put it off. If you do this, you can experience the same freedom from bondage I enjoyed and regain your wife's respect. The conviction that constantly plagues your relationship with Christ will be gone too.

There is a world of difference between addictions and hobbies. Hobbies are okay. Addictions are not. I am not suggesting that a husband must categorically give up all hobbies he enjoys, but he must give up anything that has become an addiction and hinders him from fulfilling his responsibilities as a husband and father.

Consider this example: One husband might love restoring an old car, and he spends only a few hours per month doing so. His wife doesn't mind, so for him it's a hobby that doesn't cause any problems in his relationship with his wife, children, or the Lord. Another husband spends every spare hour with his car. He is obsessed with it. His wife has grown tired of this. She tries not to walk past the garage because she doesn't want to see the car. She resents her husband because the car gets so much of his time and attention, and the two of them can't talk about it without fighting. For him, the car is an addiction.

A husband can't claim that just because the Bible doesn't forbid something that it's okay for him to do it. For example, I know two wives who felt like they were in second place to their husbands' water skiing and horses. Because the Bible doesn't forbid water skiing or horses, the husbands felt like they weren't doing anything wrong. While it's true the Bible doesn't forbid their hobbies, it does forbid making a wife feel like she is in second place. The problem isn't with the hobby, but the husband's relationship to it. The hobby isn't the sin; the sin is letting a hobby push the wife into second place.

A husband must pray, examine himself, develop discernment, and ask his wife what steps he needs to take to ensure she stays supreme. He needs to keep checking in with her to see how she's feeling about what he's doing. He might even need to make himself accountable to a mature fellow believer. With God's help, hopefully he can turn an addiction back into a legitimate hobby. If he can't, then it must be removed from his life completely.

The Ruthlessness Needed with Addictions

Sometimes a wife becomes second place to something that shouldn't be completely removed from her husband's life. For example, if a husband puts in too many hours at work, he should cut back on his hours, or perhaps even find a new job rather than stop working completely. If a husband is overly involved in his church, he needs to serve in moderation versus abandoning the church completely.

In some situations this sort of balance is reasonable, but what about when a husband has a hobby that he's unable to engage in moderately? In other words, when his hobby has become an addiction? When a husband's actions have demonstrated that he has an unhealthy relationship to a hobby and he can't engage in it in a balanced or moderate way, then it has become a sin that must be completely removed from his life—elimination versus moderation.

Jesus described the necessary severity: "If your right eye causes you to sin, pluck it out and cast it from you...And if your right hand causes you to sin, cut it off and cast it from you" (Matthew 5:29-30; see also 18:8-9). Jesus didn't expect us to do this literally. He often used figurative language, in the form of hyperbole, to make a point. In this case, He described the ruthlessness with which we should deal with sin—in this case, the sin being that of making the hobby a greater priority than the marriage relationship. If we struggle with a certain temptation, we should completely remove (cut or pluck) it out of our lives. Show it no mercy. If we have demonstrated that we can't stop a hobby from becoming an addiction, then we won't be able to keep that hobby in our life without our wife continuing to feel like she is in second place.

Too often in counseling, I have witnessed a wife's pain associated with what her husband is doing. He will say, "You're right. I'm sorry. I'll get my priorities in order and keep things in balance. From now on I will do this in moderation." The husband will start off well. His wife will be happy for a few weeks. But slowly, whatever made her feel like second place will creep back into his life as an addiction, reclaiming that position of supremacy. The husband might as well have said, because at least it would be honest, "Things are going to change superficially for a few weeks. But before long, things will be right back to the way they were before. And you'll be feeling even worse because you'll see me fail again, increasing your confidence that things will never change." The solution is for the husband to get the addiction out of his life and put his wife in her rightful place.

What is the reward when a husband obeys God's command to make his wife his greatest priority, second only to God Himself? The husband will enjoy the blessings of a prosperous and harmonious marriage, and a happy and contented wife who respects him. If they have children, he will gain their respect too. They all will appreciate the sacrifice he has made for his family.

An Important Note for Wives

If you see your husband give up something so you can be the supreme relationship in his life, be sure to encourage him. Show him respect. Communicate how much you appreciate the sacrifice he made. Let him know that you are aware that few husbands love their wives and the Lord enough to do what he is doing.

THE GREATEST "LEAVING AND CLEAVING"

God wants "a man [to] leave father and mother and be joined to his wife." Jesus wants something similar from His bride, the church. In Matthew 10:37,

He said, "He who loves father or mother more than Me is not worthy of Me." We are to leave father and mother—and everything else for that matter—for Christ!

This is the most important "leaving and cleaving" we do in marriage because when we place Christ, our Bridegroom and Head, first in our lives, we are strengthening our relationship with our spouse. Only in loving Christ and committing ourselves to Him can we become the husbands and wives God calls us to be.

C.S. Lewis put it this way: "When I have learned to love God better than my earthly dearest, I shall love my earthly dearest better than I do now. When first things are put first, second things are not suppressed but increased."[1] Having a deep and sincere love for Christ is the best way to have a deep and sincere love for our spouse.

CHAPTER TWELVE

A Wife Should Respect Her Husband

During a counseling session, as I was helping a couple who struggled a lot with fighting, the wife had an epiphany. Most couples enjoy working together, but these two always ended up disagreeing with each other. The husband explained that nothing he did was ever good enough for his wife. She always countered him with a better way to do things, and she picked apart all his decisions. She was genuinely confused about her husband's frustration because she thought she was simply trying to be helpful. It wasn't until this session that she realized her husband found her "helpful" suggestions to be disrespectful.

Though a wife might believe she has good intentions in mind, if a husband feels she is being disrespectful, that creates a big problem for two reasons. First, a husband craves his wife's respect. Second, Scripture not only commands that a wife submit to her husband, it urges her to respect him as well.

In Ephesians 5:25-32, the apostle Paul described in detail what it means for a husband to love his wife as himself, as discussed in the previous chapter. One might then expect the passage to end with parallel instructions to the wife: "Let each one of you in particular *love his own wife* as himself, and let the wife *love her own husband* as herself." Instead, Paul commanded wives to *respect* their husbands: "Let each one of you in particular so love his own wife as himself, and *let the wife see that she respects her husband*" (Ephesians 5:33).

Why the difference? First, this does not mean that men don't want to be loved. When we discussed *phileo* earlier, we reviewed this command in Titus 2:3-4: "Older women...admonish the young women to *love their husbands*." Ephesians 5:33 also doesn't say that wives don't want to be respected. First

Peter 3:7 says, "Husbands, likewise, dwell with [your wives] with understanding, giving honor to [them]." Honor is synonymous with respect. In fact, the NIV Bible translates 1 Peter 3:7 as saying "treat them with respect." Thus, it is important for wives to be respected, and it is important for husbands to be loved. But of the two—love and respect—respect is more important to husbands, and love is more important to wives:

- Husbands want to be loved, but they want to be respected even more.

- Wives want to be respected, but they want to be loved even more.

Consider how most wives covet their husbands' expressions of love, such as cards, phone calls, e-mails, or flowers. Though husbands might appreciate such gestures, what they desire more is their wives' respect. I don't need my wife to buy me flowers, call me during the day and tell me she loves me, or write me poetry. I might appreciate these things, but what I need is her respect.

In marriage counseling, when I hear wives express their frustrations about their husbands, often they say, "I don't feel like my husband loves me. I wish he loved me more. He never tells me he loves me." But when husbands express frustration, usually they say, "I wish my wife respected me more. I wish she would follow my lead. I wish she supported my decisions."

In truth, it's much easier for a wife to say she loves her husband than to show it through respect. But it is through respect that a wife expresses her love for her husband—the very fact Scripture calls a wife to respect her husband confirms this. If a wife doesn't show respect, her husband won't feel loved. A good perspective for couples to keep in mind is that feeling unloved is as painful to a wife as feeling disrespected is to a husband.

Modern research supports the biblical instruction on this topic. Marriage expert Dr. Emerson Eggerichs shares some important statistics about husbands and wives in his popular book *Love and Respect*. In one survey, 400 men were asked, "If you were forced to choose, would you prefer to feel alone and unloved or disrespected and inadequate?" Seventy-four percent responded that they would rather feel alone and unloved than disrespected and inadequate.

When Dr. Eggerichs conducted the same survey with women, a similar percentage of women responded that they would rather feel disrespected and inadequate than alone and unloved. Dr. Eggerichs sums up his findings: "[A wife] needs love just as she needs air to breathe, [and a husband] needs respect just as he needs air to breathe."[1]

Another survey asked 7,000 people, "When you are in a conflict with your spouse, do you feel unloved or disrespected?" Eighty-three percent of husbands responded with "disrespected." Seventy-two percent of wives responded with "unloved."[2] This reveals that during marriage conflicts, husbands often react because they feel disrespected and wives often react because they feel unloved.

WHAT RESPECT LOOKS LIKE TO A HUSBAND

How does a wife convey respect to her husband? Here is a basic checklist of what respect looks like to a man.

Admiration—A wife respects her husband by admiring him, looking up to him, and holding him in high regard. In the Amplified Bible, Ephesians 5:33 reads, "Let the wife see that she respects and reverences her husband [that she notices him, regards him, honors him, prefers him, venerates, and esteems him; and that she defers to him, praises him, and loves and admires him exceedingly]."

Trustworthiness—Proverbs 31:11 says of the virtuous wife, "The heart of her husband safely trusts her." A husband feels respected when he can trust his wife. When he is away, she acts in a manner that would please him just as though he were present. He's sure that she won't hide anything from him. Conversely, when a wife is untrustworthy, she communicates that she doesn't respect her husband's headship.

Protectiveness—A wife respects her husband by protecting his name and reputation. She doesn't slander him or complain about him behind his back. With the prevalence of social media, a wife's criticism of her husband can be more damaging than when she gossips to her friends. With a single click, hundreds of people can become aware of the wife's accusations against her husband.

When our church gathers, because I'm typically trying to focus on ministering to people, I'm not able to be with Katie very often. Other than the associate pastor and me, I think she's the most sought-after person in our church, especially by women. I feel very blessed that I never have to worry about what she says or how she acts when I'm not with her.

Proverbs 31:23 says of the virtuous wife, "Her husband is [respected] in the gates, when he sits among the elders of the land." Why is there a verse praising a husband in a passage that is all about a virtuous woman? How is his position a credit to her? This husband would not be respected and sitting among the elders if his wife's behavior caused others to lose respect for him. There are husbands who find it challenging to achieve respect in their circles because their wives slander and diminish them and damage their reputation behind their backs.

Appreciation—A wife respects her husband by expressing appreciation for how hard he works to care for his family and by considering the sacrifices he makes to be a good father and husband. Few attitudes communicate respect more than thankfulness, and few attitudes communicate disrespect more than ingratitude. This leads us to the next point.

WHAT DISRESPECT LOOKS LIKE TO A HUSBAND

Conversely, no matter how much a wife might profess her love, certain attitudes communicate disrespect to her husband.

Discontentment—When a wife routinely expresses frustration with her life, home, family, or possessions, inevitably she will end up disrespecting her husband. A discontented wife makes her husband feel like a failure because he is the one—at least in her eyes—who is not providing well enough to keep her content.

Katie and I have always been a single-income family. When we married, I was a schoolteacher, and then I became a pastor. We have nine children, and while God has always provided, our lives are far from glamorous. Yet if you were to listen to Katie, you would think we're well off. She has committed to being content. Like love, contentment is also a choice. The same goes for discontentment.

Disparaging speech and body language—A wife disrespects her husband when she

- talks down to him or treats him like a little boy who is in trouble

- interrupts or talks over him

- rolls her eyes, huffs and puffs, or wags her finger at him

Even worse is when such disparaging speech and actions extend to others, such as telling friends "a funny story" about a husband's inability to do something or how many times it took him to fix something.

This reminds me of a sad situation I witnessed. A man enthusiastically started sharing a story with a group of people. Those listening were enjoying what he had to say. His wife arrived, rolled her eyes, interrupted him, and said, "Let me tell you what *really* happened." The man was visibly embarrassed. Oddly enough, her account wasn't much different than his. I'm not sure what reason she had to interrupt him other than to make him look bad and draw attention to herself. When a wife treats her husband this way in public, you must wonder how much worse things are in the privacy of their home.

Second-guessing—Even when a wife thinks she is respecting her husband, she sends the opposite message when she second-guesses everything he says, offers all the reasons he is wrong, constantly corrects him, or undermines him when he makes decisions. From her perspective, she might be trying to help, but in reality, her actions communicate, "I don't trust you. You don't know what you're doing. I could do this better." Sometimes the words "I'm just trying to help" don't help.

Badmouthing Dad to the kids—One of the worst ways a wife can disrespect her husband is by belittling him in front of their children. There is absolutely nothing wrong with a wife disagreeing with her husband, but there is a right and a wrong way to do this. Disagreements between a husband and wife should be thoughtfully communicated and resolved in private. When a wife tells the children "I wish your dad would…," or "It's too bad your dad doesn't…," or "I can't believe your dad…," it diminishes him in their eyes. When a wife corrects her husband in front of the children—or worse, slanders him—she destroys his credibility and ability to lead the home. Instead, a wife should strive to instill her children with a good opinion of their father.

MEN LIVE UP OR DOWN

As a wife looks for her husband's best qualities, focuses on his strengths, speaks well of him to others, and praises him to their children, she will find her respect for him growing. Conversely, if a wife speaks badly about her husband to others—whether they be friends, neighbors, or the children—she will find her respect for him diminishing.

If a wife respects her husband and looks up to him, he'll be eager to live up to that level.

Katie thinks too highly of me. I am not the man she thinks I am. I am far from the father and husband that she tells our children and others I am. But I want to be that man. I want to live up to her praise. Yes, primarily I want to please the Lord, but secondarily, I want my wife to think well of me. I desire her respect and I want to be the man that she treats me as though I am. If Katie were to belittle or slander me, I doubt that I would be motivated to give my best.

Most men have no problem living up or down to the bar their wives set for them. If a wife disrespects her husband and treats him like he's a child, he'll have no problem living down to that level. If a wife respects her husband and looks up to him, he'll be eager to live up to that level.

ADAPTING TO YOUR HUSBAND

We will talk more about submission later in this book—for now, it is important to note that the biblical instruction for wives to submit to their husbands also includes the concept of adapting. This is captured in the Amplified Bible:

- Ephesians 5:22—"Wives, be subject (be submissive and *adapt* yourselves) to your own husbands as [a service] to the Lord."

- Colossians 3:18—"Wives, be subject to your husbands [subordinate and *adapt* yourselves to them], as is right and fitting and your proper duty in the Lord."

- Titus 2:5—"[Wives should] be self-controlled, chaste, homemakers, good-natured (kindhearted), *adapting* and subordinating themselves to their husbands."

- 1 Peter 3:1—"In like manner, you married women, be submissive to your own husbands [subordinate yourselves as being secondary to and dependent on them, and *adapt* yourselves to them]."

One of the most important ways for a wife to adapt to her husband is by learning what he finds respectful and disrespectful. After listening to hundreds of hours of my teaching, Katie often knows how I will answer questions and can even finish sentences for me. Because of this familiarity, she helps me know when *not* to say certain things. She will discreetly swipe her hand across the front of her neck, signaling, "Not a good idea." Perhaps the most common criticism I have received in response to my preaching is that I talk too quickly. During a sermon, Katie will make a hand motion that lets me know to slow down. I find these actions helpful, but Katie has had other women tell her, "I can't imagine doing that to my husband when he's talking." And I have had men ask me, "Doesn't it bother you when your wife does that?"

At the same time, there are things other men might find helpful that Katie knows I find disrespectful. This is why it is so important for wives to get to know their husbands well; this is how a wife adapts. She learns what's important to her husband and makes it important to her. Consider the following examples:

- Is your husband punctual? Work hard to be on time.

- Does he have to be up early and thus wants to be in bed by a certain time? Strive to be in bed with him by that time.

- Does it bother him when certain things are messy? Try to make sure these areas are tidy.

As my wife has shared with women: "Ladies, work hard to make your husband's priorities your own and to put your priorities second. And when you adapt to him, do not make him feel stupid for the way he desires for things to be done."

EMBRACING YOUR HUSBAND'S VISION

Scripture calls husbands to be the spiritual leaders of their homes. With that in mind, one of the best ways a wife can respect her husband is by embracing his vision for the family and doing what she can to see it fulfilled. You can do this by passing along his ideas and desires to the children. A wife who does this will have a husband who feels respected. A wife who mocks her husband about his wishes or desires will feel disrespected.

An interesting parallel to this in the military is the relationship between a platoon leader and platoon sergeant. Typically, a platoon leader is a brand-new junior officer. In contrast, the platoon sergeant may be a career soldier who is far more knowledgeable in many areas. Regardless, the platoon leader is the commanding officer responsible for developing the orders and vision for the platoon. The sergeant's responsibility is to embrace the platoon leader's plans and see that they are carried out. The relationship between leader and sergeant is not based on who is wiser or more experienced but on the chain of command. Still, a smart platoon leader will recognize his platoon sergeant's experience and wisdom and seek his thoughts and counsel.

Similarly, a wife may have more experience and wisdom in some areas than her husband, but God has still appointed the husband to be the head of the family and He expects the wife to embrace his leadership. At the same time, a husband should recognize his wife's wisdom and experience and seek her thoughts as he makes decisions and establishes the vision for the family.[3]

A PORTRAIT OF LOVE WITHOUT RESPECT

There are plenty of men who feel loved by their wives but not respected by them. Scripture provides a perfect picture of a woman who loved her husband without respecting him: Saul's daughter, Michal, the first wife of King David. Even though she was responsible for one of the strongest displays of disrespect ever recorded in the Bible from a wife toward a husband, Michal is also the only woman Scripture specifically mentioned as loving her husband: "Michal, Saul's daughter, loved David" (1 Samuel 18:20).

This is not to say other women in Scripture did not love their husbands—many of them did, but that's not emphasized. Why is that? I admit I'm being a little speculative here, but I suspect it's because—as we already discussed—the priority is for women to respect their husbands rather than love them. As a result, Scripture emphasizes a wife's respect instead of her love. Abraham's wife, Sarah, is a case in point. We will read more about her in chapter 17, but for now, it's worth noting that she is held up in the New Testament as an example for wives *not* because of her love, but her submission and respect. This also reveals why Michal, even though she is the one wife in Scripture said to love her husband, is not praised. The disrespect she showed David ruined any potential for her to serve as a positive example for women.

How was it that Michal showed disrespect to her husband? Soon after David became king of the nation of Israel, one of his top priorities was transporting the ark of the covenant to Jerusalem, the capital. The biblical account describes this as one of the most joyful moments of the new king's life. As the procession entered Jerusalem, "David danced before the LORD with all his might" (2 Samuel 6:14). Unfortunately, Michal did not share her husband's joy: "Michal, Saul's daughter, looked through a window and saw King David leaping and whirling before the LORD; and she despised him in her heart" (verse 16).

Michal thought David's behavior was terribly unbecoming. Her father, Saul, was all about appearances, and he would never have acted this way. Perhaps this rubbed off on Michal so that she found David's conduct to be below the dignity of a king. Plus, she was probably jealous of the maids who were watching David with admiration as he danced. Second Samuel 6:20 records her reaction:

> Then David returned to bless his household. And Michal the daughter of Saul came out to meet David, and said, "How glorious was the king of Israel today, uncovering himself today in the eyes of the maids of his servants, as one of the base fellows shamelessly uncovers himself!"

Her words dripped with ridicule. King David arrived home eager to share his joy with his family, but Michal was so disgusted with him that she immediately belittled him. Picture a mother reprimanding a child. You can hear the scorn and disrespect in Michal's words. Wives will want to ask themselves, "Am I like this? Do I pounce on my husband and ridicule him over something inconsequential? Do I make him feel like a little boy who is in trouble?"

Note that Michal was not the only one who handled this situation wrongly. David did not respond lovingly to his wife:

> David said to Michal, "It was before the LORD, who chose me instead of your father and all his house, to appoint me ruler over the people of the LORD, over Israel. Therefore I will play music before the LORD. And I will be even more undignified than this, and will be humble in my own sight. But as for the maidservants of whom you have spoken, by them I will be held in honor" (verses 21-22).

David harshly pointed out that God chose him over Michal's father. How do you think this made her feel? Then he added, "You think this is bad? I'll act even worse than this!" The phrase "held in honor" in verse 22 may be the clearest and simplest definition of respect in the Bible. David told Michal, "You might not respect me, but there are plenty of other women who do." For David to point out other women's feelings about him was prideful and insensitive. While I'm not at all defending the sinful actions of men who do this, how many husbands have been disrespected by their wives only to look to other women they believe will respect them?

Disrespect Can Change a Husband's Feelings Toward His Wife

This encounter between David and Michal does not end happily: "Therefore Michal the daughter of Saul had no children to the day of her death" (verse 23). I take this to mean that David no longer had sexual relations with Michal. I am not defending David's actions. God clearly commands husbands to love their wives unconditionally, and David disobeyed. As is the case in most marriage conflicts, both spouses were at fault:

- It is sinful for wives to disrespect their husbands as Michal disrespected David.
- It is sinful for husbands to punish their wives as David punished Michal.

With that said, it is important to notice how dramatically this one event changed David's relationship with Michal.

Consider what occurred only a few chapters earlier. When Saul became jealous of David, he took Michal and gave her to another man. Saul's general, Abner, defected from Saul and wanted to join David: "Abner sent messengers on his behalf to David, saying, 'Whose is the land?' saying also, 'Make your covenant with me, and indeed my hand shall be with you to bring all Israel to you'" (2 Samuel 3:12). David wasn't king over all of Israel yet, but Abner said he would help fix that. That was a wonderful offer, considering all the years David had waited to become king. Of course David would respond in the positive, but David told Abner he could join him under only one condition: "David said, 'Good, I will make a covenant with you. But one thing I require of you: you shall not see my face unless you first bring Michal, Saul's daughter, when you come to see my face'" (verse 13).

David wanted nothing to do with Michal at the end of 2 Samuel 6, but only a few chapters earlier, he made every effort to be reunited with her. Once Michal disrespected David so drastically, his attitude toward her changed just as drastically. He now resented her. His was not the right response, but it was the reality.

It is no different today. When husbands are strongly disrespected by their wives, they become resentful and distance themselves from them. That is not a right response, but it is a common fruit of disrespect. If not dealt with, the result may be a destroyed relationship, such as that between David and Michal. The biblical account of what happened between them is instructive:

- It gives wives an example of how not to treat their husbands.

- It gives husbands an example of how not to respond to their wives.

- It illustrates that wives loving their husbands is not the same as respecting them. Perhaps Michal still loved David at this point, but we can be sure that he did not feel loved because of the way she had disrespected him.

A Husband's Love and a Wife's Respect Are Not Optional

In the previous chapter, we discussed how a wife must *feel* supreme. It is not about what the husband thinks or says, but about how the wife *feels*. Similarly, a husband must feel respected. It is not about what the wife thinks or says, but about how the husband *feels*. Just as a wife's perception about being the supreme relationship in her husband's life is her reality, so, too, is a husband's perception about being respected his reality.

We also looked at how husbands are commanded to love their wives even when they don't feel like it. A husband's love should not be conditional. The same is true about a wife's respect. It should not be conditional. Ephesians 5:33 says, "Let the wife see that she respects her husband" without including the word *if.* Just as husbands are commanded to love their wives when they don't feel like it, wives are commanded to respect their husbands when they don't feel like it. As much as wives want their husbands to love them unconditionally, husbands want their wives to respect them unconditionally.

The moment any marriage becomes conditional with a husband saying, "I am not going to love my wife because she…" or a wife saying, "I am not going to respect my husband because he…," the marriage suffers. You have the recipe for a miserable marriage when each spouse's obedience is not conditional on his or her love for Christ, but rather, on the other spouse's behavior. Only when two people are equally committed to obeying God's commands unconditionally because of their commitments to Christ will a marriage experience the health and joy God desires for it.

MAKE LOVING AND RESPECTING EASIER

Even though a husband is commanded to love his wife, a wife can make it easier for him to love her. Some wives are more lovable than others. Consider the following passages:

- "Better to dwell in a corner of a housetop, than in a house shared with a contentious woman" (Proverbs 21:9; see also 25:24).

- "Better to dwell in the wilderness, than with a contentious and angry woman" (Proverbs 21:19).

These verses describe women whom even the godliest man would have trouble loving. They act in ways that a man would rather sit on the corner of a rooftop and experience terrible weather, or be in the wilderness surrounded by wild animals. Some husbands say, "I want to love my wife, but she makes it so difficult. If only you had any idea of how she acts!" Wife, make it easier for your husband to obey God's command to love you by being lovable.

Similarly, even though a wife is commanded to respect her husband, a husband ought to do what he can to make it easier to respect him. Earlier I shared about how difficult it was for Katie to respect me when I got caught up with playing World of Warcraft. I don't intend to pry into your home when I say this, but if you are doing something that causes your wife to lose respect for you, you should determine whether you need to remove it from your life or do it in greater moderation. What could be worth more than your wife's respect?

Some wives say, "I want to look up to my husband and respect him, but he makes it so difficult for me. If only you knew how he acts!" A wife finds it difficult to respect her husband when he doesn't work hard to take care of his family, mistreats their children, or looks at things he should rip his eyes away from. Part of being a loving husband is being a man who is pure, holy, and seeks to earn his wife's respect. Husband, make it easier for your wife to obey God's command to respect you by being respectable.

To make loving your wife and respecting your husband easier, keep in mind that God is for you. He wants your marriage to be a joy and blessing. After all, not only has He given you commands for your good, He also helps you to obey them. As you strive to love your spouse, you can be encouraged that "[God's] divine power has given to [you] all things that pertain to life and godliness" (2 Peter 1:3). Because your marriage is such a big part of life and godliness, how confident and encouraged can you be that God will empower you to obey these commands!

PART FIVE

UNDERSTANDING SUBMISSION

CHAPTER THIRTEEN

What Submission Does Not Mean

---

was invited to be one of the keynote speakers for a marriage conference. During one of the first planning meetings, the various speakers and the conference leaders came together to choose the topics for the messages. Many important topics were suggested, such as husbands loving their wives, intimacy, communication, and conflict resolution. Nobody mentioned submission, so I said I would preach on the subject. Immediately the tone in the room changed. While the other suggestions were met with enthusiastic responses, such as, "Sounds good...I look forward to hearing that message...That will be very beneficial," mine was met with, "Umm...Uhh...Hmm." You would've thought I had offered to speak on something completely unbiblical rather than the primary command given to wives that is very clearly repeated throughout the New Testament in Ephesians 5:22, 24, Colossians 3:18, Titus 2:3-5, and 1 Peter 3:1.

One of the other keynote speakers said, "I try not to use the word *submit*. I like to say *defer, compromise,* or *consider.*" The awkwardness continued when we filmed the promotional spots for the conference. My video probably took more time to be recorded than the rest of the speakers combined because there were repeated objections to me quoting Bible verses commanding wives to submit to their husbands. Interestingly, I did little more than simply recite the verses, letting the Bible speak for itself. I didn't interpret them or comment on them, which reveals how much discomfort there is simply associated with what God's Word says about submission.

Submission is difficult to address. Some people cringe at the word. I will be the first to say submission has been misused and abused in relationships, sermons, and counseling sessions. My desire is to approach this sensitive command in both a biblical and delicate manner. Up front, I would like to make two requests:

1. Please commit to taking the time to consider what Scripture itself says about submission and how it applies to everyday life. Clearly, the fact God made this such a *key* part of His marriage instructions means it is important.

2. Please keep in mind that as our Creator and Designer, God knows the ideal for our relationships. Not only does He *know* what is best for us, He *wants* what is best for us. For us to reject His design is to settle for less than God's best, and say we know better than Him.

ANSWERING THOSE NAGGING QUESTIONS

In any discussion of submission, some obvious and legitimate questions arise: How far does submission extend? Is there anything to which a wife should not submit? Are all women required to submit to all men? Does submission mean men can do whatever they want to their wives? What about physical or mental abuse?

As we cover the command for wives to submit to their husbands, I don't want these questions nagging you. I believe you will be more receptive to what submission involves if you first learn what it does *not* involve. Let's answer these nagging questions by considering what biblical submission does *not* mean.

Submission Does Not Mean That Wives Submit to Other Men

While Scripture is clear that God commands wives to submit to their husbands, each command is equally clear that wives are commanded to submit *only* to their husbands:

- Ephesians 5:22—"Wives, submit to *your own husbands.*"

- Ephesians 5:24—"Just as the church is subject to Christ, so let the wives be to *their own husbands* in everything."

- Colossians 3:18—"Wives, submit to *your own husbands.*"

- Titus 2:3-5—"Older women likewise…admonish the young women to…[be] obedient to *their own husbands.*"

- 1 Peter 3:1—"Wives, likewise, be submissive to *your own husbands.*"

Wives are under *their own husbands'* headship, and not under the authority of other men. Even in the church, a wife is under the authority of her husband,

and her husband is under the authority of the leadership of the church: "the head of every man is Christ, the head of woman is man" (1 Corinthians 11:3).

In Genesis 2:18, when God spoke of creating the first woman, He did not say, "I will make men [plural] helpers." He said: "I will make *him* [singular] a helper." When I want help in my life, I look to my wife or to other men God has placed in my life. I do not look to other men's wives because I know they are not my helper. Scripture clearly limits the boundaries of a husband's headship and a wife's submission to the context of a marriage relationship.

Practically, this also addresses the misconception that submission means women can only hold positions—in or out of the church—in which they are subordinate to all male associates. Such an extreme view would suggest that a woman cannot be a nurse because a male orderly might be her subordinate or that a woman could not be a teacher because a male aide or janitor might help her at times. As I mentioned earlier, when I was an elementary school teacher, most of the principals I worked for were women.

Submission Does Not Mean That Wives Submit to Abuse

What women long for is spiritual and moral leadership from their husbands—not spiritual or moral domination. While this is straightforward, because there is so much confusion about what submission is and isn't, it is vital for us to be clear on what this means. When we hear the word *abuse*, typically we think in terms of physical mistreatment. Abuse, however, can be emotional, mental, and even spiritual. There are wives whose husbands never lay a hand on them yet mistreat them so badly they are in just as bad or worse condition than women who are physically abused.

What should a woman in an abusive relationship do? She cannot divorce her husband, but she can separate from him. The apostle Paul writes, "The woman...is bound by the law to her husband as long as he lives" (Romans 7:2), and "If [a wife] does depart, let her remain unmarried or be reconciled to her husband" (1 Corinthians 7:11; see also verse 39). If the abused woman is part of a church, she should go to the pastors or elders, and they should find a safe place for her (and her children, if necessary). In the meantime, for the husband, discipline is performed, counsel is given, repentance is sought, and the biblical counsel or gospel is given time to work in his heart. An abused wife may also need to seek social or legal services, residency in a battered woman's shelter, and even help from the police, if the abuse warrants such.

That said, the abuse card can be used carelessly. I have heard women throw out the word simply because a husband didn't give his wife everything she wanted. When a wife does not get to do all that she wants to do, go all the places she wants to go, buy all the things she wants to buy, or spend all her time the way she wants to spend it, that is not abuse.

I've also heard women talk about being abused when they aren't treated with what they believe to be sufficient adoration. Having a husband who is less than perfect in this area does not constitute abuse. While God does command husbands to love their wives as Christ loved the church, no husband does this perfectly. As fallen humans, husbands will have times when they sin against their wives, but this does not necessarily mean abuse has occurred. If failing to love one's wife perfectly constituted abuse, then every wife on earth would be in an abusive relationship.

Submission Does Not Mean That Wives Submit to Sin

The account in Acts 5:1-11 of Ananias and his wife, Sapphira, is instructive. The background of this story is that early church members were selling their possessions and sharing the proceeds with the apostles and other believers who had needs. Ananias sold a possession, kept part of the money when he brought his offering to the apostles, but acted as though all the proceeds were being given to the church. As the apostle Peter declared, Ananias had every right to keep part of his profits if he wanted. But because Ananias claimed to have turned over all the funds—and thus he lied to the Holy Spirit—he dropped dead on the spot.

The correlation is that Ananias "kept back part of the proceeds, *his wife also being aware of it*" (Acts 5:2). When Sapphira showed up, not realizing her husband had died, she had the opportunity to tell the truth. Instead, she reiterated her husband's lie. This led Peter to say, "How is it that you have agreed together to test the Spirit of the Lord? Look, the feet of those who have buried your husband are at the door, and they will carry you out" (verse 9).

God's judgment on Sapphira for supporting her husband's sin shows she was as accountable as him. Peter's response indicates that if she had refused to participate in the deception, her life would have been spared. This is a perfect example of a time when a wife should not have submitted to her husband.

Let me add a caveat that the principle in question applies to being asked to engage in blatant sin. A wife should say no to a husband who demands that she participate in any kind of illegal activity, such as drug dealing, theft, adultery, or even lesser legal offenses, such as cheating on income taxes or lying to an employer. This is quite different from a husband opposing his wife's involvement in positive spiritual activities. A husband may resist his wife taking time from home and family to join a Bible study fellowship, attend church several times a week, volunteer for a Christian outreach, or participate in a church sports league. In those instances, he is not asking her to commit a sin, but simply to respect his preference. That raises an important question: What is a wife supposed to do when her husband resists her participation in activities that can contribute to her spiritual growth?

A wife can respectfully let her husband know her desire and ask if he would allow this for the benefit of their marriage, children, or family. If he is still resistant, then she should submit and pray. Assuming God wants her or the family involved in the activity, there's a possibility He will change the husband's heart. Even if a wife does not like her husband's decision or request, she should be encouraged that God will reward her submission and—assuming the husband is disobeying God by declining—hold the husband responsible for his poor spiritual leadership.

Submission Does Not Mean That Husbands Do Not Defer to Their Wives

Every healthy, joyful marriage in which a woman feels loved involves a husband who defers to his wife. Godly men are not going to thoughtlessly insist on submission. They will first seek to graciously reach an agreement with their wives. Even when an agreement can't be reached, they may still choose to defer to their wives. Let me share two examples from my marriage.

Not long ago I decided a great plan would be to surprise the family with one of my favorite foods—popcorn—and a show filled with thrills, tremendous plot lines, and edge-of-your-seat action—*Little House on the Prairie*. While I was working up an appetite doing cardio, my mom called to say, "Katie invited us to go out for frozen yogurt with all of you. When do you want us to come over?"

Now, I'm sure many husbands can relate to this. You're excited about how you would like to spend your evening, only to find out that your wife has other plans. My first thought was that Katie and I hadn't discussed getting frozen yogurt. My second thought was that the frozen yogurt shop didn't sell popcorn or show *Little House on the Prairie*.

At that moment I had two choices. I could put my foot down and say, "I've already decided we're going to have popcorn and watch *Little House on the Prairie* as a family, so that is what we're going to do." Or I could say, "You know what? I'm going to sacrifice for my wife. What she is suggesting we do could be a great way to spend the evening. I'll take the family to a frozen yogurt shop."

This might seem like a trivial example, but the point I'm trying to make is that even though wives are commanded to submit to their husbands, godly husbands look for ways to bless their wives and families, even when it means a change of plans or decisions. Ephesians 5:28 says husbands ought to love their wives as their own bodies, and at the time, my wife wanted frozen yogurt. You can guess where we ended up.

On a more serious note, at the time of this writing, our eight-month-old daughter, Lydia, stopped nursing. She also wouldn't take a bottle, eat anything, or use a pacifier. While up to this point she had been our easiest baby to care for, she couldn't be comforted, wouldn't sleep at night, and cried constantly. She started losing weight, which was even more concerning because she was already small. Katie took her to a medical clinic, but the doctor couldn't find anything wrong with her. While I was concerned about Lydia, I knew Katie was more distressed than I was. She cried regularly because we couldn't figure out what was wrong.

A few days later, Katie called me and said, "I looked in Lydia's mouth and saw something attached to the roof of it." Upon closer inspection, we could see that it was a dress-up, press-on fingernail that belonged to one of Lydia's older sisters, Charis. Somehow Lydia had gotten it, and it had become attached to the roof of her mouth. While we were thankful to finally know what was wrong, we couldn't get it out. I tried to remove it with my finger, but it wouldn't budge.

I then called someone in our church, who invited us to head over to his house, as he thought he could take it out. But Katie didn't feel comfortable with that idea. She wanted to take Lydia to the hospital in case there was an infection or the nail got lodged in her throat during the attempt to remove it. I didn't want to go to the hospital because I thought my friend could take it out. More than likely he could have, and a trip to the hospital (and the accompanying bill) would have been unnecessary. But I could see how upset Katie was and how much she wanted to see a doctor so she would know things were fine. I deferred to Katie and we went to the hospital, which gave her peace of mind as a result of knowing that Lydia was receiving all the care she needed. Deferring to my wife so she felt loved was worth the cost.

Submission Does Not Mean That Husbands Do Not Listen to Their Wives

We have already learned how God created the woman to give man a "helper comparable to him" (Genesis 2:18). I don't want to sound simplistic, but in my mind, the three greatest resources God has given a husband on this side of heaven are the Word of God, the Holy Spirit (also called "the Helper"), and his wife.

A husband who does not listen to his wife is forfeiting one of the greatest resources God has given him. In addition, consider how these three resources work together. God can use His Holy Spirit to counsel husbands through their wives. Many times, God has used Katie to warn me, correct me, encourage me, or direct me. There have been times when Katie has shared Scripture with me or given me her thoughts on a passage and she helped me to better understand God's Word.

The three greatest resources God has given a husband on this side of heaven are the Word of God, the Holy Spirit...and his wife.

Scripture gives a powerful example of how a wife's wisdom can be instructive for a husband. The context is the Roman prefect Pontius Pilate, who was sitting in judgment over the trial and crucifixion of Jesus. During the trial, Pilate's wife sent him a message: "Have nothing to do with that just Man, for I have suffered many things today in a dream because of Him" (Matthew 27:19). Pilate rejected her counsel, and we all know what happened afterward. Could there be a better example in all of history of a time when a husband should have listened to his wife?

One very significant instance in which I believe God used Katie to direct me has to do with a key transition I made as a pastor. At the time, I was an associate pastor at Grace Baptist Church in Lemoore, California. Although that was a wonderful season of life for us, Katie sensed that God had gifted me to shepherd my own church. The senior pastor agreed with Katie's assessment, so she had confirmation from him as well.

When we found out about a pastorate at Woodland Christian Church in Woodland, Washington State, Katie wanted me to take the position, but I wasn't so sure because I enjoyed my job at Grace Baptist, I don't like change, and I didn't want to say goodbye to so many people I loved. In addition, the job security at the new position didn't look promising. One of the deacons had the integrity to tell me, "Based on our savings, if the giving remains the same, we will only be able to pay you for eight months."

I say all this to make it clear how hard it was for me to change jobs. Looking back, Katie's ongoing encouragement is one of the main reasons I was able to make the move. There is one more detail to the story, but I will save that for later. For now, I simply want to share that God used Katie in that situation to give me the confidence I needed to become a senior pastor and use my spiritual giftedness in a greater variety of ways.

Submission Does Not Mean That Wives Are Inferior

A common criticism of submission sounds something like this: "If wives are supposed to submit to their husbands, then wives are not equal to their husbands. Because God made men and women equal, wives do not have to submit." Do we apply this thinking to the other kinds of relationships that require submission? Do we say that parents are superior to their children, elders are superior to their congregations, governments are superior to the people they govern, or employers are superior to their employees? Not at all. The same logic dictates that a wife's submission to her husband does not in any way make her inferior.

Perhaps the best example of this is seen in the relationship between God the Son and God the Father. Consider these verses demonstrating Jesus's submission:

- In John 5:30, Jesus stated, "I do not seek My own will but the will of the Father who sent Me."

- In John 6:38, Jesus said, "I have come down from heaven, not to do My own will, but the will of Him who sent Me."

- In Matthew 26:39, Jesus prayed only a few hours before His crucifixion, "O My Father, if it is possible, let this cup pass from Me; nevertheless, not as I will, but as You will."

Does Jesus's submission to the Father indicate that He is inferior? Absolutely not. Jesus made His equality with the Father very evident:

- In John 10:30, Jesus proclaimed, "I and My Father are one."

- In John 17:20-22, Jesus said, "I [pray]...for those who will believe in Me...that they all may be one, *as You, Father, are in Me, and I in You*...that they may be one *just as We are one.*"

Those who believe a wife's submission to her husband makes her inferior must also conclude that the Son's submission to the Father makes Him inferior. If we acknowledge that the Son is both submissive to the Father and equal with Him, we can also acknowledge that wives are submissive to their husbands while still being equal with them.

The Son's submissiveness to the Father and the unity, equality, and oneness they share is a beautiful picture of a wife's submissiveness to her husband and the unity, equality, and oneness they should share. Note the following parallel: Jesus said, "We are one," and Genesis 2:24 says, "A man shall leave his father and mother and be joined to his wife, and *they shall become one*." To make the parallel with marriage even stronger, 1 Corinthians 11:3 states, "The head of woman is man, and the head of Christ is God." Just as the Son submits to the Father and sees Him as His head, a wife submits to her husband and sees him as her head.

FOLLOWING JESUS'S EXAMPLE OF SUBMISSION

We can all be encouraged in our submission by looking at Jesus's example. In the middle of Peter's passage on submission he praised our Savior's behavior: "To this you were called, because Christ also suffered for us, *leaving us an example, that you should follow His steps*" (1 Peter 2:21). This does not apply only to wives submitting to their husbands but to any relationship involving submission. When children demonstrate submission to parents, congregations demonstrate submission to elders, believers demonstrate submission to government, and employees demonstrate submission to employers, they are demonstrating the heart of Christ. A submissive heart is a heart like Christ's. To submit is to be like Christ.

Just as Jesus is the premier example of submission, so Satan offers the premier example of rebellion. Scripture provides vivid images of Satan's original rejection of God as his head, which resulted in his being cast down and out of heaven (Isaiah 14:12-20; Ezekiel 28:12-19). Then, in the Garden of Eden, we see him as a serpent stirring up similar rebellion in Eve. Consider the parallels between the words he spoke to himself and the words he spoke to the first woman:

- "I will ascend above the heights of the clouds, *I will be like the Most High*" (Isaiah 14:14).

- "Your eyes will be opened, and *you will be like God*" (Genesis 3:5).

Satan is saying here, in essence, "You do not need to submit to God. You can have His position instead." As difficult as it is to hear this, ultimately, to be rebellious and reject the authority God has placed over us—whether parents, church leadership, government, employers, or husbands as the head of the family—is to follow Satan's example.

But let's not conclude with our focus on Satan. Let's resume "looking unto Jesus, the author and finisher of our faith, who for the joy that was set before Him endured the cross, despising the shame" (Hebrews 12:2). When we think of submission, our minds can go to

- how Jesus was willing to submit—perfectly
- what He was willing to submit to—the wrath of God that our sins deserve
- why He was willing to submit—His unimaginable love for us

Nobody has ever had as much to submit to as Jesus did. Nobody has ever submitted to any trial or suffering as well as Jesus did. We should be encouraged by the example Jesus set for us whenever we face a situation that calls for submission. We should think about all Jesus submitted to whenever we feel like we are required to submit too much. We should remember the suffering Jesus submitted to whenever we feel like our submission involves too much suffering. We should especially keep in mind that Jesus submitted "for the joy that was set before Him" so that someday, we can hear, "Well done, good and faithful servant...Enter into the joy of your lord" (Matthew 25:21). Jesus' example should encourage all us—man and woman alike—in our submission.

CHAPTER FOURTEEN

Equal-Opportunity Submission

Because we live in a fallen world—and because our fallenness resulted from Adam and Eve's refusal to submit to God—ultimately, we are prone to resist submission, unbeliever and believer alike. Our culture views submission negatively. When we become Christians, we continue to struggle with submission because we're called to submit in multiple ways that our flesh resists. Therefore, as you read this chapter, here are two key points that are vital to keep in mind:

1. The Bible speaks frequently of submission, so if you have a problem with it, you will have a problem with much of the Bible.

2. Submission—or having a submissive spirit—is spoken of positively in Scripture. If you do not want to be a submissive person, you will have a hard time following Christ.

Before we do more exploring about what the Bible says about submission in marriage, let's talk about submission in other areas of life.

SUBMISSION IS NOT ONLY FOR WIVES

Often when we hear the word *submission*, the first thing that comes to mind is God's command for wives to submit to their husbands. But wives are far from the only believers commanded to submit. In fact, every Christian is called to submit in a variety of ways. Later we will examine 1 Peter 3:1-6, which commands wives to submit to their husbands, but before Peter instructs wives, he first addresses submission in other relationships:

- First Peter 2:13-17 commands believers to submit to government (see also Romans 13:1-7).

- First Peter 2:18-25 commands slaves to submit to their masters; in our society, the equivalent is employees submitting to employers (see also Ephesians 6:5-8).

- First Peter 5:5 commands congregations to submit to their elders (see also Hebrews 13:17).

In Ephesians 6:1, the apostle Paul commands children to submit to their parents (see also Colossians 3:20). He also instructs wives to submit to their husbands in Ephesians 5:22, but one verse earlier, in Ephesians 5:21, he commands believers to submit "to one another in the fear of God." This calls us to have a submissive spirit that is willing to give up rights and desires unity in the body of Christ. We see this described more clearly in Philippians 2:3-4: "Let nothing be done through selfish ambition or conceit, but in lowliness of mind *let each esteem others better than himself.* Let each of you look out not only for his own interests, but also for the interests of others."

Our spiritual liberty is not only about freedom but about giving up—that is, submitting—our rights for others. If a brother or sister in Christ would be offended or stumble on account of exercising our liberties, we submit to that person by laying down our rights (Romans 14:14-23; 1 Corinthians 8:9-13). Paul says in Romans 12:18, "If it is possible, as much as depends on you, live peaceably with all men." Hebrews 12:14 reiterates, "Pursue peace with all people." Establishing this peace, whether in the marriage union or any other relationship, involves submission. It involves making sacrifices in deference to others.

THE WAY WE SUBMIT IS AS IMPORTANT AS SUBMITTING

When I taught elementary school, I told students on the first day of class that the *way* in which they did what I asked was as important as *doing* what I asked. For example:

- If I instructed a student to take out a book and the student slammed it defiantly on his desk, he would be in as much trouble as if he had not taken out the book at all.

- If I told a student to push in her chair but she pushed it in with a bad attitude, she would be in as much trouble as if she had not pushed in the chair at all.

The way we submit—whether students to teachers, children to parents, congregations to elders, believers to government, employees to employers, believers to one another, or wives to husbands—is as important as submitting itself. If we submit with a bad attitude, we are not really submitting. We may think of submission as an outward action, but it starts with a right inward attitude. To put it simply: Submission is an issue of the heart.

It's noteworthy that the New Testament Greek word translated "submit"—*hypotasso*—is a military term that means "to arrange (troop divisions) in a military fashion under the command of a leader." This reminds me of a lesson I will never forget from my time in the Army. A superior officer asked those of us under his command, "What do you do with every command you receive?" We gave any number of answers:

- "Make sure you know exactly what you are being asked to do."

- "Learn from the order."

- "Carry out the request as quickly as possible."

Nobody had the response the officer was looking for. Finally, he said, "Take the order and make it your own."

What he meant was that any time we were given a command, we should do it as though we wanted to do it. If a soldier moaned, groaned, rolled his eyes, complained, or argued with his commander when asked to do something, he would be considered insubordinate. To say the commander would frown upon his response is an understatement. Likewise, from a Christian perspective, we should recognize how much God frowns upon us when we submit with a poor attitude. This also applies to

- students when they submit to their teachers

- children when they submit to their parents

- employees when they submit to their bosses

- wives when they submit to their husbands

And this applies to husbands when they demonstrate their love for their

wives. Will a wife feel blessed if her husband sighs and complains while changing a diaper or washing the dishes?

OBEY THE BIBLE, NOT THE WORLD

These days we often hear about the "redefinition" of marriage. Such discussions typically refer to marriage as being something other than the union
of one man and one woman for life. But there is another way society has rede-
fined marriage, and that is in relation to the roles and responsibilities of husbands and wives. Consider this: Even non-Christian friends and neighbors have
no issue discussing husbands loving their wives, but mention male headship or
submission, and you can count on facing fierce opposition. Here is what self-
proclaimed feminist Cath Elliot said about biblical womanhood:

> Unfortunately, as in any movement for social change, there are those
> who remain resistant to their own [freedom]: a tiny minority of
> women who have been so indoctrinated by religious conditioning
> that they continue to see themselves as men's subordinates…Bib-
> lical womanhood does exactly what it says it does: it sends women
> back to the dark ages. At the [True Woman] Conference, for exam-
> ple, the Christian sisters launched their new manifesto, inspiringly
> titled "The True Woman Manifesto," where they resolved to culti-
> vate "such virtues as purity, modesty, submission, meekness, and
> love" and where they affirmed their calling as women "to encourage
> men as they seek to express godly masculinity, and to honor and sup-
> port God-ordained male leadership in the home and in the church."
> It's encouraging to see that only three thousand women have signed
> this terrible charter, but it's also depressing to think that three thou-
> sand women think so little of themselves and their daughters that
> they're prepared to endorse such illiberal, anti-woman nonsense.[1]

Ms. Elliot's perception of biblical submission is that it enslaves women and
ruins their lives. She is not alone in thinking that way. This is the prevailing view
of secular society regarding the biblical roles of husbands and wives.

In support of the biblical view of submission, Dr. Jay Adams, founder of the
Institute for Nouthetic Studies (INS), the National Association of Nouthetic
Counselors (NANC) (now known as ACBC, or the Association of Certified
Biblical Counselors), and the Christian Counseling and Educational Founda-
tion (CCEF), explained:

Submission does not remove freedom; it allows for it. When is the train freer? When it is bumping over the hillside off the track? Or when it is smoothly running along the track, confined or restricted, if you will, to the track? It is freer when it is where it ought to be, doing what it was intended to do…Freedom in God's world never comes apart from structure. When one is free to live as God intended, he is truly free indeed. We hear much about women's liberation today. I want you to be liberated. Here is the path of genuine liberation for a woman: submission. Submission allows her to run on the track; it allows her to make beautiful music in her home.[2]

Dr. Adams's point, which is equally true for husbands, is that true freedom is experienced when we live in obedience to God. True freedom comes when we strive to be husbands and wives as God commanded rather than as society defines. Jesus said, "You shall know the truth, and the truth shall make you free" (John 8:32). This is why we need to embrace what Scripture says. Real freedom and joy—whether for young, old, male, female, single, or married—comes from embracing the Bible's teachings. Disobedience always leads to frustration and bondage.

Whenever we read the Bible, we face two choices:

- We can shape Scripture to fit our desires and beliefs.
- We can allow Scripture to shape us and our thinking.

As Christians, we will undoubtedly say we want the latter, but the real difficulty is that we live in a world that strives to shape us. What's wrong with being shaped by the world? Jesus said the devil is "the ruler of this world" (John 12:31; 14:30; 16:11). John said, "The whole world lies under the sway of the wicked one" (1 John 5:19).

For this reason Paul instructed, "Do not be conformed to this world, but be transformed by the renewing of your mind, that you may prove what is that good and acceptable and perfect will of God" (Romans 12:2). Paul alerted us to the fact the world desires to conform us, and he said that instead, we are to be transformed by letting our minds be renewed. If we were reading this verse for the first time, we would probably expect Paul to use the same word twice: "Do not be *conformed* to this world, but be *conformed* by the renewing of your mind," or "Do not be *transformed* to this world, but be *transformed* by the renewing of your mind." Instead, Paul used two different words, and if we understand them both, then we can understand the verse.

The Greek word translated "conformed" is *syschematizo*, which means "to conform one's self to another's pattern." It's related to the English word *schematic* because it's describing the way society shapes us to follow its patterns. The Greek word translated "transformed" is *metamorphoo*, from which we get our English word *metamorphosis*. Picture a caterpillar bursting from its cocoon, transformed into a beautiful butterfly. This is what should occur with us: If we resist the world's conforming influence, we can be transformed as our minds are renewed by God's Word.

Allowing this transformation to happen can be difficult when we choose to disagree with what Scripture says. When our beliefs are challenged, it is at those moments that we must choose to submit to God's Word instead of the world. Unless we think we are wiser than God, we can trust that He knows best. As you read this book, my hope is that you will make the decision to let the Bible transform your view of marriage. Otherwise, you will end up being conformed to the world's ways of thinking. This is especially important when it comes to the matter of submission, a teaching that is firmly rejected by society and, sadly, even by some churches.

THE NEED FOR SUBMISSION

An examination of basic leadership structures makes clear that submission is an important principle in every area of human interaction. No organization can be successful without authority or headship. Businesses have CEOs, sports teams have coaches, governments have presidents or prime ministers, and schools have principals.

Just as we recognize the need for a leader, or a head, we also recognize that there cannot be two heads. We do not see two head coaches, two presidents, two senior pilots, or two lead surgeons. Imagine how uncomfortable you would feel flying on a plane in which two senior pilots are arguing over the flight plan. Imagine being operated on by two lead surgeons quarreling over the proper procedure. That is why we always see a head coach and an assistant coach, a president and a vice president, a pilot and a copilot, a principal and an assistant principal. The second-in-command is expected to submit to the authority of the leader, or head.

Because we recognize the wisdom of and need for orderly leadership in all other areas of life, we should recognize the wisdom of and need for the same in a marriage relationship and appreciate how clear God makes this point in Scripture. Consider the following:

- In the New Testament, wives are instructed five times to submit to their husbands (Ephesians 5:22; 5:24; Colossians 3:18; Titus 2:3-5; 1 Peter 3:1). The repetition makes this one of the more common commands in God's Word.

- Every New Testament passage that discusses the marriage relationship commands wives to submit. In other words, there's no discussion of marriage without discussing a wife's submission. A wife's role is inextricably linked to and contingent on her submission to her husband. God does not see wives' relationships to their husbands separately from their submission to their husbands.

- Despite all the New Testament verses we have looked at that instruct believers to submit toward various individuals—employers, elders, government, parents, husbands—it's significant that there is no verse specifically instructing husbands to submit to their wives.

Because Ephesians 5:21 says to "[submit] to one another," the passage is sometimes used to argue that husbands and wives should submit equally to each other. There are a few problems with that interpretation:

- Ephesians 5:21 does not refer to the marriage relationship. Rather, it is talking about believers' mutual responsibilities toward each other. Paul does not transition to the subject of marriage until verse 22, when he begins addressing wives directly.

- As we saw earlier in chapter 6, at least two husbands—Adam and Ahab—were rebuked for submitting to their wives (Genesis 3:17; 1 Kings 21:25).

- Paul cannot be teaching that husbands should submit to their wives because that would conflict with the instruction that immediately follows in verses 22 and 24 for wives to submit to their husbands, as well as similar instruction in Colossians 3:18, Titus 2:3-5, and 1 Peter 3:1.

Submission When a Wife Disagrees

One of the most common arguments I have heard from wives who don't want to submit to their husband is, "I would submit to my husband if I agreed with him." Can we see the problem with this logic? The command for a wife to submit to her husband is especially relevant when she disagrees because that is when she has the most trouble embracing her husband's leadership. When a wife agrees with her husband, she has a much easier time submitting to him.

Perhaps a husband and wife have discussed a decision together, presented their ideas, shared their thoughts, and tried to come to an agreement. But they cannot. At this point, what do they do? How do they decide? Do they flip a coin or play rock-paper-scissors? Just as in all the other authority structures we have discussed, there is a clear answer that God has decreed: For the marriage to be able to move forward and maintain harmony, the husband has been designated to make the final decision.

When couples make a decision, a husband should do his best to hear his wife's counsel and take her thoughts into consideration. In doing so, he fulfills his calling to love his wife. Yet these two points should be kept in mind:

- Although it is ideal for a decision to be made only after a husband has given his wife ample time to share her thoughts and opinions, some situations might not allow for lengthy discussions. If, for whatever reason, time is limited and a presentation of both sides is not feasible, wives are still called to submit to their husbands.

- As much as a husband should make every effort to hear his wife's thoughts, a wife should not make every effort to exasperate her husband in the hopes that he will simply give up and give in.

As difficult as submission may be at times for the wife, she needs to remember this: If her husband is wrong, he will be held responsible for the outcome. The decision is on his shoulders. Her responsibility ends at submitting, not at making the final decision. Marriage counselor and author Wayne Mack explains it this way:

> Submission means a wife sees herself as part of her husband's team. She has ideas, opinions, desires, requests, and insights, and she lovingly makes them known. But she knows that in any good team someone must make the final decision. She knows the team members must support the team leader, his plans and decisions, or no progress will be made and confusion and frustration will result. Fifty-fifty marriages [where the husband leads half the time and the wife leads half the time] are an impossibility. They do not work.

They cannot work. In marriage someone must be the final decision maker, and God has ordained that this should be the husband.[3]

Yes, submission is difficult. It is tough for husbands to lead spiritually, and it is tough for wives to submit. Wives should be encouraged and find submission easier by keeping two things in mind: First, a willingness to submit doesn't necessarily mean supporting the idea. Instead, submission means supporting the man behind it. And second, when wives submit, they are doing it for their husband, but even more importantly, they are doing it for the Lord Himself: "Wives, submit to your own husbands, *as to the Lord*" (Ephesians 5:22). A wife submits to her husband because she wants to submit to Christ.

A Husband Can Make Submission Easier, but He Can Never Make It Easy

Earlier we discussed how a husband can make it easier for a wife to respect him, but making it easier to submit to him is a different issue. Generally, a wife has trouble *respecting* her husband if there is sin in his life, and she has trouble *submitting* to her husband if he is not a spiritual man. It is difficult for a wife to trust a man to lead when he doesn't pray, read the Bible, isn't involved in the church, or doesn't have a heart for God. The reason should be obvious: If a husband isn't fulfilling his spiritual callings, a wife will have little confidence in his ability to make the right decisions for the family.

A woman wants a man who is guided by the Lord. When a wife knows her husband is spending time regularly in prayer and in God's Word, she will have a much easier time placing her life and the lives of her children in his hands. She will feel confident in his judgment and decisions. There are plenty of reasons for a husband to pray and read Scripture, and one of them is so that his wife can say, "I have concerns about the decision my husband is making, but I trust him because he is receptive to God's will and he wants what the Lord wants. I know this because his spiritual life makes it obvious." Being a man of prayer and of the Word is the greatest way for a husband to make his wife's submission easier.

To bring some balance to this discussion, you will notice I said a man who fulfills his spiritual responsibilities makes submission *easier* rather than *easy*. It will always be difficult for wives to submit to their husbands. As we saw earlier, God told Eve, "Your desire shall be for your husband" (Genesis 3:16). This refers to a desire for wives to control their husbands. It might help for a man to be loving and godly, but because of the curse, wives are going to struggle with submission regardless of whether their husbands are living a spiritually yielded life or not.

Being a man of prayer and of the Word is the greatest way for a husband to make his wife's submission easier.

While a wife might insist that she would submit to her husband if only he were more like Christ, this is not a valid argument because Christ loves all wives perfectly, and they still fall short of submitting perfectly to Him. To tie this together: Husbands can make submission easier for their wives by being godly men, but as part of the curse, a wife will have times when she struggles with submitting even to the godliest man.

WHAT IS REVEALED ABOUT A WIFE WHO SUBMITS TO HER HUSBAND?

When a wife submits to her husband, it reveals she is discerning enough to reject worldly philosophies and cultural pitfalls that plague other women. Unlike them, she recognizes the wisdom of God's design for marriage, and her faithfulness is a tremendous testimony: "[She is] obedient to [her] own husband, that the word of God may not be blasphemed" (Titus 2:4-5).

The wife who submits to her husband can have peace because she has put her life and marriage in God's hands. Just as a willingness to submit to headship provides peace, harmony, and progress in businesses, organizations, and teams, so too do they provide the same in marriages. A wife who submits to her husband reveals her commitment to the health and joy of the relationship. Through her devotion to her husband, and most importantly to Scripture, she reveals her desire to have a marriage God's way.

CHAPTER FIFTEEN

Putting Your Husband in a Position to Lead

Most people who have heard me preach know that wrestling is my favorite sport, and I like to say that it's God's favorite sport too. He wrestled with Jacob (Genesis 32:24-26). He warns that we will "wrestle...against principalities, against powers, against the rulers of the darkness of this age, against spiritual hosts of wickedness in the heavenly places" (Ephesians 6:12). He wrestles with sinners' hearts.

Most wrestlers will tell you basketball is wrestling's biggest opponent because the two seasons take place at the same time. One thing basketball has going for it is the movie *Hoosiers*. Even as a wrestling fan I must admit that it's a great movie.

In the movie, Gene Hackman plays Normal Dale, the new head coach. Nobody knows him, and he's disliked because he does things differently than the previous coach. Dennis Hopper plays Shooter Flatch, who knows much about basketball, but everyone has written him off because he's also the town drunk. Coach Dale upsets people even more when he decides to make Shooter the assistant coach. When Shooter shows up at the first game, he's clean-cut, sober, and wearing a nice suit, but he looks terrified.

Coach Dale wants to give Shooter a chance to prove to the townspeople—and more importantly, to himself—that he is valuable, has potential, and can coach. The problem is there's one thing standing between Shooter and that opportunity, and that's Coach Dale. A basketball team—like any business, organization, or marriage—can only have one person leading.

With one of the most important games on the line, Coach Dale intentionally gets himself kicked out of the game. As he's about to leave the gymnasium, he walks over to Shooter, hands him the playbook, and says, "It's up to you now." The camera zooms in on Shooter's face, revealing his fear. The team is looking to him to lead them during this crucial moment, but they understandably doubt his ability. Some of the players lower their heads and look at the floor. Shooter didn't want to be in this position, but Coach Dale removed himself from being in charge, and Shooter had no choice but to lead. He pulled himself together and came up with the game-winning play.

Why am I sharing this? This illustrates a key point for us: When wives do as Coach Dale did and remove themselves from leading, they put their husbands in a position where they must lead. Some husbands don't lead because their wives are already doing so.

Other husbands don't lead because they believe their wives are going to fight whatever decision they make. As a result, they don't even bother to lead, or they don't take their responsibility seriously. Some wives say they want their husbands to lead, but what they really mean is "I want my husband to do what I want."

This brings me back to my story about accepting the senior pastoral position at Woodland Christian Church. In that situation, Katie put me in a position to lead.

Though Katie encouraged me to take the position, she could see I was hesitant. I remember her saying, "If this move ends up being a mistake and we went there because of me, I couldn't live with that. The only way I can feel good about this decision is if *you* make it. I respect your leadership, and I believe God will direct you. Whatever you decide, I will support you."

I knew how hard it was for Katie to say this because of how much she wanted me to take the position. The fact she put the responsibility so squarely on my shoulders made me take the decision even more seriously. In some ways, it was easier for me when Katie was telling me what she wanted. But the moment she told me I had to be the one to decide, I could feel the burden settle on me.

When a wife says, "I will support whatever you decide," a husband has no choice but to lead. Some husbands do not feel the weight of the responsibility God has given them because their wives act in ways that take the mantle of leadership upon themselves. Some wives even take charge and then complain, "I am so tired of not being able to count on my husband to make decisions."

In marriage counseling sessions, wives have told me, "I have to do it because if I don't, it won't get done." I often respond, "How do you know? Maybe your husband would lead if he knew you would not. Your husband might be so used to you taking matters into your own hands that he simply goes along with it." When a wife recognizes the wisdom of stepping out of the way and placing the responsibility to lead squarely on her husband's shoulders, she increases the likelihood her husband will take his leadership calling more seriously.

If a wife really wants her husband to lead, she should get behind him, encourage him, and make him feel responsible. Then, when a husband starts to lead, a wife must ensure she doesn't complain about his decisions or criticize him for not doing things the way she wants. She needs to embrace the decisions he makes and resist the temptation to take over. Helen Andelin, founder of the Fascinating Womanhood Movement for promoting biblical marriage, writes,

> When a woman hands back the [reins] to her husband, she must let go completely. She must turn her back on it, come what may. If he makes a mess of it, let him suffer the consequences. Refer all [questions] to him. Don't shield him in any way. He must suffer. That is the only way he will learn [to lead].[1]

When a wife steps back to let her husband lead, there's a very real possibility things might go poorly at first. I don't want to give the impression that following biblical principles means everything works out perfectly. Undoubtedly, some things will fall through the cracks. If a husband has never led, he probably won't hit the ground running. Though we hope a husband will quickly step up if a wife doesn't take over, he might not. When a husband is not used to being in the driver's seat, he might be all over the road at first. But the wife needs to decide: "The driver's seat is not mine. It belongs to my husband." Regardless of how well or poorly a husband leads, the responsibility still belongs to him, and ultimately, he is accountable to God for what he does.

If a wife communicates this reality through her actions, she can be confident that at some point her husband will figure out, "Wow, she expects me to be in charge. She isn't going to take over. I'd better get my act together."

EMBRACING YOUR HUSBAND'S LEADERSHIP STYLE

A wife should not embrace sin in her husband's life, but she should embrace who he is as a person. This is the man she chose to marry. His personality is not something she should try to change because that is the way God created him. Because men have different personalities, they will do things differently, which is to say they'll lead differently. There is nothing wrong with that because there isn't always only one right way to lead.

The greatest men in Scripture had different personalities and, as a result, they led differently. King David was a military-minded man. First, he was a soldier, then a general, and even as a king he still often led his men into battle. In contrast, David's son, King Solomon, was another great leader, but there is no record of him fighting even one battle. The prophets were also different from each other. Elijah was a loner, but his successor, Elisha, was more social.

The judges delivered the people of Israel from their oppressors, but they accomplished that goal in a variety ways:

- Ehud used his left-handedness to conceal a dagger and assassinate the king of Moab.

- Samson used brute strength to defeat his enemies.

- Jephthah was diplomatic, sending messengers to Israel's enemy.

Each of these judges was a successful leader, but each one worked differently.

- What if Jephthah's wife had said, "Instead of sending those messengers, why don't you try to be like Ehud and assassinate the king of Ammon?"

- What if Ehud's wife had said, "Why are you so sneaky? Why don't you be a real man like Samson for a change?"

Even if a wife could change her husband, she would encounter just as many frustrations with her "new" man as she had with the "old" one. For example, imagine a wife has a very consistent, steady husband who is predictable. She wishes he were more adventurous, had more creative ideas, and didn't take so long to think about things. Then her husband becomes that kind of man. At first it seems great. They jump in the car for a spontaneous trip without bothering to plan out the details. He leaves his job for one that sounds more exciting, which means the family has to be uprooted and moved. Now she believes her husband is being too spontaneous and hasty, and she is longing for her formerly steady, predictable husband.

Or the reverse can happen. A wife has a strong and decisive husband, but she wishes he listened better and didn't make up his mind so quickly. Then imagine she gets her more consistent, patient husband. She loves this at first. But soon she's frustrated because he takes so long to make up his mind. When the kids misbehave, he isn't as quick to discipline them. She even wishes he was more of a leader because she finds it harder to respect him. In time, she will miss her determined, decisive husband.

The point is, every husband's personality has advantages and disadvantages. While a wife might wish her husband were different in certain ways, those differences would come with their own accompanying frustrations. For this reason, a wife should look for and encourage her husband's strengths and try not to dwell on his weaknesses.

This is one reason a wife should not encourage her husband to be like other men. Instead, she should be thankful for the way God created him. When God fashioned women as comparable helpers for their husbands, He did not make all wives the same any more than He made all husbands the same. Women have different strengths that work to complement their husbands' needs and weaknesses. Similarly, the type of leadership style God gives each husband is meant to complement the needs of his wife and family.

RECOGNIZING A HEART FOR GOD IS MORE IMPORTANT THAN LEADERSHIP STYLE

In Scripture, kings were said to be good if they were like King David:

- 1 Kings 15:11—"Asa did what was right in the eyes of the LORD, *as did his father David.*"

- 2 Kings 18:3—"[Hezekiah] did what was right in the sight of the LORD, *according to all that his father David had done.*"

- 2 Kings 22:2—"[Josiah] did what was right in the sight of the LORD, and *walked in all the ways of his father David.*"

And kings were said to be bad if they were like King Jeroboam:

- 1 Kings 16:19—"[Zimri] committed in doing evil in the sight of the LORD, in *walking in the way of Jeroboam.*"

- 1 Kings 16:25-26—"Omri did evil in the eyes of the LORD...For *he walked in all the ways of Jeroboam.*"

- 1 Kings 22:52—"[Ahaziah] did evil in the sight of the LORD, and *walked...in the way of Jeroboam.*"

When Scripture says a king is like David, does that mean he was a shepherd or that he slew giants? No, it means that king had a heart for God, like David, who was a "man after [God's] own heart" (1 Samuel 13:14; Acts 13:22).

When Jeroboam became king, he set up golden calves that led the people of Israel away from worshipping God (1 Kings 12:25-33). When Scripture says a king is like Jeroboam, does it mean that he built idols? No, it means that king was evil like Jeroboam was.

Biblically speaking, men have never been good or bad leaders because they led a certain way. Rather, men have always been good or bad leaders because they had hearts for God or they did not. That was the case in the Old Testament, and the same is true today.

Regardless of personality or leadership style, every godly man is called to do certain things. He must pray with his family, be a student of the Word, disciple his children, and serve the body of Christ. While there is flexibility regarding how men lead their homes, no man has the liberty to say,

- "I don't pray with my family because that's not my leadership style."

- "I don't take my family to church because that's not my personality."

- "I don't read the Bible with my family because I'm not into reading."

If a man is not doing these things, he is failing as a spiritual leader regardless of his leadership style or personality. Every husband should keep two things in mind:

- No matter how many good things a man does for his family, he cannot be a great husband without being a great spiritual leader. No number of family vacations, completed projects around the house, or amount of time with the wife and children can take the place of the greatest call God has on a husband's life.

- Whatever a husband does in the church pales in comparison to what he needs to be doing in the home. First Timothy 3:5 states, "If a man does not know how to rule his own house, how will he take care of the church of God?" While it is wonderful for a man to serve his brothers and sisters in Christ, God states that it is even more important for him to serve his wife and children by leading them well spiritually.

*Men have always been good or bad leaders because
they had hearts for God or they did not.*

MAKING YOUR HUSBAND'S SPIRITUAL LEADERSHIP EASIER

When Katie and I first dated, I really wanted to impress her. So, during one of our first Bible studies, I decided to look at the Assyrian siege of Jerusalem to show her the relationship between these three passages of Scripture: Isaiah 36, 2 Kings 18, and 2 Chronicles 32. It was probably the most confusing Bible study ever taught. Let's just say that by the time we finished three hours later, I did not look impressive—I simply looked weird. Later that day, however, I overheard Katie on the phone telling a friend, "I am so thankful to have met a man who will read the Bible with me."

You can imagine how encouraged I was to hear that. Sadly, I have met husbands who are reluctant to read the Bible or pray in front of their wives because they are afraid of the wife's reaction if they do not measure up to a well-known pastor or Bible teacher. Wives, let me give you some hints for making it easier for your husband to fulfill his role as the spiritual leader of your marriage and family.

Be Encouraged to...

Thank your husband when he takes the family to church—Unfortunately, this is more than many men do. There are women who would give just about anything to have a husband who worships the Lord with them on Sundays. Ladies, do not take for granted a husband who is willing to go to church!

Encourage your husband when he prays or reads Scripture with you—He might fumble every word he says, but you should still thank him for his spiritual leadership. Recognize that you are among a small percentage of wives whose husbands engage in these disciplines with their wife. Hold his hand when you pray and thank the Lord for giving you a man who desires to be godly.

Support your husband with the children—Help get the kids together for times of worship. When your husband reads the Bible with the family, set an example to your children by being attentive. Encourage the children to express appreciation for a father who is willing to do what few men do.

Be Discouraged from...

Needless debate—This is a tough issue because I don't want to discourage wives from asking their husbands questions, or even disagreeing when their husbands say something that is wrong. But if your husband concludes he is going to face an argument every time you open the Bible together, you are going to end up with a husband who does not open the Bible with you.

Katie and I once counseled a couple whom we finally persuaded to read the Bible together. Later, when I asked the husband how it was going, he told me they had stopped and he wouldn't read the Word with her again. When I asked why, he said that whenever they read together, his wife constantly challenged everything he said.

Needless comparisons—Wives, I implore you to never, under any circumstances, compare your husband negatively with another man. Your husband is the man you chose to marry. Be thankful for him. If he does not have the gift of teaching, which is a spiritual gift the Holy Spirit gives to some believers and not to others, then he is probably already nervous about reading or praying in front of you and the kids. A man who does not have the gift of teaching is not inferior or less spiritual, but simply has different spiritual gifts. Some of the godliest men I have known struggle terribly when they have to teach in front of others.

The last thing any husband needs is to hear that he doesn't sound like a well-known pastor. Don't expect an eloquent sermon when your husband opens the Bible with you. The power is in God's Word and not in your husband's teaching ability. If your husband is reading Scripture to the family, trust that it is washing over the family members and doing its work of bringing spiritual cleansing and sanctification, as stated in Ephesians 5:26.

BEING YOUR HUSBAND'S BIGGEST SUPPORTER

Imagine a husband who has been reading this book and feels convicted about being a better spiritual leader. He has not been reading the Bible with his family, but he knows he should. Understandably, he is nervous about doing so. He does not know how his family is going to respond. He is asking himself, *What if I don't know what to say? What if they ask me a question I can't answer? Where should I start? What if I don't sound like Pastor Bill?*

All day at work he has been summoning up his courage, and he has decided that today is the day. As soon as dinner is over, he is going to ask his wife and children to get their Bibles. Fast-forward a few hours. Dinner is over and the husband's heart is racing, but he still manages to say, "Tonight, we're going to do something different. Why don't we all grab our Bibles and read a passage together?"

Now imagine his wife says,

- "Do we have to do this right now? I wanted to get the table cleaned up."

- "Is that the version of the Bible we're going to use? Can we use this instead?"

- "Is this the passage we're going to read? Why did you pick this one?"

- "Is that how you pronounce his name?"

- "When I was listening to the pastor on the radio, that's not what he said about this verse."

- "I don't think that's right."

- "Can you ask Mike if that's correct?"

- "Wow, this first Bible study sure is long!"

Will this husband ever want to read the Bible with his family again? Probably not.

Now imagine this: Same husband, same conviction, same nervousness all day. Dinner is over. He tells his wife and children to get their Bibles, and his wife says,

- "I am so excited!"

- "This is such an answer to prayer."

- "I am very proud of you!"

- "Not many men do this with their families. I feel blessed to have you as my husband."

Imagine his wife says to the children,

- "Isn't this great? What a wonderful daddy you have!"

- "Let's go get our Bibles. Don't worry about the dishes. We'll take care of them later." This statement alone will get the kids excited!

Imagine that, after the study is over and everyone takes turns praying, the wife says, "Lord, I am so thankful to have such a godly man. Thank You that he will read the Bible with us. We are so blessed. Help him lead our family. What a huge responsibility he has. You have called me to be his helper, so please help me to help him." These sorts of encouragements from a wife will diffuse a husband's fears and infuse him with the confidence he needs to be a good spiritual leader.

Wife, be your husband's biggest supporter. Encourage him when he prays and reads the Word with the family. Husband, do these things that God has called you to do, and you will gain your family's respect.

PART SIX

A WIFE'S BEAUTY AND A HUSBAND'S TREATMENT (1 PETER 3:1-7)

CHAPTER SIXTEEN

Winning Over Your Husband

Through my ministry Living God's Way, I put on marriage conferences across the country. In between sessions I'll meet with people. They almost always ask me questions that are difficult to answer, and oftentimes they hope that I can help fix a problem they've been experiencing for years in a five-minute answer.

For example, a wife will ask, "My husband won't lead our family spiritually. What can I do to get him to pray and read the Bible with us?" If a woman married an unspiritual man, what are the chances that I can tell her something that will encourage him to be spiritual?

A husband will ask, "My wife disrespects me at home and she's rude to me in front of my friends. What am I supposed to do?" If a man married a rude and obnoxious woman, how can I tell him, in a brief conversation, how to have a gentle, respectful woman?

These kinds of dilemmas typically take hours of counseling to resolve.

There is one question I get asked at almost every conference, and ironically, it's one of the easiest to answer: "Should I submit to my spiritually immature or unbelieving husband?" Why is this so easy to respond to? Because the answer is spelled out in Scripture: "Wives, likewise, be submissive to your own husbands, that even if some do not obey the word, they, without a word, may be won by the conduct of their wives, when they observe your chaste conduct accompanied by fear" (1 Peter 3:1-2).

These verses are directed to wives and once again deal with submission—but with a new twist. We have established that wives are not expected to submit to abuse, sin, or even other men. But is a spiritually mature wife expected to submit to a spiritually *im*mature husband? According to 1 Peter 3:1-2, submission is called for not only to a spiritually immature husband, but also to a spiritually bankrupt husband—or more specifically, an unbeliever.

How do we know that unbelieving husbands are what Peter had in mind? Each human author of the Bible has a recognized style of writing. When Peter mentioned husbands who "do not obey the word," we know that he was referring to unbelieving husbands because he used similar terminology for non-Christians elsewhere. For example, in 1 Peter 1:2, he described believers as "elect according to the foreknowledge of God the Father, in sanctification of the Spirit, *for obedience*." Peter equated obedience with salvation, and rightly so. While obedience is not what saves us, Scripture makes it clear that believers should be obedient. In 1 Peter 2:8, he similarly described unbelievers as "being *disobedient* to the word." Because Peter used "obedience" to refer to believers and "disobedient" to refer to unbelievers, we can know that when he wrote about men who "do not obey the word," he was referring to unbelieving husbands.

Now, just because a man is an unbeliever doesn't mean he is a scoundrel. He may be kind, affectionate, and hold to a high moral standard. However, if he has not taken the first step of obedience—that is, the obedience of faith, which leads to salvation in Christ—then he is properly identified as disobedient.

A wife whose Christian husband is not as spiritually mature as she would like should be encouraged, because although submitting to an immature believing husband may be difficult, it's not as difficult as submitting to an unbelieving husband. Because God's Word commands wives to submit to unsaved husbands (within the parameters discussed in chapter 13), how much more willing should wives be to submit to spiritually immature believing husbands? A Christian husband might not be as spiritually mature as his wife longs for, but at least she can be thankful that he is indwelt by the Holy Spirit.

WHAT IF YOU ARE MARRIED TO AN UNBELIEVER?

For wives who find themselves in marriages with unbelieving husbands, Peter offers encouragement and hope. Through a wife's example of godly submission, her husband may be won to faith in Jesus. In a parallel passage found in 1 Corinthians 7:13-16, Paul explains why a believing wife is called to submit to her unbelieving spouse rather than leave him to find a spouse more compatible with her spiritual commitment:

> [If] a woman…has a husband who does not believe, if he is willing to live with her, let her not divorce him. For the unbelieving

husband is sanctified by the wife, and the unbelieving wife is sanctified by the husband; otherwise your children would be unclean,
but now they are holy. But if the unbeliever departs, let him depart;
a brother or a sister is not under bondage in such cases. But God
has called us to peace. For how do you know, O wife, whether you
will save your husband? Or how do you know, O husband, whether
you will save your wife?

Paul's teaching here is twofold. First, a believing spouse is called to remain
in marriage to an unbeliever. "Sanctified" means "set apart" or "holy." By
staying married, the believing spouse can have a spiritual influence on the
unbelieving spouse, who is "set apart" due to constant exposure to the believing spouse's faith. This can help open the door for the unbelieving spouse to
come to faith as well. Logically, we understand that one of the best ways for
unbelievers to come to salvation is through relationships with believers. An
unbeliever could have no more intimate relationship with a believer than
through marriage.

Likewise, the children in that family are far more likely to be exposed to
godly living when the believing spouse remains in the home and creates a Christian environment. The alternative breaks up the home, possibly leaving the children in the custody of the unbelieving parent. In 1 Corinthians 7:13-16, this
issue is directed primarily at the believing wife—perhaps because at the time
Paul was writing, husbands had sole legal possession of any children born within
a marriage. A believing wife who abandoned the marriage would also be abandoning her children to the custody and sole influence of an unbelieving husband. As Paul concluded, a believer staying in the marriage may provide just
the influence necessary to bring an unbelieving spouse or child to faith. It is not
guaranteed, though, for Paul wrote, "How do you know…?," pointing out that
this a possibility and not a promise.

The second matter Paul addressed was that of an unbelieving spouse choos-
ing to leave the believing spouse. While believers are instructed to stay in the
marriage and be an influence to win their spouse to faith, they can't force an
unbelieving spouse to remain. This is especially pertinent when a wife or husband comes to Christ after getting married—an unbelieving spouse may end
up rejecting a spouse who becomes a Christian.

Notice what Paul's instruction is based on: "God has called us to peace." If
the conversion of one spouse to Christianity has become the source of continued conflict, then the believing spouse should not quarrel over the unbelieving

spouse's departure. This would be antithetical to the Christian's calling to peace. In addition, unbelievers are never won to Christ through heated arguments. It is more important to be true to the Christian testimony of peace than to attempt to keep an unbeliever in a marriage by force or argumentation. This elevates the Christian faith above even an unstable marriage. It's better to let the unbeliever depart than to sully Christ's reputation.

This brings us to an important point: Paul's permission for Christians to allow an unbelieving spouse to "depart" should not be interpreted as permission to divorce. As we already discussed in connection with abuse, a separated spouse is commanded to remain single while seeking reconciliation: "If [a wife] does depart, let her remain unmarried or be reconciled to her husband. And a husband is not to divorce his wife…A wife is bound by law as long as her husband lives" (1 Corinthians 7:11, 39; see also Romans 7:2). The principle is that even when separated from an unbelieving or sinful spouse, a believer may still be an influence for change and repentance through faithfulness to the unsaved person. God's design is always reconciliation and never divorce.

I will be the first to acknowledge that marriage can be difficult enough for two people who are already believers—and much more so for believers married to unbelievers. But how tragic it is—and disobedient to God's Word—for Christians to divorce an unbelieving spouse when that believer constitutes the unbeliever's greatest chance to be drawn to faith. I have heard Christians talk about wanting to leave an unbelieving husband or wife, usually because of how terrible that spouse is. I don't doubt what they say, but in my mind I am thinking: *Yes, this sounds terrible, but the worse you make the person sound, the more obvious it is just how much your spouse needs Christ. And that person needs to be exposed to Christ through you!*

A WIFE'S NAGGING AND A HUSBAND'S STUBBORNNESS

Let's take a closer look at two important contrasting points in 1 Peter 3:1: "[Husbands], without a word, may be won by the conduct of their wives." Wives are told

- how *not to* try to win their husbands—with words.

- how *to* try to win their husbands—with their conduct.

In Genesis 3:16, God told Eve, "Your desire shall be for your husband, and he shall rule over you." This verse reveals two struggles husbands and wives face because of the fall. As we learned earlier, the first half of the verse speaks of wives' desires to control their husbands. This often manifests itself as nagging, which we find described in Proverbs:

- "The contentions of a wife are a continual dripping" (Proverbs 19:13; see also Proverbs 21:9, 19; 25:24).

- "A continual dripping on a very rainy day and a contentious woman are alike; whoever restrains her restrains the wind, and grasps oil with his right hand" (Proverbs 27:15-16).

Not only is the tendency to nag ongoing, but as Proverbs 27:15-16 confirms, it's virtually impossible to stop. When a man responds to a nagging or contentious woman, she usually becomes more contentious and argues and nags even more.

The second half of Genesis 3:16, "and he shall rule over you," reveals the corresponding struggle men have with stubbornness. God created men to be leaders in the marriage relationship, so by nature there may be times when they are less receptive to what their wives say to them. Let me illustrate through two incidents that occurred in my relationship with Katie.

For the first few years of our marriage, every couple weeks I would grow a beard, then shave it off. At some point I asked Katie, "Do you think I should grow a beard?" She said, "Why do you ask me that? You know you're never going to keep one. You grow a beard for a couple weeks, but then shave it." I've had—and kept—a beard since that conversation!

One day I was putting wood in our fireplace. One piece was rather big and should've been split into two or three smaller pieces. Katie said, "You're not going to be able to get that big piece of wood into the fireplace." I was determined to prove her wrong and almost pulled a muscle or burst a vein when I lugged that piece of wood, but you can be sure I got it into the fireplace.

When husbands are told not to do something, frequently their all-too-human response is to do it anyway because they are inclined to be stubborn:

- Katie: "You're not going to grow a beard."

- Genesis 3:16 in action: "I'm going to grow the longest beard you've ever seen."

- Katie: "You're not going to get that piece of wood into the fireplace."

- Genesis 3:16 in action: "I don't care if I have to hold one end of this piece of wood outside the fireplace as the other end slowly burns and I push it in over the next few hours—it's going in there."

Two realities about our fallenness make the tension between husbands and wives even worse:

- Husbands seem to struggle with stubbornness even more when they feel they are being nagged.

- Wives seem to struggle with nagging even more when they feel their husbands are being stubborn.

This can create a vicious cycle that sucks the joy out of a marriage. God is aware of this, so He has revealed how to bring such contention to an end—not with words, but with godly behavior.

If you are a believing wife, most likely there are certain activities you want your husband to do, such as pray and read the Bible with you. Perhaps you also want your husband to do things of a less spiritual nature, such as finish a couple of projects around the house or take the family on a trip he promised years ago. There might also be things that you want your husband to stop doing, such as watching ungodly movies or spending too much time on a certain activity.

The truth is, nagging your husband won't bring him any closer to being the man you desire him to be or increase the likelihood that he'll do what you want. On the contrary, because men are stubborn, nagging will probably make him less inclined to do what you want and could possibly even push him in the opposite direction. What a wife needs to do instead is obey Peter's command to win over her husband not with words, but with godly conduct.

The Line Between Helping and Nagging

Earlier, I shared about my addiction to World of Warcraft right after Katie and I got married. One reason I felt so convicted about my behavior was that I had married a wonderful woman, and even at the worst of my addiction, Katie continued being a godly wife. If she had nagged me, I wouldn't have felt as bad.

Now, don't get me wrong. Katie let me know how much it bothered her that I was playing; I already mentioned that she had a little breakdown over it. But she spoke to me honestly out of her pain instead of in anger; she didn't nag me. Part of the conviction I felt came from being married to such a godly woman who deserved better than a husband addicted to a video game. Had she nagged me, she would not have seemed like a woman who deserved better. Katie's godly conduct while I was being a lame husband helped convict me of my selfishness.

Hopefully you see the balance I'm pointing out here: I'm not advising wives to refrain from ever asking their husbands to do or not do certain things, or from giving their husbands reminders. After all, God created a wife to be a helper to her husband. Sometimes husbands forget things, and a reminder (or two) can be a blessing.

Also, sometimes husbands are not aware of how much they may have hurt their wives, children, or friends. It's common for men to be oblivious to how others feel about what they're doing, and wives can help their husbands to see what they themselves don't see. There have been times Katie and I were driving home from spending time with people, and she said, "When you said that, it sounded rude," or "He was talking, and you interrupted him." Was Katie nagging me? Not at all! She was helping me grow. But there *can* come a point when attempts to be helpful can turn into nagging.

When wives share with their husbands what they want and how they feel, they should keep two points in mind:

- The frequency with which a wife says things is important. At some point, a request made a few times moves from being a reminder to nagging.

- The way a wife makes requests is important. Yelling and disrespecting a husband will not convict him. Lovingly and respectfully petitioning him about the way he is acting and the pain he is causing will. When a wife speaks to her husband with grace and patience, he will likely feel terrible for mistreating such a wonderful woman.

Husbands, in turn, need to let their wives know when they have moved from being helpful to nagging, but do so in a gentle and loving manner. Husbands who respond stubbornly to their wives are not going to help their wives stop nagging. When a husband stubbornly raises his voice at his wife or gets angry with her he is sinning, and he is also pushing her to yell and nag in response.

A Warning About Winning

It's possible for a wife to win over her husband yet not necessarily in a positive way. We have already looked at two examples of this:

- Sarah convinced Abraham to take Hagar as a concubine.
- Jezebel convinced Ahab to steal Naboth's vineyard.

Scripture gives another example of a man who made a habit of allowing the women in his life to win him over with their words, with disastrous consequences. Ironically, Samson was the strongest man in history, but he was easily overcome by the persistence of two women who could be called the Queens of Nagging.

Samson, an Israelite, disobeyed God's command forbidding intermarriage when he chose a Philistine for a wife. During the wedding festivities, he posed a riddle to 30 men from his bride's town. If they didn't solve the riddle, each one would have to supply him with a set of clothing. If they solved it, he would supply each of them with a set. Wanting the answer, the men secretly went to Samson's wife, who agreed to help her fellow Philistines. For seven days she wept and complained, "You only hate me! You do not love me! You have posed a riddle to the sons of my people, but you have not explained it to me" (Judges 14:16).

Samson's new bride "pressed him so much" (verse 17) that he finally told her the answer, and she, in turn, told the Philistine men. Feeling betrayed, Samson rejected his wife, and she went on to marry one of the 30 men (verse 20).

Sadly, Samson did not learn from his mistake. Sometime later he fell in love with another Philistine woman, Delilah (Judges 16:4). By this time, the Philistines were furious over Samson's successful attacks against them. They offered Delilah a large reward if she would find out the source of Samson's great strength so they could defeat him.

Delilah nagged Samson, and he lied to her on three separate occasions (Judges 16:6-14). Each time she would wait until Samson was asleep, then she would call the Philistines and act on the lie he had told her. Because Samson was lying, he was able to easily defeat the Philistines who came against him. Finally, Delilah played the victim: "How can you say, 'I love you,' when your heart is not with me? You have mocked me these three times, and have not told me where your great strength lies" (verse 15).

Does this sound familiar? It is almost identical to what happened with Samson's first wife. Delilah "pestered him daily with her words and pressed him, so that his soul was vexed to death" (verse 16). She made Samson so miserable with her nagging that he wished he would die. He then finally admitted, "No razor has ever come upon my head, for I have been a Nazirite to God from my mother's womb. If I am shaven, then my strength will leave me, and I shall become weak, and be like any other man" (verse 17).

Samson knew that Delilah would turn him over to the Philistines, but he told his secret to her anyway. This is a strong testament to the power of a woman's nagging. In a scene that is painful even to read, Delilah cut off Samson's hair while he slept, and when he awoke, he discovered his strength was gone. The Philistines captured him, put his eyes out, and turned him into a slave. He remained in captivity until his last-ditch stand that resulted in his death along with the deaths of 3,000 Philistines.

The lesson here is that some wives will attempt to manipulate their husbands like the two women in Samson's life. They will play the victim and act as though they are being mistreated. They will nag until their husbands' soul, like Samson's, is vexed to the point where death feels like a better alternative. Their words can eventually wear down their husbands until they give in. They win over their husbands, but they do so in the wrong way

Winning by Godly Conduct

As 1 Peter 3:1-2 states, husbands "without a word, may be won by the conduct of their wives, when they observe your chaste conduct accompanied by fear." Wives are not called to win over their unbelieving husbands by what they say, but by their lifestyle. The gracious submission of a Christian woman to her unsaved husband is the strongest evangelistic tool she has.

What does this look like in practical terms? Comparing 1 Peter 2:18 with 1 Peter 3:1-2 can help with the answer because of the parallel language that appears in the verses:

- "Servants, be submissive to your masters" is similar to "Wives...
  be submissive to your own husbands."

- "Not only to the good and gentle, but also to the harsh" is similar
  to "even if some do not obey the word."

- "With all fear" is similar to "your chaste conduct accompanied
  by fear."

With both passages, it is important to understand Scripture is *not* speaking of servants or wives submitting out of fear to their masters or husbands, but rather, out of fear and reverence for God. The NIV translation says, "Slaves, *in reverent fear of God* submit yourselves to your masters." First Peter 1:17 supports that this is the intent in both passages—there, Peter used similar terminology when he wrote to believers as a whole: "If you call on the Father...conduct yourselves throughout the time of your stay here *in fear*." When an unbelieving husband sees his believing wife's heart for God, that will serve as a powerful witness. His wife's godly behavior will convict him of his need to be a godlier husband. Her life will speak louder to him than any words.

No unspiritual husband can watch a wife's godly example without feeling ashamed.

If a wife wants her husband to read God's Word more, pray more, or be a more godly man, rather than nagging him, she herself should read God's Word more, pray more, and be a more godly woman. Wives should be encouraged by Jesus's promise in John 16:8, which says, "When [the Holy Spirit] has come, *He will convict the world of sin*." Notice the emphasis is on the Holy Spirit doing the convicting. This includes husbands, unbelieving or otherwise! Wives are not supposed to take over the Holy Spirit's role in their husbands' lives. Wives should pray, and then trust the Holy Spirit to do the work of convicting their husbands.

No unspiritual husband can watch a wife's godly example without feeling ashamed. A husband might pretend that he is not convicted, and his wife might not be able to tell by looking at him that he feels convicted, but he does. In contrast, when a wife is angry, nagging, and unsubmissive, the husband does not see God through her, and, as a result, avoids feeling convicted.

JESUS SETS THE EXAMPLE OF GODLY CONDUCT VERSUS WORDS

Jesus is the greatest example—not just for wives, but for all of us—of demonstrating godly conduct with actions versus words. Consider His silence before His unbelieving accusers:

- "He was oppressed and He was afflicted, yet *He opened not His mouth*; He was led as a lamb to the slaughter, and *as a sheep before its shearers is silent*, so *He opened not His mouth*" (Isaiah 53:7; see also Acts 8:32).

- "While He was being accused by the chief priests and elders, *He answered nothing*" (Matthew 27:12).

- "Who committed no sin, *nor was deceit found in His mouth*"; who, when He was reviled, *did not revile in return*; when He suffered, *He did not threaten*, but committed Himself to Him who judges righteously (1 Peter 2:22-23).

These verses point to Jesus's conduct during the unjust trials that led up to the crucifixion. He was willing to endure the shame and eventually the cross for our sake. While we were yet unbelieving and lost in sin, Jesus willingly laid down His life to win our salvation. This is the example to which we are called, whether wives or husbands. We are to be willing to live in such a way that unbelieving spouses may be won to salvation through our Christlike conduct.

CHAPTER SEVENTEEN

A Woman's Greater Beauty

What makes a woman beautiful? Is it her physical appearance, such as her hair and face? Is it her mental acuity, such as her intelligence and education? Does it have to do with her emotions, such as her personality, or her spirituality, such as her heart for God? The apostle Peter answers this question for us, stating from a biblical standpoint what it is that makes a woman beautiful to God. That kind of beauty, of course, is the kind that a Christian woman should pursue and a Christian man should value.

As we read in the previous chapter, 1 Peter 3:1-2 makes the point that a wife's greatest asset for winning over her spiritually immature or unbelieving husband is godly character. Then in the verses that follow, Peter lays out what such a godly woman looks like. He begins with her physical appearance because that is a good indicator of her spiritual health. It wouldn't be too much to say that what comes forth on the outside is produced from the inside: "Do not let your adornment be merely outward—arranging the hair, wearing gold, or putting on fine apparel—rather let it be the hidden person of the heart, with the incorruptible beauty of a gentle and quiet spirit, which is very precious in the sight of God" (1 Peter 3:3-4).

The Greek word translated "adornment" is *kosmos*, which is related to the English word *cosmetic*. *Kosmos* is an umbrella term that encompasses everything related to the physical appearance—clothing, makeup, and jewelry. Note that Peter's instruction does not forbid outward adornment—his use of the word "merely" indicates a woman's beauty should not come only from her outward appearance. The NASB and Amplified Bible render the passage this way: "Your adornment must not be merely external." Scripture is not instructing women to neglect their appearance. All of us, as Christians, do want to give attention to our physical appearance because every one of us—male or female, young or old—is an ambassador of Christ. We should care about what kind of Christian testimony we are presenting to others. Yet Peter says outward beauty should not be a woman's primary focus.

WHAT ABOUT JEWELRY AND MAKEUP?

If you have ever been made to feel guilty about any form of external beautification, let me point out that Scripture makes positive references to jewelry and fine clothing. Proverbs 25:12 states, "Like an earring of gold and an ornament of fine gold is a wise rebuker to an obedient ear." Gold jewelry is compared to the way an obedient ear accepts instruction. If outward adornments such as earrings were immoral, Scripture would not compare them to wise behavior. Likewise, the beautiful bride in Song of Solomon is complimented on her jewelry: "Your cheeks are lovely with ornaments, your neck with chains of gold. We will make you ornaments of gold with studs of silver" (Song of Solomon 1:10-11). If jewelry were wrong, Solomon's bride wouldn't be complimented on hers.

Also consider the virtuous wife of Proverbs 31—she was not complimented on her outward simplicity or plainness. Instead, she was applauded for the way she adorned her family and herself: "All her household is clothed with scarlet. She makes tapestry for herself; her clothing is fine linen and purple" (Proverbs 31:21-22). In that time, scarlet, fine linen, and purple were costly materials, which indicates this virtuous wife cared about her family's appearances.

Isaiah 61:10 beautifully compares salvation and righteousness with fine clothing, ornaments, and jewelry:

> I will greatly rejoice in the LORD; my soul shall be joyful in my God; for He has clothed me with the garments of salvation, He has covered me with the robe of righteousness, as a bridegroom decks himself with ornaments, and as a bride adorns herself with her jewels.

God would hardly compare salvation and righteousness with outward adornment if the latter were immoral. An even stronger positive reference comes from God's proclamation in Ezekiel 16:11-13, where He describes His chosen people, Israel, as a beautifully dressed bride:

> I adorned you with ornaments, put bracelets on your wrists, and a chain on your neck. And I put a jewel in your nose, earrings in your

ears, and a beautiful crown on your head. Thus you were adorned
with gold and silver, and your clothing was of fine linen, silk, and
embroidered cloth.

We can be sure that God would not outwardly adorn His people as a gift if such
adornment were ungodly.

Having said this, we still need to strike a right balance—it's fine to look nice,
but we don't want to be overly preoccupied with our appearance. In 1 Timothy 2:9, the apostle Paul gives instructions parallel to those found in 1 Peter 3:3:
"Women [should] adorn themselves in *modest apparel, with propriety and moderation*, not with braided hair or gold or pearls or costly clothing." Again, the
emphasis is not on forbidding women from adorning themselves. Rather, they
are told *to* adorn themselves, but in a modest and not an extravagant way. The
Bible speaks positively of outward adornment while also commanding moderation and decency. Women must exhibit self-control with regard to their outward beautification. Focusing too much on one's physical appearance reveals an
unhealthy preoccupation, or worse, an obsession. A woman who wears excessive jewelry, makeup, or extravagant clothing can be as distracting as a woman
who has made no effort to take care of her appearance.

OUTWARD APPEARANCE IS A REFLECTION OF THE HEART

Women should examine what they wear and why they wear it. Is the motivation to attract attention, or to be a good representative of the Lord? When a
woman dresses immodestly, whether she is aware of it or not, she makes herself into a walking temptation who shows no regard for her brothers in Christ.
A woman might dress immodestly because she is insecure, desperate for attention, or does not respect herself. Regardless of the reason, even though immod-
esty manifests itself externally, it begins in the heart. The way a woman looks
outwardly says a lot about the way she looks inwardly.

The more modestly a married woman dresses, the more attractive she will be
to her husband because more is reserved for him alone. Conversely, the more
immodestly a wife dresses, the more she makes herself suggestively noticeable
to other men, and the less she reserves for her husband.

GREATER BEAUTY IS FOUND INWARDLY

In 1 Peter 3, there is a strong relationship between what is said in verses 3
and 4. Verse 3 describes the natural human tendency to be overly focused on

outward appearance: "Do not let your adornment be merely outward—arranging the hair, wearing gold, or putting on fine apparel." Then in verse 4, Peter encourages women to be more focused on the inward: "*rather* let [your adornment] be the hidden person of the heart, with the incorruptible beauty of a gentle and quiet spirit, which is very precious in the sight of God."

Women should give attention to their outward appearance, but they should give even more attention to their inward appearance. God is more concerned with the way a woman's heart looks than with the way her face, hair, makeup, or clothing look.

Today's culture tells women to "put it all out there" and to be concerned chiefly with outward beauty at the expense of inward beauty. That is how society measures whether a woman is beautiful. Tragically, this reduces women into superficial creatures with no dimensions of personality or inner worth. Contrast this with the phrase "hidden person," which inspires women to have an inner or unseen beauty that requires looking and searching to find. To see and appreciate this beauty requires time and energy.

Inward Beauty Is Incorruptible

In 1997, 2.1 million cosmetic surgeries were performed in the United States; in 2011, 9.2 million were performed.[1] In a 15-year-period, the number more than quadrupled. One particularly excessive example took place with a celebrity named Heidi Montag. After ten plastic surgeries in one day, she complained about the scars they left behind: "Parts of my body definitely look worse than they did pre-surgery. This is not what I signed up for!…I wish I could jump into a time machine and take it all back. Instead, I'm always going to feel like Edward Scissorhands."[2]

Even ten plastic surgeries did not give Ms. Montag the beauty she wanted, to say nothing about obtaining beauty that would last the rest of her life. CNN reported:

> What recession? Despite record unemployment, rising health care costs and sinking home values, Americans shelled out more than $10 billion on cosmetic surgeries and other procedures in 2010…Almost half of Americans have less than $10,000 saved for retirement, but millions are running off to the plastic surgeon…What does it mean that despite the worst recession since the Great Depression, Americans spent more than $10 billion on cosmetic procedures last year?[3]

What this tells us is that plenty of women—and men too—are pursuing a beauty that does not change with time. The problem is that physical beauty is corruptible. True, incorruptible beauty can't be found outwardly. Inward beauty is the only kind that never fades because it doesn't come from physical appearance; therefore, it doesn't diminish with time or age. Proverbs 31:30 expresses it this way: "Charm is deceitful and beauty is passing, but a woman who fears the LORD, she shall be praised." In other words, physical beauty fades, but spiritual (found in a woman who fears God) does not.

Popular Christian writer J.R. Miller observes,

> Only in Christ can women find that rich beauty of soul, that gemming of the character, which shall make her lovely in her husband's sight, when the bloom of youth is gone, when the brilliance has faded out of her eyes, and the roses have fled from her cheeks. Only Christ can teach her how to live so as to be blessed, and be a blessing in her married life![4]

Inward beauty does not require any makeup, jewelry, or accessories to be attained. Conversely, when a woman does not have inward beauty, no amount of makeup, jewelry, or outward adornment can make her beautiful. A woman who lacks inner beauty might look attractive at first, but that will disappear quickly when the inward unattractiveness is revealed. Proverbs 11:22 says, "Like a gold ring in a pig's snout is a beautiful woman without discretion" (ESV). Just as a gold ring cannot make a pig beautiful, physical beauty cannot make an inwardly ugly woman beautiful.

Inner beauty radiates outward with an attractiveness that transcends anything we can do to our external looks.

Simply consider any book or movie with a male character who falls in love with a woman. The woman is typically presented as jovial, pleasant, and good-tempered as opposed to angry, unkind, or selfish. Why is that? Even the secular world recognizes inward beauty makes women outwardly attractive, while inward ugliness makes women outwardly unattractive.

Ultimately, there is a ceiling to what any of us can do with our outward appearance. No matter how well we care for ourselves physically and work on how we look, we will still be limited by factors beyond our control, such as our genetic material and aging.

In contrast, as Peter points out when he talks about a woman's appearance, every woman has the potential to develop inward beauty, which is able to grow over time. Such inner beauty radiates outward with an attractiveness that transcends anything we can do to our external looks.

That brings us to an obvious question: What produces this inward beauty? It comes from the next quality described in 1 Peter 3:4.

The Source of Inward Beauty

The phrase "gentle and quiet spirit" can be puzzling to women who have more extroverted or talkative personalities, or who are gifted to lead and teach (such as my wife, Katie). But when Peter uses the term "quiet spirit," he is not suggesting that women not speak at all. Consider the description of the virtuous wife in Proverbs 31:26: "She opens her mouth with wisdom, and on her tongue is the law of kindness." She is applauded for speaking. God created women with varying personalities and gifts, and we can be certain His instructions will not conflict with His own creation. Even women who are extroverted, talkative, and have the gift of teaching can possess a gentle and quiet spirit.

If Peter is not discouraging women from speaking, what is he saying? He is discouraging women from speaking *a certain way*. The Greek word translated "gentle" is *prays*, which means "mildness of disposition, gentleness of spirit, meekness." The word appears only two other places in Scripture:

- "Blessed are the meek [*prays*], for they shall inherit the earth" (Matthew 5:5).

- "Behold, your King is coming to you, lowly [*prays*], and sitting on a donkey, a colt, the foal of a donkey" (Matthew 21:5).

Looking at the three uses of *prays*, we see it is used to describe (1) those who will inherit the earth, (2) the Messiah's own disposition, and (3) a godly woman's true beauty. The use of this term in 1 Peter 3:4 describes the way a woman should handle herself and respond to situations in life. She is calm and in control. She is not easily wrought or stirred up.

In 1 Peter 3:4, the Greek word translated "quiet" is *hesychios*, which means "tranquil and peaceful." The only other place this term appears is 1 Timothy 2:2, where believers are encouraged to "lead a quiet and peaceable [*hesychios*] life." Women should not seek the limelight or intentionally draw attention to themselves.

How does a woman develop this type of spirit? Peter provides the answer in verse 5: "In this manner, in former times, *the holy women who trusted in God* also adorned themselves." A woman develops a gentle and quiet spirit by trusting in the Lord. Holy women of the past who demonstrated gentle and quiet spirits did so through their relationships with Him. When a woman trusts God, her spirit will be peaceful and at rest. And when she's not trusting Him, she will be filled with anxiety and worry. In this way we can see that while outward beauty is achieved through physical means, inward beauty is achieved through spiritual means.

God's View of Inward Beauty

A key reason women should be motivated to pursue inward beauty is that, as 1 Peter 3:4 says, it "is very precious in the sight of God." The word translated "precious" is *polyteles*, which means "very costly, excellent, of surpassing value." The word appears only two other times in Scripture. The first example is in Mark 14:3, which says, "As [Jesus] sat at the table, a woman came having an alabaster flask of very costly [*polyteles*] oil of spikenard. Then she broke the flask and poured it on His head." The second example is in 1 Timothy 2:9, which has an important parallel with 1 Peter 3:4:

- "Women adorn themselves in modest apparel, with propriety and moderation, not with braided hair or gold or pearls or costly [*polyteles*] clothing" (1 Timothy 2:9).

- "Rather let it be the hidden person of the heart, with the incorruptible beauty of a gentle and quiet spirit, which is very precious [*polyteles*] in the sight of God" (1 Peter 3:4).

Polyteles is used in both verses, but in 1 Timothy 2:9 it refers to outward adornment, while in 1 Peter 3:4 it refers to inward beauty. It's as though God is saying: "Don't pursue outward, fading, expensive beauty, because it is your inward beauty that is truly precious and valuable in My sight." This should encourage women to keep these two truths in mind:

- It is possible to be beautiful in man's eyes and ugly in God's eyes.

- It is possible to be plain or even unattractive in man's eyes and very beautiful in God's eyes.

First Samuel 16:7 confirms, "The LORD does not see as man sees; for man looks at the outward appearance, but the LORD looks at the heart." To rephrase this verse specifically for women, we could say, "The LORD does not see as man sees; for man looks at the outward adornment—arranging the hair, the wearing of gold, or putting on fine apparel—but the LORD looks at the hidden person of the heart, with the incorruptible beauty of a gentle and quiet spirit, which is very precious in His sight."

JESUS WAS NOT BEAUTIFUL TO THE WORLD

A wonderful way for us to conclude our look at true beauty is by considering what Scripture says about our Savior's appearance: "He has *no form or comeliness*; and when we see Him, there is *no beauty* that we should desire Him" (Isaiah 53:2). By worldly standards, Jesus was humble in appearance. The Hebrew word translated "comeliness" is *hadar,* and it means "splendor, majesty, honor, or glory." Jesus had none! He veiled His beauty when He became a man. While few people would intentionally try to be unattractive, modern society has made physical beauty something to worship. We should keep in mind that Jesus was able to succeed in perfectly pleasing and obeying His Father without it.

Many of the images or portrayals we see of Jesus in art or books or movies don't represent what a first-century Jewish man looked like and put too much emphasis on physical attractiveness. According to Isaiah 53:2, there was nothing outstanding about Jesus' outward appearance that would draw people to Him. He wanted people drawn to Him for other reasons, such as His humility, love, compassion, and—most importantly—the sacrifice He would make for them.

When we think of the inner beauty brought about by a gentle and quiet spirit, how can we not think of Jesus? Isaiah 53:7 goes on to say, "He was oppressed and He was afflicted, yet *He opened not His mouth*; He was led as a lamb to the slaughter, and as a sheep before its shearers *is silent*, so *He opened not His mouth.*" When Peter wrote about the same event in Christ's life, only a few verses before describing a woman's gentle and quiet spirit, he similarly praised Him: "When He was reviled, [He] *did not revile* in return; when He suffered, He *did not threaten*, but committed Himself to Him who judges righteously" (1 Peter 2:23).

Christ's gentle and quiet spirit is what compelled Him to go to the cross. He truly depicted the greatest manifestation of inward beauty, one that was "very precious in God's sight." His example encourages all believers to imitate Him.

CHAPTER EIGHTEEN

The Bible's "Perfect" Wife

W hen it comes to learning how we can grow as Christians, being told what to do can be instructive, but being shown what to do can be even better. This is why examples are so helpful. When I taught elementary school, I would tell my students what to do, then I would also try to give them an example of how to fulfill my request. The apostle Peter takes this approach in the New Testament. He finishes his instruction to women by lifting a woman out of the Old Testament—Abraham's wife, Sarah—and using her as an example for church-age wives. Sarah demonstrated the submission and inner beauty Peter describes in 1 Peter 3:1-4. He writes, "In this manner, in former times, the holy women who trusted in God also adorned themselves, being submissive to their own husbands, as Sarah obeyed Abraham, calling him lord, whose daughters you are if you do good and are not afraid with any terror" (1 Peter 3:5-6).

That Sarah was chosen as an example should serve as an encouragement to wives for two reasons. First, they should consider who Sarah submitted to: Abraham. It might be tempting for women to say, "I wouldn't have any trouble submitting to my husband if I was married to Abraham!" While Abraham was indeed one of the greatest men of faith in Scripture, the truth is that being his wife was difficult. God's call on Abraham's life required him to leave a comfortable city life in Ur to become a wandering nomad (Genesis 12:1-5; Hebrews 11:8-10). How many places did Abraham and Sarah live? How many times did they have to move?

In addition, Abraham made some foolish decisions. Twice he told Sarah to say she was his sister instead of his wife because he was afraid someone coveting her beauty might murder him in order to seize Sarah. He was willing to endanger his wife to protect himself:

> [Abraham] said to Sarai his wife, "Indeed I know that you are a
> woman of beautiful countenance. Therefore it will happen, when
> the Egyptians see you, that they will say, 'This is his wife'; and they
> will kill me, but they will let you live. Please say you are my sister,
> that it may be well with me for your sake, and that I may live because
> of you" (Genesis 12:11-13; see Genesis 20:2 for the second instance).

As a result, Sarah ended up in a pagan king's harem twice, which must have
been terrifying for her. Worse yet, Abraham didn't do anything to save her. In
contrast, when his nephew Lot was captured, he organized a war party to res-
cue him:

> When Abram heard that [Lot] was taken captive, he armed his
> three hundred and eighteen trained servants…and he and his ser-
> vants attacked them…and also brought back his brother Lot and
> his goods, as well as the women and the people (Genesis 14:14-16).

How would that make a wife feel? Far from being a strong, brave husband
to whom it would be easy to submit and follow, at times Abraham was a cow-
ardly, compromising husband. More than likely, Peter chose Sarah as an example for wives because of how difficult and terrifying it was at times for her to
submit to Abraham.

A second reason women should be encouraged by Sarah as an example is
that she was not always a picture of submission and faith. If Sarah had been
the perfect wife, it would be discouraging for women to think they needed to
emulate her. But Sarah had her own struggles. We know that she failed to trust
God when she convinced Abraham to fulfill God's promise of a son and heir
through her handmaid Hagar. Sarah sought to control her husband, and the
result ended up being a disaster on several levels. She also failed when God vis-
ited Abraham to tell him she would have a child the following year at age 90.
Sarah laughed because of her lack of faith, and then she lied when God confronted her about it (Genesis 18:12-15).

In light of these incidents, we could almost wonder why Sarah was chosen as an example of a godly wife, but Peter tells us the answer: "Sarah obeyed
Abraham, calling him lord" (1 Peter 3:6). Despite Sarah's mistakes, for the most
part, she was a woman who respected her husband and submitted to him. The
title "lord" was used often in the Old Testament to show reverence for someone. The closest comparable English expression would be addressing a man as
sir. This doesn't mean today's wives need to address their husband as "lord," but

the principle still applies that God calls wives to respect and submit to their husbands in the same way Sarah did to Abraham.

WIVES SUBMIT WHEN THEY FEAR BECAUSE THEY TRUST GOD

The final part of 1 Peter 3:6 offers wives a special title. They can be identified as "[Sarah's] daughters" if they "do good and are not afraid with any terror." The Greek word translated "terror" is *ptoesis*:

- In Luke 21:9, Jesus used the verb form when He told His disciples, "When you hear of wars and commotions, do not be terrified [*ptoeo*]."

- In Luke 24:37, the adjective form is used when Jesus appeared to the disciples after His resurrection and "they were terrified [*ptoeo*] and frightened, and supposed they had seen a spirit."

Terror is stronger than ordinary worries, anxieties, or even fears. Terror is what people feel on a plane about to crash, or when a doctor announces they have cancer, or when they receive a call that one of their children has been in an accident. And apparently, terror is also what wives might feel when it comes to submitting to their husbands! A wife today probably won't experience the same terror that Sarah experienced when she ended up in a king's harem, but there are still plenty of legitimate terrors a woman may face when she submits to her husband. She may find herself asking,

- "What happens if this decision ruins our family?"
- "What happens if he is unable to pay these bills?"
- "What happens if we can't afford to eat?"
- "What happens if he shouldn't take this job?"
- "What happens if we move there and it ends up being a disaster?"

How can wives be "Sarah's daughters" and handle the terror they experience when they submit to their husbands? They can consider Sarah's example and how she handled the terror she felt while submitting to Abraham, and how the other holy women of God handled the terror they felt when they submitted to their husbands. We are told they "*trusted in God...being submissive to their own husbands*" (1 Peter 3:5). Sarah was able to submit to Abraham's poor decisions because she trusted God and believed He was in control.

It's important to notice *why* Sarah and the other holy women of the Old Testament submitted to their husbands. It wasn't because they trusted their husbands, thought they were perfect, or expected them to make the right decisions. They submitted because they "trusted God." A wife's submission to her husband has less to do with her relationship with her husband and more to do with her relationship with the Lord. A woman's trust in God combats the fear—or terror—she experiences when she submits to her husband.

In marriage counseling sessions, I often hear women say, "It would be easier for me to submit to my husband if I could trust him," or "I do trust God. I just don't trust my husband." A wife is not expected to submit to her husband because she trusts him. Rather, she is expected to submit because she trusts God. When a wife submits to her husband, she is showing she trusts God. Conversely, when a wife does not submit, she is showing she does not trust God. Why is this the case? God is the one who commands wives to submit to their husbands. When wives obey God in this way, they are showing that they trust the one who gave them the command.

Reading both accounts of Abraham asking Sarah to say that she was his sister should be a great encouragement for women because they reveal Sarah's trust was well placed. God protected her and kept her captors from consummating a relationship with her:

- Genesis 12:17—"The LORD plagued Pharaoh and his house with great plagues because of Sarai, Abram's wife."

- Genesis 20:3—"God came to Abimelech in a dream by night, and said to him, 'Indeed you are a dead man because of the woman whom you have taken, for she is a man's wife.'"

In both instances, Sarah was rescued from captivity and her deliverance came from God's direct intervention. In the end, Sarah's submission produced blessing not just for her but for her husband as well:

> Abimelek brought sheep and cattle and male and female slaves and gave them to Abraham, and he returned Sarah his wife to him. And Abimelek said, "My land is before you; live wherever you like." To Sarah he said, "I am giving your brother a thousand shekels of silver. This is to cover the offense against you before all who are with you; you are completely vindicated" (Genesis 20:14-16 NIV).

Sarah experienced difficult circumstances because of her submission to Abraham, but God vindicated her, and blessed her and her husband as a result.

Encouraged by Sarah's Example of Trusting God

Wives should keep Sarah's example in mind when they fear their husband is making a wrong decision. This isn't to say that God will bless every wife's submission the same way He blessed Sarah's, but a wife can keep two things in mind: First, just as God was in control of Sarah's circumstances, He is in control of the wife's circumstances. Second, just as He worked through Sarah's submission to bring about the best end, He will work through the wife's submission to bring about the best end.

Encouraged by Jesus's Example of Trusting God

Wives should also be encouraged by Jesus's example, because He, too, submitted by trusting God. In Hebrews 2:13, He said, "I will put My trust in Him," and 1 Peter 2:23 (NIV) says Jesus "entrusted himself to him who judges justly." Just as wives must put themselves in God's hands, Jesus put Himself in His Father's hands.

These verses reveal how much Jesus fully identified with us at the incarnation. The reality of His humanity was demonstrated by going so far as to also live by faith. R.C.H. Lenski said, "Although Jesus was Himself God and omnipotent, in His humiliation and in His human nature here on earth He depended on God in complete trust."[1] When wives struggle to trust God, they can find encouragement in Jesus as a role model because He, too, relied upon God during His earthly life.

---

*The willingness to submit reveals a strong,
godly woman filled with faith.*

WIVES SUBMIT BY KEEPING THEIR STRENGTH UNDER CONTROL

Submission involves trusting God and overcoming fear (and even terror). This reveals two things about women who submit: They're spiritually strong, and they're brave.

Contrary to what culture says, submission is not a sign of weakness. Rather, it's a sign of strength. Submission isn't a sign of faithlessness, but of faithfulness. The failure to submit to the husband—and ultimately, to the Lord—reveals weakness and fear. The willingness to submit reveals a strong, godly woman filled with faith.

Let me share a story that illustrates this point. The summer after I finished eighth grade, my parents flew me from California to upstate New York to work on my uncle's dairy farm. Being 13 years old and having no friends in the area, I had to find things to do to entertain myself. My uncle had a bull that stood at the end of the barn staring straight ahead all day. One day I thought it would be fun to try to get him to move. As I stood before the bull, he brought his head up underneath me and launched me into the air. Think of a cowboy thrown off a bull during a rodeo, and you have the correct imagery. Fortunately, the barn's ceiling was high, so I did not slam into it, but I did come crashing down onto the cement floor.

A man who worked on the farm saw what happened and ran to me. He screamed, "You could have gotten yourself killed! Do you see that little chain around the bull's neck? That's all that's holding him there. He could break it at any moment!"

My first thought was, *They need to put a bigger chain around the bull's neck!* My second thought was, *That bull has so much strength, but he allows himself to be subdued by so little.*

Submission is a choice; it is voluntary and deliberate. Husbands know a wife can choose to rebel rather than submit. A wife can "break" her husband's headship, "launch him into the air," and send him crashing back down to earth. When a wife chooses to willingly submit to her husband, she is exhibiting great strength that is subdued and kept under control.

THE PREMIER DEMONSTRATION OF STRENGTH UNDER CONTROL

Think of the immense strength Jesus had that allowed Him to control demons and nature: "With authority and power He commands the unclean spirits, and they come out…He commands even the winds and water, and they obey Him!" (Luke 4:36; 8:25). Compare that to what Jesus said when a mob came to arrest Him and Peter took out his sword to defend Him: "Put your sword [away]…do you think that I cannot now pray to My Father, and He will provide Me with more than twelve legions of angels?" (Matthew 26:52-53). Jesus had immense power and authority at His disposal, but He subdued it so that He could "[lay] down his life for us" (1 John 3:16). Nobody took Jesus's life from Him:

> I am the good shepherd. The good shepherd *gives His life* for the sheep…As the Father knows Me, even so I know the Father; and *I lay down My life* for the sheep…Therefore My Father loves Me, because *I lay down My life* that I may take it again. *No one takes it from Me, but I lay it down of Myself. I have power to lay it down*, and I have power to take it again. This command I have received from My Father…Greater love has no one than this, than to *lay down one's life for his friends* (John 10:11,15,17-18; 15:13).

Nobody has ever had greater power, authority, and strength than Jesus, but He kept it under control so that He could die for our sins. When wives struggle to keep their strength under control, they should be encouraged by Jesus's example.

HUSBANDS ARE GOING TO MAKE WRONG DECISIONS

The fear (or terror) a wife can experience when she submits to her husband comes from realizing the possible consequences if it turns out he has made a wrong decision. After reading up to this point, a wife might be tempted to ask, "If I am supposed to submit to my husband because God commands it and I should trust Him, then doesn't this mean God will also make sure my husband makes the right decision?" Because we humans are fallen and imperfect creatures, the inevitable reality is that a husband will sometimes make a wrong decision even as his wife chooses to submit to him. Sarah is a good example. She submitted to Abraham when he made a wrong decision—on more than one occasion.

That brings us to our next questions: How should a husband respond when he realizes he has made a wrong decision? And how should a wife respond?

How Husbands Should Respond

A husband who makes a wrong decision should acknowledge his mistake without making excuses. If he wants to be his wife's hero, he should admit, "You were right, and I was wrong." If he deliberately did not listen to his wife because he was being prideful and stubborn, he should realize those are sinful attitudes and say, "I am sorry. Will you please forgive me? I was being prideful and stubborn."

When a husband responds this way, these are the positive results:

- He blesses his wife.

- He encourages his wife to submit to him in the future.

- He sets a good example for his wife and children. Husbands need to lead not only by making decisions for the family, but also by the example they set.

Earlier in chapter 9, we looked at how a husband's behavior can influence the way his wife and children act:

- If a husband makes excuses, justifies himself, or blames his wife or children, he will likely end up with a wife and children who follow his example and make excuses, justify themselves, and blame others.

- If a husband humbles himself, takes responsibility for his actions, admits when he is wrong, and asks for forgiveness, he will encourage his wife and children to accept responsibility for their actions, admit when they are wrong, and ask for forgiveness.

Let me give a personal example. When Katie and I moved to Washington, I decided to rent our California house to a woman we knew. Katie told me, "Do not rent to that woman. She is not going to take care of our home." I rented to her anyway, and soon she invited her boyfriend to move in with her. Even though we had stipulated they were not supposed to have pets, they ended up bringing eight dogs and four cats into the home. The neighbors on both sides called me in Washington to complain about the barking and garbage. I received letters from the city threatening to fine me if the messes outside were not cleaned up.

When the woman's lease was up, Katie said, "Thankfully she'll finally be out." I, however, decided to try to recoup some of our losses by extending the woman's rental agreement. Katie thought I was crazy. The realty company that was handling the property advised me to take legal action to have the woman's wages garnished. I chose not to because the woman claimed to be a Christian and Scripture forbids taking fellow believers to court (1 Corinthians 6:5-7). Because a lack of rental payments meant no income for the realty company, they were upset with me too. By the time the woman, her children, her boyfriend, and their animals moved out, the house was trashed. I had lost thousands of dollars in rent, and I had to pay thousands of dollars in repairs so we could make the house inhabitable again.

There were several excuses I could have given Katie to justify my actions: "She was a family friend and single mother. I wanted to help her. There was no way of knowing this would happen." (Even though Katie seemed to know!) Ultimately, though, there was only one correct response: "I am sorry. You were right, and I was wrong."

How Wives Should Not Respond

A wife must resist two temptations when she willingly submits to her husband and he ends up being wrong. First, she may find herself thinking, *I knew it was going to turn out this way. I should have kept arguing with him. If I hadn't submitted to him, this never would've happened. I'm never going to submit to him again!* Wives must instead remind themselves that they were still right for making the choice to submit.

Second, she will find herself tempted to say these four little words: "I told you so!" Whether these words come from a wife, husband, child, parent, pastor, friend, or anyone else, they are always fleshly, prideful, and obnoxious. A vindictive attitude will only do damage to a marriage relationship, whereas forgiveness will bring healing and hopefully motivate the husband to be more careful when he makes decisions.

RESPONDING RIGHTLY TO WRONG DECISIONS

If a husband genuinely considers his wife's feedback and is truly prayerful as he makes a decision he believes is best for his family, should he be made to feel bad if his decision turns out to be a mistake? No.

The reality is that when a husband has made an effort to be spiritually right before God and has the best of intentions for his family yet still makes a wrong decision, more than likely he already feels bad enough about what he has done. At this point, what a husband needs most is his wife's encouragement and grace. When a husband has the humility to admit he was wrong, a godly wife should say, "Thank you for saying that. We all make mistakes. You did what you thought was best."

Now, obviously, some husbands do not have the humility to admit they have made a wrong decision. Even then a wife should resist the urge to tell her husband, "I told you so." Instead, she should pray for God to convict her husband of his stubbornness or pride and grant him humility and repentance.

Let me illustrate this point with a situation from my own marriage. When I was teaching elementary school, I learned of another position that would allow me to take better financial care of my family. During the drive to the interview, I prayed God would let me receive the job if that was the best next step for me. Before I left the interview, the position was offered to me, which I took as confirmation that this was God's will.

The one drawback of accepting the job was that I lost my secure, tenured position at my former district. Soon after, a recession hit, and school districts cut back on new teachers. As a result, even though I had already been teaching almost ten years, I was laid off. I had to go home and tell Katie, who was pregnant at the time, that I had lost not only my job, but our wonderful medical insurance. You can imagine I was feeling terrible about myself and my decision-making. I even felt frustrated with God for letting me take on a job that I would lose so quickly.

At this low point, Katie could have said, "You had a good, secure teaching position. Why didn't you stick with that? You say that you prayed about this? Next time, pray a little harder! You're supposed to be the spiritual leader of our family, and your prayers end up with you unemployed? You're supposed to provide for our family, but you don't have a job or insurance?"

Here is how Katie responded instead: "I am so excited to see what God is going to do!"

Katie was right. God did have a plan. This is when Grace Baptist, the church where I was working part-time, decided to hire me full-time. Even though they stepped out in faith because the budget was not sufficient to support me, the church grew, and the annual giving exceeded expenses. I will always remember the way God provided and Katie supported me. That was what I needed more than anything else. My wife not only did not make me feel worse about my decision but was a constant encouragement to me.

Let me conclude with this: Husbands, when we're wrong (not *if* we're wrong, but *when* we're wrong), let's be humble and admit it. If we were being proud and stubborn, let's ask for forgiveness. We owe that much to our wives and especially to God. Wives, when your husband is wrong, don't say, "I told you so." And don't make him feel worse. Encourage him. Be the helper God designed you to be for him.

CHAPTER NINETEEN

A Husband Treats
His Wife Well By...

here's a story about a pastor who, when he preached on 1 Peter 3:1-7, he told his congregation that he didn't know why there were six verses for wives but only one verse for husbands. After the service was over an elderly, wise woman came up to the pastor and said, "It's because women can remember six verses, but men can only remember one."

Whether that's true or not, Peter packs so much into the one verse for husbands that it could be multiple verses: "Husbands, likewise, dwell with [your wives] with understanding, giving honor to the wife, as to the weaker vessel, and as being heirs together of the grace of life, that your prayers may not be hindered" (1 Peter 3:7).

In verses 1 through 6, Peter instructed wives to submit to their husbands, and then in verse 7, he taught husbands how to treat their wives to ensure they didn't abuse the authority entrusted to them by God. The first six verses describe a godly wife, and then verse 7 correspondingly describes how a godly husband treats his wife.

LEARNING ABOUT HER

Let's begin with a look at the New Testament Greek words Peter chose when he admonished husbands about their conduct. Earlier we learned about the different Greek words for love, and there are also different Greek words that translate to "know" or "knowing." *Epistamai* means "to put one's attention on or to fix one's thoughts on." This is an intellectual knowledge that comes by observing, but it lacks personal relationship or experience. On the other hand, *ginosko* means "to learn, get a knowledge of, feel." This is a knowledge that comes from personal relationship or experience. Here are two examples of how these terms can be applied:

- I know what rugby is even though I have never played it; therefore, I know it intellectually, or *epistamai*. On the other hand, I have played and coached football, which means I know it experientially, or *ginosko*.

- I know of (*epistamai*) Abraham Lincoln historically, but I know (*ginosko*) my wife, Katie, relationally.

Husbands are told to "dwell with [their wives] with understanding," and the Greek word translated "understanding" is *gnosis*, which is related to the word *ginosko*. It describes a close intimacy—the same word is used in Luke 1:34, where Mary said, in response to the angel who told her she would give birth to the Messiah, "How can this be, since I do not know [*ginosko*] a man?"

Peter commands husbands to develop an intimate knowledge or understanding of their wives that comes through personal relationship or experience. We talked earlier about a wife learning about her husband: what his needs and strengths are to be a "comparable helper" to him, what he finds respectful and disrespectful. Similarly, husbands need to get to know their wives and learn about and understand them.

Do wives want husbands who make a priority of learning about and understanding them? Definitely! Wives feel loved by being understood. A lot of wives wish their husbands knew as much about them as they know about sports, cars, television shows, friends, food, music, video games, you name it.

Now, what exactly are husbands supposed to know about their wives? Everything that is important to them. If it's important to the wife, it is vital that the husband know about it. This means knowing what she likes and doesn't like, enjoys and doesn't enjoy, desires and despises. A husband ought to know as much as he can about the woman who will be at his side for the rest of his life.

If it's important to the wife, it is vital
that the husband know about it.

Respecting Him and Understanding Her

In chapter 12, we learned about God's command for wives to respect their husbands. Then in chapter 14 we looked at the importance of obeying the Bible versus obeying the world.

Because we live in a fallen, sinful world, we can fully expect culture to contradict the Bible. So if God commands wives to respect their husbands, what is the world going to do? It's going to try to convince wives to disrespect their husbands. How does today's culture do this? One way is by making men look like they're not worthy of respect. Whether it's commercials, shows, movies, music, books, or general counsel from ungodly women, men are consistently made to look bumbling and foolish. Husbands are presented as incompetent and inept, to the point a wife has no choice but to take matters into her own hands. There's no way she can trust her husband to lead or do what needs to get done. Consequently, Christian wives need to realize that when they choose to disrespect their husbands, they're supporting society's agenda instead of obeying God.

Similarly, if God commands husbands to learn about and understand their wives, what is the world going to do? It's going to try to convince men that it's impossible to do so: "You can't understand women!" Again, think of what we frequently see in the media. Women are shown to be complicated or confusing, so there's no reason to even bothering trying to understand them. Christian husbands must realize that when they act as though they can't understand their wives, they're supporting society's agenda instead of obeying God.

Living with Her According to Knowledge

In 1 Peter 3:7, the word "dwell" (most Bible versions say "live") communicates being together physically, but it means more than just occupying the same house. Sadly, some marriages look like little more than two roommates, and the spousal relationship is little more than a business partnership. Peter puts the responsibility on husbands to prevent this from happening. A man must make his wife his true companion in all that life offers. God didn't design for a marriage to be two people living independently of each other spending most of their time "doing their own thing."

Let's connect the dots. Together, the words "understanding" and "dwell" command husbands to develop knowledge of their wives and then live with them according to that knowledge. What good would it do if a husband learned about his wife but didn't apply that knowledge to his daily life with her? To put it simply, a husband should understand what makes his wife feel loved and seek to love her that way; he should know how she wants to be treated and strive to care for her that way.

Dwelling with our wives in an understanding way also means dealing tenderly with them; we don't treat them the same way we do our male friends. This is especially applicable regarding our wives' weaknesses. Katie has given me permission to share here the ways she appreciates me gently addressing two of her struggles based on the knowledge I have of her:

- My wife is a visionary, creative woman with many plans and thoughts. She likes to think months, years, or even decades in advance. On the other hand, I generally have one focus each week: making sure Sunday goes well. I count time by the number of days until the sermon must be completed. When Sunday is over, the countdown begins again. I rarely think eight days ahead (much less eight months or eight years). As a result, Katie appreciates me listening to her ideas no matter how far they look into the future, and regardless of whether there is much chance they will come to fruition.

- Most strengths have a corresponding weakness, so even though Katie has many plans, she also has trouble finishing things she starts. Some of her favorite words to say to herself come from Ecclesiastes 7:8: "The end of a thing is better than its beginning." In other words, finishing is better than starting. Because Katie knows this about herself, she has asked me to do two things for her: encourage her to finish whatever she starts, and discourage her from beginning new projects until previous ones are completed.

These are simple yet important ways Katie wants me to "dwell with [her] with understanding." Each wife is different, which means each husband must learn how his wife wants him to dwell with her in an understanding way.

VALUING HER FEMININITY

Next, Peter urges husbands to "[give] honor to the wife," and the Greek word translated "honor" is *time*, which means "a valuing by which the price is fixed." Eight times in Scripture, the Greek word *time* is translated as "price" because it refers to the value of something. Here are two examples of its use:

- "The chief priests took the silver pieces and said, 'It is not lawful to put them into the treasury, because they are the price [*time*] of blood'" (Matthew 27:6).

- "Peter said, 'Ananias, why has Satan filled your heart to lie to the Holy Spirit and keep back part of the price [*time*] of the land for yourself?'" (Acts 5:3).

Peter's message to husbands is clear: Recognize the value of your wife, and as a result, honor her.

The phrase "to the wife" has an interesting application as well. The Greek word translated "wife" is *gyne*, occurring 221 times in the New Testament. The word is used twice in 1 Peter 3: "Wives [*gyne*], likewise, be submissive...In former times, the holy women [*gyne*]" (verses 1, 5). But the phrase "to the wife" is only one word in the Greek text, *gynaikeios*, and this is the only place it appears in Scripture. While *gyne* is a noun, *gynaikeios* is an adjective meaning "of or belonging to a woman, feminine."

Peter is not commanding husbands to honor their wives simply for the sake of honoring them. Instead, he's urging them to honor their wives for being feminine—that is, being the woman God created her to be. A man should find value in his wife's feminine nature and praise her for it. If we allow Scripture, versus the world, to define femininity for us, we can develop a good understanding from the passages we've covered, such as Proverbs 31:10-31, 1 Timothy 2:9-15, and 1 Peter 3:1-6. Completing the picture for us is Titus 2:3-5, which reveals what God expects of feminine women whether they are older or young:

> Older women [should] be reverent in behavior, not slanderers, not given to much wine, teachers of good things—that they admonish the young women to love their husbands, to love their children, to be discreet, chaste, homemakers, good, obedient to their own husbands, that the word of God may not be blasphemed.

A wife who lives out these verses is manifesting biblical femininity, which should prompt the husband to see her value and honor her as a result. Sadly, because the secular feminist movement discourages women from being feminine in the way God designed them to be, it destroys their value. Feminists encourage women to move away from what God says gives them honor.

Ladies—young or old, single or married—should celebrate their femininity and enjoy the beauty God has given them. Husbands should encourage their wives in their femininity. Parents should raise their daughters to be feminine, as this is what will allow them to be honored by their husbands in the future.

PROTECTING HER

Next, Peter says wives are "the weaker vessel," but this does *not* mean they are weaker morally, intellectually, or spiritually. Some women are stronger than their husbands in these areas. This is speaking of men being stronger physically. The Amplified Bible puts it this way: "honoring the woman as [physically] the weaker." Studies have shown that physiologically, women are approximately 40-50 percent weaker than men in the upper body and 30-40 percent weaker in the lower body.[1, 2]

It is also important to notice that Peter said "weaker" instead of "weak." Men are physically weak too. They get sick. They can be injured. They are susceptible to aging and eventually die. A man's physical weakness should be a reminder to him to be sensitive to his wife's physical weakness.

Why did God make men physically stronger? Primarily so men can protect women! One of the evilest tragedies is when men use their strength to hurt women. God gave men greater strength so they could be protective. James 4:17 describes the sin of omission: "To him who knows to do good and does not do it, to him it is sin." When men physically abuse women, they're doubly sinning:

- They're committing a sin of commission through their behavior.

- They're committing a sin of omission by failing to use their strength for the reason God gave it to them.

Treating our wives as the weaker vessels means making our wives feel safe and protected. Colossians 3:19 instructs, "Husbands, love your wives and *do not be harsh with them*" (NIV, see also ESV). Wives should not have to fear verbal, emotional, or physical abuse. Rather, every wife should be confident that her husband will step up and protect her from conflict or danger. Every husband, as best as he can, should put himself between his wife and anything that might threaten her physically, mentally, emotionally, or spiritually.

Even though women are physically "weaker," when we bring that together with the next words in 1 Peter 3:7—"heirs together of the grace of life"—we see that Peter prevents his readers from thinking wives are at all inferior to their husbands because the word "heirs" speaks of equality. In the ancient Roman world, only males were heirs. In contrast, the gospel makes women fellow heirs and co-inheritors, which was a radical concept in that era. The fact wives are "heirs together" reminds husbands that even though they are given headship, their wives are still identical to them in terms of spiritual privilege and importance. Husbands who see their wives in this way will protect them because they recognize they're married to daughters of the King.

KEEPING HIS PRAYERS FROM BEING "CHOPPED DOWN"

If the world isn't trying to feminize men by completely discouraging them from using their distinctively masculine traits, then it's trying to push them to the other extreme, or chauvinism and hypermasculinity that values physical strength above all else. God wants husbands to resist both extremes and be strong spiritual leaders. It is for this reason that 1 Peter 3:7 ends with a sobering warning that should cause any Christian husband to treat his wife well: "that your prayers may not be hindered." Scripture teaches that sin hinders our prayers:

- "When you spread out your hands, I will hide My eyes from you; even though you make many prayers, I will not hear. Your hands are full of blood" (Isaiah 1:15).

- "If I regard iniquity in my heart, the Lord will not hear" (Psalm 66:18).

- "God does not hear sinners; but if anyone is a worshiper of God and does His will, He hears him" (John 9:31).

First Peter 3:7 specifies one sin that prevents God from hearing the prayers of husbands—the sin of mistreating their wives. The Greek word translated "hindered" is *ekkopto*, which means "cut off; of a tree."[3] The Amplified Bible renders this passage "in order that your prayers may not be hindered and cut off." Elsewhere in the New Testament, Jesus used the word twice in connection with cutting down a fruit tree:

- "Every tree that does not bear good fruit is cut down [*ekkopto*]" (Matthew 7:19).

- "Look, for three years I have come seeking fruit on this fig tree and find none. Cut it down [*ekkopto*]" (Luke 13:7).

Why would God use a word that speaks of cutting down a fruit tree to describe a husband's prayers being hindered? The intended imagery is that of a husband's prayers being fruitless or "chopped down." For a husband to be a good spiritual leader, he needs to have God hear his prayers. In 1 Peter 3:7, God is saying that, to Him, it is so important that husbands treat their wives well that He will not hear them if they disobey in this area. The only prayer God will hear from husbands when they mistreat their wives is a prayer of repentance: "I am truly sorry for the way I treated my wife." I am ashamed to say there have been days when I left for the office only to have to turn around and head home to make sure things were right with Katie. I realized I had not treated her the way I should, and I knew that unless I made things right, God would not hear me when I prayed.

The nineteenth-century preacher Charles Spurgeon said, "To true believers prayer is so invaluable that the danger of hindering it is used by Peter as a motive…in their marriage relationships."[4] Sadly, some men have such a low regard for prayer that this warning does not cause them to treat their wives any differently. One reason this attitude is so terrible is that the passage, 1 Peter 3:1-7, is largely about wives submitting to their husbands, and wives will have a much easier time submitting to spiritual men who are fearful of having their prayers hindered. A wife who has a husband who values having his prayers heard by God will have a much easier time submitting to him.

I believe it is safe to say that one of the best motivators for a husband to treat his wife well is to keep his prayers from being "chopped down."

TREATING HER WELL

So far, we have looked at how husbands should treat their wives. Now we will look at two examples—from Scripture—of how husbands should *not* treat their wives.

A Husband Mistreats His Wife When He Responds in Anger

Jacob married two sisters, Rachel and Leah (Genesis 29:15-28), which in itself was a problem. You may wonder why biblical patriarchs took multiple wives for themselves, but realize that God never condoned this. The Old Testament passages that mention polygamy are descriptive in nature, not prescriptive. This practice of marrying multiple women portrays the sad reality of ancient cultures. Jesus said, "Wisdom is justified by all her children" (Luke 7:35). There, "justified" means "declared right." The wisdom of a person's decisions is shown to be right (justified) by what's produced from them (the children). The "wisdom" of polygamy is shown to be foolishness because whenever it took place, it only produced problems. All instances of polygamy in the Bible are characterized by turmoil and strife instead of peace and harmony. That was the case with Jacob's marriages to Rachel and Leah.

Rachel was the more beautiful of the two sisters, and Jacob loved her the most (Genesis 29:17-20, 30). Upon seeing Jacob's lack of love for Leah, God opened Leah's womb and gave her a total of six sons and at least one daughter (Genesis 29:31-35). In that era, being infertile was a great shame for a woman. You can imagine how Rachel felt when she was unable to bear children, but her husband's other wife, who also happened to be her sister, was able to have so many. Genesis 30:1 says, "When Rachel saw that she bore Jacob no children, Rachel envied her sister, and said to Jacob, 'Give me children, or else I die!'" This account is instructive not only for husbands but for wives as well. Women can learn two lessons from Rachel's response to her predicament.

First, consider whom Rachel held responsible for her suffering: her husband. Was it really Jacob's fault that she could not have any children? Clearly not, because he had been able to have children with Leah. Instead of blaming Jacob, Rachel should have taken her problem in prayer to God. A wife reading this could ask herself: "When I'm suffering, do I hold my husband responsible? If I'm upset, do I get frustrated with those around me? When I'm having a bad day, do I make sure my husband—or the rest of my family—has a bad day too?"

Second, Rachel's anger stemmed from the fact Leah was the only one having children. Her anger was not motivated by something her husband had done, but by her own sins: jealousy and discontentment. A wife reading this could ask herself: "Am I jealous of other women? Do I covet what they have? Am I discontent with my lot in life? Is this planting a root of bitterness in my heart as it did with Rachel?"

Even so, Jacob had the opportunity to be a loving, sensitive husband. In the spirit of 1 Peter 3:7, he should have asked himself, "After all that I've learned about my wife, how can I respond to her so I'm dwelling with her in an understanding way? Part of her femininity is a desire to have children, so she has a reason to be upset. How can I honor her when she's feeling this way? We are heirs together in the grace of life, so how would God have me treat her right now so my prayers will not be hindered? I need to go to her and say, 'I am so sorry you have not been able to bear any children. This must be difficult. Can we pray together and bring this matter to God?'"

But that wasn't Jacob's response. Instead, according to Genesis 30:2, "Jacob's anger was aroused against Rachel, and he said, 'Am I in the place of God, who has withheld from you the fruit of the womb?'" Other Bible versions translate this even more strongly: "Jacob's anger was kindled" (ESV) and "Jacob's anger burned" (NASB).

Jacob's words were true enough; he was not in control of whether his wife conceived and had children. But we as husbands can be right and wrong at the same time: We can be right in what we say, but wrong because of the way we say it. When wives are upset or emotional, it can be tempting for husbands to get angry in return. Instead, a husband should strive to learn why his wife is upset so he can respond in a loving, compassionate way.

A Husband Mistreats His Wife When He Responds Insensitively

Elkanah also had two wives, Hannah and Peninnah. Like Jacob and his wives, Peninnah could have children, but Hannah could not. What made Hannah's situation even worse was Peninnah's cruelty toward her:

> [Hannah's] rival [Peninnah] also provoked her severely, to make her miserable, because the LORD had closed her womb. So it was, year by year, when she went up to the house of the LORD, that [Peninnah] provoked her; therefore [Hannah] wept and did not eat (1 Samuel 1:6-7).

Twice we're told that Peninnah was cruel to Hannah to emphasize how difficult Hannah's barrenness must have been for her. Sadly, Elkanah didn't make matters any better. First Samuel 1:8 records, "Elkanah her husband said to her, 'Hannah, why do you weep? Why do you not eat? And why is your heart grieved? Am I not better to you than ten sons?'" Husband, when your wife is upset, do not use Elkanah as a model! In one short response, he made two common mistakes.

First, Elkanah asked insensitive questions that leave only two possibilities about his state of awareness in this situation: He really didn't know why his wife was grieving, which makes him look like a completely oblivious man. More than likely he knew exactly why she was so upset. This means Jacob's questions gave the impression that his wife's hurt was illegitimate; at the least, he showed that her reasons weren't good enough for him. His actions communicated, "You shouldn't be upset about this!" Husbands should learn from this example and avoid questions that make their wives feel bad about being upset, such as, "Why are you crying?"

Second, Elkanah made the king of all prideful statements: "Is not being married to me better than all the children you could have?" He rebuked Hannah for crying, and then added, "Why are you upset about not having any children when you already have me?" Today's equivalent would be to tell your wife, "Aren't you glad you are married to me? You are one lucky lady. Think of all I do for you, and you won't be sad!"

There is a difference and a similarity between Jacob and Elkanah. The difference is that while Jacob became angry with his wife, Elkanah at least tried to encourage his wife—even though he failed spectacularly in doing so. The similarity is that their actions showed they didn't know how to dwell with their wives in an understanding way. Proverbs 25:20 says, "Like one who takes away a garment in cold weather, and like vinegar on soda, is one who sings songs to a heavy heart." When people are hurting, they don't want someone to come alongside and encourage them with clichés and platitudes. Instead, they want a caring person to listen and be with them. This is known as the ministry of presence, and after talking about what husbands shouldn't do, this helps us to see what husbands should do.

How Should a Husband Respond to His Wife's Hurt?

In the years that I've been a pastor, many people have told me, "I know someone who is hurting. I want to encourage that person, but I don't know what to say." I frequently tell them they already have the right response to the situation: "If you don't know what to say, there's less chance of saying something you shouldn't. If you can't improve on silence, don't!" Of all the times I've been with grieving people, I can't think of one instance that someone asked me a difficult question that would have been helped with any kind of profound response. Instead, people simply wanted a listening ear during their grief. We see this illustrated by Job's friends—at least at the beginning of his suffering:

> When Job's three friends heard of all this adversity that had come upon him, each one came from his own place...For they had made an appointment together to *come and mourn with him, and to comfort him.* And when they raised their eyes from afar, and did not recognize him, they lifted their voices and wept; and each one tore his robe and sprinkled dust on his head toward heaven. So they sat down with him on the ground seven days and seven nights, and *no one spoke a word to him, for they saw that his grief was very great* (Job 2:11-13).

How did they comfort him in the beginning? They did what Romans 12:15 encourages: "Weep with those who weep." They comforted him with their silent presence. When did they stop comforting him? When they opened their mouths!

This is instructive for husbands. You should respond with sympathy to your wife by listening well and then saying something like, "I am very sorry. I can see this is difficult. What can I do for you? Would you like me to pray with you?"

Husbands, when our wives are upset, let's make sure we don't respond in anger like Jacob because we lack patience, or insensitively like Elkanah by pointing out the reasons we think they should be in a good mood. When we respond in such ways, we disobey 1 Peter 3:7, which calls us to dwell with understanding with our wives. We should study and learn about our wives so we can respond in gentle, caring ways.

CONCERNED WITH THE RESPONSIBILITIES

Most military officers will say one of the biggest days of their life was when they were commissioned. Fittingly, you choose someone important to you to administer the oath. I chose a retired general who mentored me and taught some of my college classes. Because he outranked everyone at the ceremony, he felt the liberty to deliver a small, unexpected speech. Although he spoke directly to me, his words applied to all the cadets who would soon be second lieutenants. He read the speech from a paper that he later gave to me, and afterward, I framed it and put it on my wall.

The general began by extolling the advantages that would be ours because of our authority as officers. As you can imagine, we all enjoyed this part of the speech that caused us to feel good about ourselves, our positions, and the fact that we were not lower-ranking soldiers. But toward the end of the speech, he began talking about the huge weight on our shoulders and he concluded with a quote that has stuck with me since: "You need to be more concerned with your responsibilities than your privileges." What seemed like a speech meant to encourage us clearly became one meant to somber us to the task ahead.

Husband and brother in Christ, let me address you personally like the general did with me. I have listened to enough sermons to know that many pastors shy away from preaching on submission, or they soften the message so much it removes the pointedness and conviction it could bring. They leave out portions they believe will offend people or add enough qualifiers that nobody thinks the Scripture text applies to them. When I started writing *Your Marriage God's Way,*

I was committed to being faithful to Scripture regardless of whether it would be popular. I would like to think that in the last few chapters I have encouraged wives to take their role seriously by being straightforward and honest with them about God's instruction to them. And I know this: however high the bar is for wives, because God has commanded husbands to be the head of the relationship, it is even higher for us.

This is the conclusion for the chapter, but because this chapter concludes our look at the biblical content directly aimed at husbands, it is also the final part of this book's instruction for husbands. I wish I could speak to you face to face and share just how important it is that we be faithful. It's not to say that you don't know this, but we need to be reminded, myself included. With our role comes authority, but we must be more concerned with our responsibilities. While I could say that I am charging you to take your role seriously, that would mean little. Instead, we must keep in mind that *God* charges us to take our role seriously. Of all the stewardships in our lives as men, none are more important than that of husband, and "it is required in stewards that one be found faithful" (1 Corinthians 4:2).

Biblically speaking, the opposite of faithful is treacherous. In the Old Testament, the priests were the spiritual leaders of the nation. Consider this strong rebuke God had for them: "The LORD has been witness between you and the wife of your youth, with whom you have dealt treacherously; yet she is your companion and your wife by covenant. But did He not make them one, having a remnant of the Spirit?...Therefore take heed to your spirit, and let none deal treacherously with the wife of his youth" (Malachi 2:14-15). God has made us one with our wives with His Spirit between us. Let us pursue our wives in such a faithful way, lacking treachery, that God would be pleased with how we are caring for His daughter.

In the military there are many benefits to having competent, disciplined, skilled leaders. It wouldn't be too much to say that there are many similarities with marriage. Little in this world has as much potential to affect positive change for the kingdom of God than spiritually strong, competent, disciplined, skilled leaders who are aware that they will stand before God and give an account. As husbands, let's faithfully love and cherish our wives, not just for their sake, but for the sake of Christ, who gave Himself for us (Titus 2:14).

PART SEVEN

A BIBLICAL VIEW
OF INTIMACY
(1 CORINTHIANS 7:1-6)

CHAPTER TWENTY

The Case for Intimacy

How do we determine the important topics in Scripture? I frequently tell my congregation that God does not use highlighting, italics, boldface, or underlining for emphasis. Instead, He uses repetition when He wants to make sure we don't miss something.

Sexual intimacy is discussed several times in the Old and New Testaments. One entire book—Song of Solomon—is dedicated largely to the topic. When God's Word addresses a subject repeatedly because it is important, we must make it important in our lives by learning what Scripture has to say. If we don't do this, we are more likely for our understanding of that subject to be shaped by the world. When it comes to sexuality, we definitely want to know what the Bible teaches, for secular society has a thoroughly corrupt view of it. So let's take a closer look at God's intended design for intimacy in marriage, starting with three key truths.

GOD'S DESIGN FOR MARITAL INTIMACY

Intimacy in Marriage Is Blessed by God

Hebrews 13:4 says, "Marriage is honorable among all, and the bed undefiled; but fornicators and adulterers God will judge." The word "bed" is a euphemism for sexual activity, and within marriage, God calls this activity "undefiled," which means "pure." The same New Testament Greek word is used earlier in Hebrews 7:26 to describe Jesus, our High Priest, as "holy, harmless, undefiled." God wants us to know there is absolutely nothing sinful or compromising about sexual activity between a husband and wife.

When it comes to wrong thoughts about sexuality, we typically think of the devil tempting people to disobey the second half of Hebrews 13:4 and engage in sexual activity outside of marriage. But what about when he tempts people to disobey the first half of the verse? He leads them to believe sexual intimacy *is* defiled, or impure.

I once counseled a man in his fifties who was addicted to pornography. I mention his age only because pornography is more typically considered a struggle for young, single men. But it can enslave men—and women—of any age, in any season of life. Let me say up front this man's actions were sinful; there is no minimizing the wickedness of what he was doing. That said, after months of counseling, it became apparent that one reason for his addiction was a wrong view of intimacy. His mother told him at a young age that sex was filthy, and he was never able to rid himself of that belief. He told me, "I look at porn because at least then I'm not involving my wife in a dirty activity." Though I tried to convince him otherwise, he never seemed to be able to shake himself free of his mother's incorrect teaching.

In the Song of Solomon, the couple consummate their relationship in chapter 4, and we read of God's approval in 5:1: "Eat, O friends! Drink, yes, drink deeply, O beloved ones!" This invitation is meant to encourage husbands and wives in their sexual activity. Not only should intimacy in marriage *not* be thought of as neutral, amoral, or nonspiritual, it should be thought of as good, spiritual, and blessed by God.

Intimacy in Marriage Is for Enjoyment as Much as for Procreation

God's purpose for intimacy goes far beyond simply having children. Yes, God created sex so couples can fulfill His command in Genesis 1:28 to "be fruitful and multiply," but He also gave intimacy as a gift for marital pleasure. The Song of Solomon is filled with passages that describe the ways a husband and wife can enjoy each other physically. Consider these verses:

- "Let him kiss me with the kisses of his mouth—for your love is better than wine" (1:2).

- "A bundle of myrrh is my beloved to me, that lies all night between my breasts" (1:13).

- "Like an apple tree among the trees of the woods, so is my beloved among the sons. I sat down in his shade with great delight, and his fruit was sweet to my taste" (2:3).

- "Your two breasts are like two fawns, twins of a gazelle, which feed among the lilies" (4:5).

These verses (with perhaps the exception of the last one!) are discreet, but they describe the physical pleasure the husband and wife experience during sexual activity. They truly enjoy discovering each other and opening themselves up to each other. Within the marriage relationship there is a sexual liberty and freedom that God wants couples to experience.

Intimacy in Marriage Is Commanded

I have counseled couples who have not been intimate for months, and in a few cases, even years. During the first counseling session with one such couple, I assigned them homework: have sex before our next counseling session one week later. They came back and still hadn't been intimate. I gave them the same homework, but they still didn't do it. You would think this wasn't that difficult of an assignment, but it is for some couples. Was I out of line for encouraging them to have sex? Not according to the apostle Paul. In 1 Corinthians 7:1-3, he wrote:

> It is good for a man not to touch a woman. Nevertheless, because of sexual immorality, let each man have his own wife, and let each woman have her own husband. Let the husband render to his wife the affection due her, and likewise also the wife to her husband.

The phrase "touch a woman" is another euphemism for sex. Paul commands single people to abstain, but then says that it is equally bad for married people to abstain. Just as the devil wants to encourage sex outside of a marriage (fornication and adultery), he equally wants to discourage sex within a marriage. While we generally recognize that intimacy outside of a marriage is wrong, so we should also recognize that withholding intimacy in a marriage is equally wrong. Paul instructs married people to "render" to their spouses the "affection" or intimacy that is "due." The Greek word translated "due" is *opheilo*, which means "to owe, be in debt for." Here are two other places this term is used in the New Testament:

- "That servant went out and found one of his fellow servants who owed [*opheilo*] him a hundred denarii; and he...threw him into prison till he should pay the debt [*opheilo*]" (Matthew 18:28-30).

- "There was a certain creditor who had two debtors. One owed [*opheilo*] five hundred denarii, and the other fifty" (Luke 7:41).

Spouses owe affection—or intimacy—to each other. Withholding intimacy out of anger or to be vindictive or manipulative is not only unloving and sinful, it is also dangerous, as we'll see in the upcoming verses.

Your Body Belongs to Your Spouse

The apostle Paul continues in 1 Corinthians 7, "The wife does not have authority over her own body, but the husband does. And likewise the husband does not have authority over his own body, but the wife does" (verse 4). We discussed in previous chapters a husband's authority in the marriage relationship, so it is significant to see that with regard to intimacy, husbands and wives have equal authority over their spouse's body. This makes sense because when it comes to marital intimacy, our goal should be to willingly please our husband or wife.[1]

Should You Ever Abstain?

While a husband and wife should not deprive one another of sexual intimacy, the Old Testament mentioned some circumstances during which couples should abstain from sexual activity. For example, when the Israelites gathered at Mount Sinai to receive the Ten Commandments, they were commanded to abstain as part of their preparations to meet God (Exodus 19:10-14). A more ordinary period of abstinence took place after a woman gave birth. She was considered unclean for seven days following the birth of a son, and two weeks following the birth of a daughter (Leviticus 12:1-5). A similar restriction of seven days occurred when a woman was menstruating (Leviticus 15:19-24; 18:19; 20:18). The original purpose of these commands to abstain is found in an understanding of the sacredness of blood in the Old Testament: "The life of the flesh is in the blood, and I have given it to you upon the altar to make atonement for your souls; for it is the blood that makes atonement for the soul" (Leviticus 17:11). Forbidding contact with a menstruating woman revealed the value placed on blood.

The obvious question for us today is, Should husbands and wives abstain on account of these Old Testament commands? Some couples choose to abstain because they believe these commands still apply. Others believe the ceremonial portions of the law—under which these commands fall—are no more binding than the commands to offer blood sacrifices at the temple. Romans 14:5 provides some latitude for couples as they address these types of questions: "Let each be fully convinced in his own mind." Couples should agree together regarding the circumstances under which they choose to abstain. Unless both husband and wife agree to abstain, they should not do so. This is supported by the apostle Paul's words as he continues his instruction in 1 Corinthians 7:5-6:

> Do not deprive one another *except with consent* for a time, that you may give yourselves to fasting and prayer; and come together again so that Satan does not tempt you because of your lack of self-control. But I say this as a concession, not as a commandment.

Even when the New Testament discusses abstinence, it is for the purposes of "fasting and prayer," as opposed to observing Old Testament commands. Paul also makes the point that couples do not have to abstain. Rather, he says they can do so if they choose to for the reasons mentioned. If a husband and wife go their entire marriage without ever abstaining, that is perfectly acceptable. If they do agree to abstain, the words "for a time" and "come together again" indicate the abstinence should be for a determined, limited season. The words "so that Satan does not tempt you" reveal the reason: There is greater potential for succumbing to sexual temptation while abstaining. In 1 Corinthians 7:9, Paul writes, "If they cannot exercise self-control, let them marry. For it is better to marry than to burn with passion." First Corinthians 7:5 and 7:9 both teach that when people refrain from physical intimacy, their self-control is tested.

Husbands and wives must recognize that when they deprive their spouse in a sexual sense, they put their partner in a spiritually precarious situation. They risk making their spouse feel, once again, like a single person "[burning] with passion." A man or woman who looks at pornography or commits adultery cannot blame the sin and lack of self-control on the spouse, but it is important to understand that husbands and wives who withhold affection are making their spouses more vulnerable to temptation. Knowing that fact, as well as the teaching that our body belongs to our spouse, makes us realize how committed we should be to satisfying our husband or wife—not just to obey God's commands, but to help our spouse avoid temptation.

UNDERSTANDING *EROS*

Recall for a moment what we learned earlier about the fact New Testament

Greek has various words for love—*phileo, storge, agape,* and *eros. Eros* is the type of love specifically related to sexual intimacy between husband and wife.

One of the important principles we looked at earlier is that love is not so much an emotion as it is actions: "Love suffers long and is kind" (1 Corinthians 13:4). In contrast, *eros* is more of a feeling than a demonstration of loving action toward someone. It describes the sensation people experience when they are physically attracted to someone. The word *eros* is the root of the English word *erotic.*

While the word *eros* does not appear in Scripture, we can see this kind of love on display. *Eros* is what Samson felt in Judges 14:2 when he told his parents, "I have seen a woman in Timnah of the daughters of the Philistines; now therefore, get her for me as a wife." *Eros* is how King David found himself in the worst trouble of his life when he stepped out on his rooftop and spotted "[Bathsheba] bathing, and the woman was very beautiful to behold" (2 Samuel 11:2). Song of Solomon gives a clear depiction of *eros* as it describes the strong physical attraction the man and woman feel toward each other.

Eros is self-centered in the sense it relates to the way a person feels and what a person wants. Little to no consideration is given to the object of one's *eros.* Unlike *agape, eros* is conditional and will not move a person to be forgiving or sacrificial, which is why it's important not to base a marriage on *eros,* or physical attraction. Many couples find themselves wanting to get married because of strong feelings of *eros* toward each other, but when the *eros* wears off, they will find themselves frustrated and uninterested.

That, of course, is the problem with *eros:* It can wear off. It can change with time, age, or physical appearance. When *eros* is the main reason for a relationship, couples often find out their union has no foundation at all. If a relationship is based on *eros* alone, then when *eros* is gone, the relationship is also gone. For a true and lasting relationship, the thrill and excitement of *eros* must be supported by a deeper, unchanging love and commitment. *Eros* must be based on the other types of love we discussed earlier—the sacrificial love of *agape* and the abiding affection and friendship of *phileo.*

That doesn't mean *eros* is immoral or sinful. In fact, it is an important part of a marriage relationship. It is part of the attraction husbands and wives should feel for each other.

Now, what if we lack *eros* for our spouse? Let me give you three recommendations. First, pray for God to restore, and even increase, your *eros.* It is a wonderful request, and one that you can be confident God wants to answer. Second, practice *agape,* because that will cause *eros* to follow. As we discovered earlier, *agape* is a choice versus a feeling. Making the choice to exercise *agape*, which means unconditionally sacrificing and loving your spouse, will grow your *eros*, because feelings follow actions. Proverbs 16:3 says, "Commit your works to the Lord, and your thoughts will be established." Do what's right, and your emotions will follow your behavior. Third, read the Song of Solomon with your spouse, because the example set by the couple can help you both to enjoy the physical aspects of marriage.

God gave us sex as a gift, but as sinful people in a fallen world, we have the potential to ruin anything good God gives us.[2] Let's look at three of the most common threats to *eros*.

Selfish Attitudes Threaten *Eros*

Husbands and wives should be committed to satisfying each other, but a Scripture passage must also be balanced in light of other Scripture passages. If 1 Corinthians 7 were the only passage we were to consider in relation to sexual intimacy, we can easily get the impression it is okay for us to demand that our spouse satisfy our desires regardless of the way he or she feels. But we have looked at other passages—such as Ephesians 5 and 1 Peter 3—that mandate love, gentleness, compassion, and deference in marriage. While it would be unhealthy and even sinful to sexually deprive our spouse for selfish reasons, it can also be equally unhealthy and sinful to be sexually demanding or insensitive toward our spouse.

Although Paul listed fasting and prayer as possible reasons for abstinence, common sense and simple consideration dictate there are other acceptable reasons—including sickness, pregnancy, and grief. When a spouse is suffering or struggling, he or she might find intimacy unattractive. Because sex should be an enjoyable experience for both the husband and the wife, couples should strive to ensure there is a mutual level of comfort and interest regarding intimacy. Love and respect require caring about how the other person feels. Selfish and unkind attitudes threaten the joy and pleasure God desires for couples.

Impurity Threatens *Eros*

Of all the gifts God has given us, sex might be the one that is the most frequently abused and perverted. This fact is even more tragic when we consider that intimacy is most enjoyed when couples have pure hearts and minds. People who reserve all their desires and passions for their spouse will have the healthiest and happiest sex lives, which is why impurity is one of the greatest threats to intimacy.

We should rip our eyes and minds away from anything that provokes feelings of *eros* for anyone other than our spouse. Primarily, we should do this because God commands it as part of living a holy life: "This is the will of God, your sanctification: that you should abstain from sexual immorality" (1 Thessalonians 4:3). Secondarily, we should do this because failing to do so destroys the *eros* in a marriage. Individuals who give themselves over to pornography or lust find very quickly that they have no *eros* for their spouses.

People who reserve all their desires and passions for their spouse will have the healthiest and happiest sex lives,

---

Anytime impurity is an issue in a marriage, pornography almost always plays a role. My son Ricky recently shared with me how amazed he was that a bull can be controlled by a ring through its nose. He could not believe that a creature so big and powerful could be led around by something so small and insignificant. This is what pornography does with people: it does not matter how powerful or significant they are, when they introduce pornography into their lives, it enslaves and controls them.

We must also be concerned with what we set our hearts, thoughts, or feelings on. While there is nothing wrong with having friendships between genders, we should be cautious of becoming too close with people of the opposite sex. Even if your feelings for someone are pure and healthy, you cannot control how that person may feel toward you, and you don't want to become the object of someone else's misplaced affection.

When it comes to interactions with the opposite sex, it is best to err on the side of caution and avoid becoming "the good listener" or "shoulder to lean on." This is especially true with married friends who should be looking to their own spouse as a listener or shoulder to lean on. At the time of this writing, I learned of three prominent ministry leaders who experienced moral failure because of relationships with the opposite sex. More than likely, each situation began with casual friendships that escalated after the individuals became too close to each other.

Much of marital faithfulness has to do with contentment. Many in secular society view contentment as they view love—as a feeling or emotion over which they have no control. The Bible, however, presents contentment the same way it presents love—as a decision. In marriage, we choose to be content or discontent with our spouse. This is illustrated in Proverbs 5:18-19:

> *Let* your fountain be blessed,
> And *rejoice* with the wife of your youth.
> As a loving deer and a graceful doe,
> *Let* her breasts satisfy you at all times;
> And always *be* enraptured with her love.

Several words in that passage reveal the pleasure God wants us to experience with our spouse: "blessed...satisfy...enraptured." Several other words and phrases reveal we have the choice to feel these ways toward our spouse: "Rejoice...Let her...satisfy you at all times...always be enraptured with her." These are commands we can obey or disobey. Husbands and wives can choose to be content with their spouses, and this will go a long way in protecting their marriage and preserving their sexual purity. The couple in Song of Solomon had eyes and feelings only for each other. They were completely content with each other. As a result, their physical intimacy was healthy and joyful.

Mismatched Desires Threaten *Eros*

Because no two people are the same, marriages always involve many differences that have the potential to cause disagreements or problems when it comes to matters like finances, parenting, organization, and promptness. Among these differences are mismatched desires for physical intimacy. There will inevitably be times when one spouse desires sex and the other does not.

Let me present a situation that can happen in any marriage. Spouse A desires intimacy while Spouse B does not. While there are no contradictions in Scripture, there can be situations when biblical commands appear to compete. For example:

- Spouse A might quote from 1 Corinthians 7 that spouses should not deprive each other sexually, and may even be insensitive enough to say, "I know you don't want to do this, but I don't care. You need to obey God and recognize your body belongs to me!"

- Spouse B might then respond, "Why don't you flip forward a few chapters and read about love in 1 Corinthians 13? And go to Philippians 2, which says you're not supposed to look out for your own interests but to esteem others above yourself!"

So, should Spouse A's desire for physical intimacy be satisfied, or Spouse B's desire for no physical intimacy? We have seen in Scripture how God established a husband's headship and a wife's submission to break a stalemate so the relationship can go forward, but we have also seen that husbands and wives have equal authority over each other's bodies. As a result, unlike most impasses in marriage, it is not as easy as simply going with the husband's decision. For lack of a better way to say it, "Who wins?"

Boiling any conflict down to the simple question "Who wins?" is not only selfish, but will always cause problems. When I do marriage counseling, I try to avoid being a referee. That makes a marriage look like a competition, with husbands and wives placing themselves on opposing teams competing against each other. This could not be further from God's desire when He joins two people together and makes them one flesh.

SEEKING TO PLEASE THE OTHER

Rather than seeking to win, a better approach for each spouse is to seek to die to self and please the other. If both spouses have this attitude, this is what will happen:

- Spouse A will appreciate the effort Spouse B makes to satisfy Spouse A's desire for intimacy even when Spouse B does not want to be intimate.

- Spouse B will appreciate when Spouse A puts Spouse B's feelings ahead of Spouse A's own desires for intimacy.

This approach allows couples to have a strong relationship and usually allows mismatched desires to resolve themselves. With that said, let me add an important disclaimer. If I had to suggest erring on one side or the other, I would recommend erring on the side of satisfying your spouse. Why? First Corinthians 7 commands husbands and wives to satisfy each other, and there are no competing scriptures telling believers that they do not have to satisfy their spouse. Yes, we have considered biblical instruction about being loving, compassionate, and considerate toward our spouse, but those verses have to do with the bigger picture of how we are to act and are not directly aimed at the subject of marital intimacy. While we have a direct command to please our spouse, any verses we might think give us an out from pleasing our spouse must instead be inferred; they don't specifically apply to intimacy. A direct command carries more weight than verses that require inferences or indirect application.

Consider the results of both courses of action. The potential consequences of not satisfying your spouse far outweigh the "consequences"—if you want to call it that—of satisfying your spouse. There are not many drawbacks to pleasing your husband or wife, but when a spouse goes without physical intimacy, he or she becomes more vulnerable to temptation (1 Corinthians 7:5).

Let me conclude this section on marital differences with this encouragement: We are prone to think that the best marriages exist between people who are the most identical, whether it's their views on parenting, finances, sexual intimacy, or other important areas of life. But even the most compatible couple will have a miserable marriage if the spouses are selfish and insensitive. The healthiest relationships exist between people who recognize their differences—no matter how great—and are committed to moving beyond those differences and being giving, selfless, and sacrificial. This applies to every area of marriage, including intimacy. This "put the other person before self" mindset is one of the main ingredients for a joyful, Christ-centered marriage. And what does this have to do with Christ? Only through our relationship with Him can we enjoy this sort of relationship with our spouse.

INTIMACY THAT PLEASES GOD

As I have said multiple times in the previous chapters, God is for our marriages, and that includes our physical intimacy. Just as God wants other areas of our relationships to be strong, healthy, and joyful, He wants the same for our sex lives. At the same time, however, we have responsibilities. If we stay within God's design for intimacy, we can experience God's best for us. Should we stray outside that design, we bring hurt, division, and pain into the marriage and our personal lives. We must be proactive about anything that would threaten the *eros* for our spouse. Selflessness and purity can ensure we have the fullest kind of intimacy with our spouse, while selfishness and impurity destroy one of God's most beautiful blessings for marriage.

PART EIGHT

A STRONG FOUNDATION
(MATTHEW 7:24-27)

CHAPTER TWENTY-ONE

Building on Christ

S oon after Katie and I moved from California to Washington, my parents moved so they could live closer to us. Pretty quickly, they found what seemed like the perfect house. It was beautiful, near us, and the price was low. I wondered, *How had this house remained on the market for so long?*

Come to find out, there was a crack in the foundation. The house was so unstable no bank would even back a loan. On one hand I thought, *How sad that such a beautiful house has lost so much value because of a poor foundation!* On the other hand, I thought, *How valuable is a house with such a poor foundation that it could fall at any moment?*

Homes and buildings are not the only things that need strong foundations. Jesus taught an entire parable making this point:

> Whoever hears these sayings of Mine, and does them, I will liken him to a wise man who built his house on the rock: and the rain descended, the floods came, and the winds blew and beat on that house; and it did not fall, for it was founded on the rock. But everyone who hears these sayings of Mine, and does not do them, will be like a foolish man who built his house on the sand: and the rain descended, the floods came, and the winds blew and beat on that house; and it fell. And great was its fall (Matthew 7:24-27).

The Greek word translated "house" is *oikia*, and it can refer to a physical dwelling or a family or household. For our purposes, think specifically of a married couple. I would like to conclude our journey through *Your Marriage God's Way* with a look at this parable for two reasons:

- Jesus brought the Sermon on the Mount to a close with this teaching. He wanted to make sure His listeners put into practice what they heard. My prayer is that you will put into practice what you have read in this book.

- This teaching makes clear that there is only one true foundation for healthy, joyful relationships: Jesus Christ.

THE FOUNDATION FOR OUR LIVES—AND MARRIAGES

Let's back up to get some momentum into this point. The Old Testament looked forward to Jesus:

- Luke 24:27—"Beginning at Moses and all the Prophets, [Jesus] expounded to them in all the Scriptures the things *concerning Himself.*"

- John 5:39—"[Jesus said], 'You search the Scriptures...and these are they which *testify of Me.*'"

There are many titles for God in the Old Testament, and the New Testament reveals Jesus is the true and greater fulfillment of them. For example, in the Old Testament, God is called:

- Shepherd (Psalm 23:1-4; Ezekiel 34:11-24), and in John 10:11, Jesus said: "I am the good shepherd. The good shepherd gives His life for the sheep."

- Redeemer (Psalm 19:14; Isaiah 41:14), and Galatians 3:13 says, "Christ has redeemed us from the curse of the law."

- Deliverer (2 Samuel 22:2; Psalm 144:2), and 1 Thessalonians 1:10 says, "Jesus...delivers us from the wrath to come."

- Judge (Genesis 18:25; Ezekiel 34:17), and in John 5:22 Jesus said, "The Father...has committed all judgment to the Son."

- The strength of His people (Psalms 18:1; 28:7), and in Philippians 4:13 Paul said he "can do all things through Christ who strengthens [him]."

There are plenty of other Old Testament titles for God that have their fulfillment in Jesus, and there's one that is particularly relevant to our focus in this chapter, and that's Rock:

- Deuteronomy 32:4—"He is the Rock, His work is perfect."

- 1 Samuel 2:2—"...nor is there any rock like our God."

- Psalm 144:1—"Blessed be the LORD my Rock."

In the New Testament, this title finds its fulfillment in Jesus. First Corinthians 10:4 identifies Jesus as the Rock that was with Israel in the wilderness: "They drank of that spiritual Rock that followed them, and that Rock was Christ." Jesus was there providing spiritually for the nation of Israel as the people traveled to the Promised Land.

Jesus is also the Rock for the church. In Matthew 16:18, Jesus told Peter, "On this rock I will build My church." Though the verse is a play on Peter's name, which means "rock," Jesus was not referring to Peter himself, but to Peter's profession of faith in Christ and the way the church would be a group of people with that same profession.

When it comes to building a foundation, the first stone laid is what enables all the rest to be set correctly, and this stone is given a special name—cornerstone. The New Testament identifies Jesus as the cornerstone:

- Acts 4:11—"The 'stone which was rejected...has become the chief cornerstone.'"

- Ephesians 2:20—"...Jesus Christ Himself being the chief cornerstone."

- 1 Peter 2:6—"Behold, I lay in Zion a chief cornerstone."

Just as Jesus was the Rock for Israel and is the Rock for the church, He can also be the Rock—or foundation—for our marriages.

THE STORMS WILL COME

Why is it so important to have a strong foundation in your marriage? In His parable of the builders, Jesus described what is inevitable in every life: "The rain descended, the floods came, and the winds blew" (Matthew 7:25). You have probably seen on the news—or perhaps personally experienced—what can happen to a house under the onslaught of a powerful storm, hurricane, tornado, or tsunami. Jesus was not teaching that the weather will be unpleasant or chilly and we might need an umbrella or coat to protect ourselves. Rather, He was speaking of the trials of life—trials that will batter us, wear us down, and attempt to make us fall.

Jesus didn't present these storms as possibilities that only some people will be unfortunate enough to experience, because trials are inevitable in every person's life. That is made clear in the following Bible passages:

- James 1:2—"Count it all joy *when* you fall into various trials."

- Acts 14:22—"We *must* through many tribulations enter the kingdom of God."

- 1 Thessalonians 3:3—"No one should be shaken by these afflictions; for you yourselves know that we *are appointed* to this."

- John 16:33—"In the world you *will have* tribulation."

- 1 Peter 4:12—"*Do not think it strange* concerning the fiery trial which is to try you, as though some strange thing happened to you."

We don't know when we will experience storms, but we do know they will come. In the same way that physical storms have the potential to destroy a house, life's storms have the potential to destroy a marriage; they can make us feel as though we are going to collapse. How many people have said, "I can't do this anymore! I don't know if I can stay in this relationship one more day"?

The words "beat on that house" in Matthew 7:25 are analogous to the daily struggles that wear on a marriage—such as a health care or financial issue, rebellious child, job loss, sleepless nights with a baby, or betrayal from a friend. The storms can even become unrecognizable because they happen so regularly. Couples may have found themselves to have honorably endured great trials—such as adultery and addictions—but then floundered when they discovered they were too weak to endure the smaller, daily ones.

In November 2015, Czech pilot Zbynek Abel was forced to perform an emergency landing of his Aero L-159 Alco subsonic attack jet when it collided with a bird. The aircraft was armed with powerful weapons that could destroy other planes and attack cities, but it was downed by a bird hundreds of times smaller that had no powerful engine, deadly weapons, or skilled pilot. In the same way, small, daily trials can do a lot of damage to marriages, making them as dangerous as the large trials we fear most.

As we look at Matthew 7:24-25, let's note what Jesus was *not* teaching. He was not saying that obeying Him keeps marriages from experiencing storms. Sometimes we think that if we are "good Christians," then God will prevent trials from coming our way. But note that Jesus said the storm was beating on a house that *was*, in fact, built on the strong foundation of His teaching.

If obeying Jesus's teaching does not enable couples to avoid the storms of life, then what is the benefit of obedience? The promise Jesus was making is that our obedience to Him enables our relationships to survive even the worst trials: "The rain descended, the floods came, and the winds blew and beat on that house; and *it did not fall, for it was founded on the rock*" (Matthew 7:25). While spouses who obey Jesus's teachings will not *avoid* the storms of life, they will *survive* those storms.

Perhaps you have witnessed a Christian couple experiencing terrible suffering and thought, *How can they handle that? I don't know what I would do if that were me!* The great encouragement to take away is that if you are obeying Jesus's teachings, you can be assured that you, too, will be able to withstand difficult trials.

THE IMPORTANCE OF OBEDIENCE

When I was a schoolteacher, anytime I gave instructions to the students, I would encourage them to carry them out on their own. Then I would walk around the room looking over shoulders, and it would be evident that even though all the students had received the same guidance, they generally fell into two groups: some applied what they heard, and others did not.

When I coached wrestlers, I spent part of each practice session teaching new moves. I would explain the technique step by step and then put the wrestlers in pairs to apply what I had taught. Again, even though all the athletes had watched the same demonstration, some put into practice what I taught, while others did not.

Jesus also knew His hearers would fall into two categories: Some would hear what He said and apply it, while others would not. This is evident by the fact He said, "Whoever hears these sayings of Mine, *and does them*, I will liken him to a wise man who built his house on the rock" (Matthew 7:24).

The importance of going beyond hearing (or reading) to obeying is a regular theme in Scripture. Jesus said, "My mother and My brothers are these who hear the word of God *and do it*...If you know these things, blessed are you *if you do them*" (Luke 8:21; John 13:17). We do not learn God's Word simply for the sake of knowing it. We learn it so that we can apply it.

James 1:22 urges us to "be doers of the word, and not hearers only, *deceiving yourselves*." This verse reveals a common mistake people make. They learn God's

Word and believe they have done enough and end up falling short of applying it to their lives. Husbands and wives do this when they believe they have a marriage built on Christ simply because they know what the Bible teaches, read Christian marriage books, and attend Christian marriage conferences. But none of their learning will have any effect if they are not obeying Scripture's instructions. As believers, our responsibility goes much further than simply obtaining information. We must obey what we have learned.

If we are not building on Christ—which is to say we are not obeying the commands in Scripture—then we should not have much confidence that our marriages will survive the storms of life. Jesus made that clear when He said, "The rain descended, the floods came, and the winds blew and beat on that house; and *it fell. And great was its fall*" (Matthew 7:27). Jesus's words are strong, but was He being harsh? Just the opposite! He was being gracious and loving. He wanted to convince His hearers to build their lives on Him, the solid Rock. When we do that, our marriages will become stronger and will remain standing when the storms come.

The Sermon on the Mount is filled with incredible teaching for every believer, but those who familiarize themselves with its teachings without obeying them are no better off than those who have never heard or read the teaching. You are nearly finished reading an entire book that has presented the Bible's commands for husbands and wives, but if you do not obey those commands, your marriage will be no different from the marriages of those who have never read what Scripture says about marriage relationships. Christ is the strong foundation we need in our lives so that we can experience a strong marriage, but that requires us to *do* what He says, and not merely *hear* Him.

Response Determines Outcome

The accounts of the wise builder and the foolish builder are almost identical:

- They both seem to be talented builders.

- There was nothing to indicate any difference in their houses; they both achieved the goal of building a strong, sturdy house.

- They faced the same storms; verses 25 and 27 say that "the rain descended, the floods came, and the winds blew and beat on that house."

This is why the two widely differing results are so shocking: "it did not fall" versus "it fell. And great was its fall." The builders had nearly identical circumstances, but completely different outcomes. The only noteworthy difference was the foundation under each house.

A couple's response to Jesus's teaching determines whether their house will stand up to life's storms.

Similarly, it is not the marriage itself, nor the number or intensity of trials suffered, that leads to different outcomes for couples. At the church I pastor, we have celebrations for people who reach 50 years of marriage. Did they stay married that long because their marriages were free from troubles? Are we celebrating how God graciously gave them five decades without storms? No. It is not the absence of trials that enables couples to stay married for any number of years. It is the foundation they have built upon. A couple's response to Jesus's teaching determines whether their house will stand up to life's storms.

Wisdom and Foolishness Revealed

We typically think of wisdom and foolishness in terms of knowledge. People are considered wise because they have some measure of knowledge or they are foolish because they lack knowledge. But a lack of knowledge doesn't necessarily lead to foolishness. More accurately, it leads to ignorance. This is why, when the apostle Paul wrote to people who were ignorant, he gave them knowledge.[1]

If foolishness isn't the absence of knowledge, then what is it? A good definition of foolishness is "failing to apply knowledge." A good definition of wisdom is "making sure to apply knowledge." Consider the builders in the parable. They both heard the same teachings of Jesus, which means they had the same knowledge. The wise builder was deemed wise because he applied what he heard, and the foolish builder was deemed foolish because he did not. The questions facing you and your spouse are:

- Are you going to be wise, or are you going to be foolish?
- Are you going to apply the knowledge you've gained?
- Are you going to build your marriage on a strong foundation, or are you going to build on sand?

Your wisdom or foolishness is not shown by what you know or by how many Christian marriage books you have read. Rather, it is shown by whether you obey Christ's teaching, which is to say your wisdom or foolishness is shown by whether you build on Christ. Here's the simple yet crucial truth: Marriage God's way means having Christ's teaching as the foundation of your relationship. This gives us not only the assurance that our relationships will survive any of the storms we face, but that we can experience all the blessings God has for us.

THE PRAYERS FOR YOU

As I wrote this book, I prayed repeatedly for everyone who would read these chapters. I will continue to pray for every reader—including you—for years to come. But the greatest encouragement you could possibly receive is knowing that, at all times, Jesus is "[making] intercession for [you]" (Romans 8:34). You can be sure that His intercession includes your marriage because it is a depiction to the world of His own relationship with His bride. Nobody wants your marriage to reflect the beauty of that divine relationship more than Jesus Himself. And by the power of the gospel at work in your life, you can follow the guide in Scripture that enables you to experience a healthy, joyful, Christ-centered relationship.

Notes

CHAPTER 1—YOUR MARRIAGE REFLECTS YOUR RELATIONSHIP WITH CHRIST

1. Chapter 13 addresses the "What ifs?" of submission: What about an abusive husband? When does a wife not need to submit?

CHAPTER 3—GOD'S ESTABLISHMENT OF ADAM'S HEADSHIP

1. Homosexual marriage, transgenderism, and bisexuality are simply extreme forms of egalitarianism because in every case, ultimately they require people to blur the lines between the genders.

2. James Fowler, "Women in the Church," Christ In You Ministries 1999, http://www.christinyou.net/pages/womeninchurch.html (accessed March 7, 2016).

3. Read more about this in chapter 13.

4. David Guzik, "Genesis 1," Enduring Word Media, 2013, https://enduringword.com/bible-commentary/genesis-1/.

CHAPTER 4—MALE LEADERSHIP IS GOD'S PATTERN

1. Wayne Grudem, *Evangelical Feminism & Biblical Truth* (Wheaton, IL: Crossway, 2012), 82.

2. John Piper and Wayne Grudem, *Recovering Biblical Manhood and Womanhood* (Wheaton, IL: Crossway, 2006), 217.

3. Grudem, *Evangelical Feminism & Biblical Truth*, 134.

CHAPTER 5—THE HELP A MAN NEEDS

1. Let's consider the exceptions Paul discussed. In 1 Corinthians 7:7-9 he wrote:

> I wish that all men were even as I myself. But each one has his own gift from God, one in this manner and another in that. But I say to the unmarried and to the widows: It is good for them if they remain even as I am; but if they cannot exercise self-control, let them marry. For it is better to marry than to burn with passion.

While Paul calls marriage a gift, it almost sounds as though he is saying singleness is better than marriage. The only way to understand these verses is by considering Paul's words at the end of the chapter, where he explains why singleness was a gift for him and can be a gift for others. In 1 Corinthians 7:32-34, he wrote:

> I want you to be without care. He who is unmarried cares for the things of the Lord—how he may please the Lord. But he who is married cares about the things of the world—how he may please his wife. There is a difference between a wife and a virgin. The unmarried woman cares about the things of the Lord, that she may be holy both in body and in spirit. But she who is married cares about the things of the world—how she may please her husband.

Paul is referring to people being without the responsibilities that come with having a spouse. Every married person—especially those with children—recognizes that a family takes a lot of time and energy that could be committed directly to serving the Lord. I pastor a church, but my most important ministry is to my wife and children. If I were unmarried, I would be able to commit even more time to studying, meeting with people, teaching, and so on. The apostle Paul himself is a good example. He had a ministry that a man with the responsibilities of a family could not have fulfilled. He wanted others to be able to serve the Lord with the same singleness of mind he was able to have.

Paul further clarifies his view of marriage in verses 27-29, where he points out:

> Because of the present crisis, I think that it is good for a man to remain as he is. Are you pledged to a woman? Do not seek to be released. Are you free from such a commitment? Do not look for a wife.

But if you do marry, you have not sinned; and if a virgin marries, she has not sinned. But those who marry will face many troubles in this life, and I want to spare you this. What I mean, brothers and sisters, is that the time is short (NIV).

When Paul was writing, the early Christians were facing increasing persecution that led to one of the darkest eras in church history. It culminated with the Roman emperor Nero throwing Christians to the lions while committing many other atrocities against them. Paul knew these Christians could get married but then find themselves fleeing for their lives. This is not a safe situation for anyone starting a family. Jesus made a similar statement when forecasting the coming destruction of Jerusalem in AD 70: "Woe to those who are pregnant and to those who are nursing babies in those days!" (Matthew 24:19).

Paul's advice might apply today to a missionary heading into an area of the world too dangerous to take a family or to a young couple risking discovery in an underground church in a closed country. The important point to notice is Paul's words were never meant to imply that singleness is somehow superior or more spiritual than being married.

In fact, when Paul wrote to his son in the faith, Timothy, he warned, "In latter times some will depart from the faith, giving heed to deceiving spirits and doctrines of demons" (1 Timothy 4:1). Paul then gave two examples of these demonic doctrines, one of which is forbidding people to marry (verse 3). When we consider the problems caused by people attempting to remain single who are not called to singleness, we can see why demons desire this. Marriage should be viewed as the normal, healthy pattern for all men and women save those few who have the gift of singleness as Paul did.

2. Read more about this in chapters 19 and 20.

3. Richard and Sharon Phillips, *Holding Hands, Holding Hearts* (Phillipsburg, NJ: Presbyterian & Reformed, 2006), 26-27.

4. Campbell, Nancy, "Do You Feel Downgraded?," *Above Rubies*. February 12, 2015, http://aboverubies.org/index.php/ar-blogs/entry/do-you-feel-downgraded (accessed March 7, 2016).

5. J.R. Miller, *Secrets of Happy Home Life: What Have You to Do With It?* (New York: Thomas Crowell, 1894), 12.

6. Daniela Lup, "Something to Celebrate (or Not): The Differing Impact of Promotion to Manager on the Job Satisfaction of Women and Men," *Work, Employment and Society* 32 (2). 407-425 (2018), Middlesex University, https://eprints.mdx.ac.uk/21841/3/WES%2520manuscript%2520for%2520mdxrepository.pdf (accessed September 18, 2019).

7. Betsey Stevenson and Justin Wolfers, "The Paradox of Declining Female Happiness," May 2009, IZA, http://ftp.iza.org/dp4200.pdf.

CHAPTER 9-A HUSBAND SHOULD AGAPE HIS WIFE

1. John MacArthur, *The Fulfilled Family* (Nashville, TN: Thomas Nelson, 2005), 78.

CHAPTER 10—SPIRITUALLY STRONG HUSBANDS

1. One of the more common mistakes people make when it comes to God's Word is they fail to consider how a principle communicated via physical examples can be applied spiritually. When it comes to Jesus's teachings, it is helpful to recognize that what He said about the physical realm often pictures what He wants to do for us spiritually. For example:

- When Jesus physically healed the blind, this didn't mean He would heal every blind person. But He does want to heal our spiritual blindness so we can see spiritually.

- When Jesus physically healed the deaf, this didn't mean He would heal every deaf person. But He does want to heal our spiritual deafness so we can understand spiritual truths.

- When Jesus physically healed the paralytics, this didn't mean He would heal every paralyzed person. But He does want to heal our spiritual lameness so we can walk with God: "We…should walk in newness of life" (Romans 6:4).

- When Jesus physically raised the dead, this didn't mean He would physically raise us from the dead the moment we die. We are spiritually raised when we die: "To be absent in the body and to be present with the Lord" (2 Corinthians 5:8; see also Philippians 1:23). But our physical resurrection awaits us in the future. Instead, Jesus has achieved victory over sin and death, and He wants to give us eternal life.

- When Jesus physically calmed the storm, this didn't mean He would calm every physical storm that occurs. But He does want to calm the spiritual storms that rage in our hearts: "The peace of God, which surpasses all understanding, will guard your hearts and your minds through Christ Jesus" (Philippians 4:7).

CHAPTER 11—PROTECTING YOUR MARRIAGE

1. C.S. Lewis, *The Collected Letters of C.S. Lewis, Volume 3: Narnia, Cambridge, and Joy 1950–1963* (New York: HarperOne, 2007), 1952.

CHAPTER 12—A WIFE SHOULD RESPECT HER HUSBAND

1. Emerson Eggerichs, *Love and Respect: The Love She Most Desires, the Respect He Desperately Needs* (Nashville, TN: Thomas Nelson, 2004), 36.
2. Eggerichs, *Love and Respect*, 160.
3. Read more about this in chapter 13.

CHAPTER 14—EQUAL-OPPORTUNITY SUBMISSION

1. Cath Elliot, "Beware the anti-feminists," *The Guardian*, January 28, 2009, http://www.theguardian.com/commentisfree/2009/jan/28/women-gender (accessed March 7, 2016).
2. Jay Adams, *Christian Living in the Home* (Phillipsburg, NJ: Presbyterian & Reformed, 1972), 74-75.
3. Wayne Mack, *Strengthening Your Marriage* (Phillipsburg, NJ: Presbyterian & Reformed, 1999), 14.

CHAPTER 15—PUTTING YOUR HUSBAND IN A POSITION TO LEAD

1. Helen Andelin, *Fascinating Womanhood* (New York: Random House Publishing group, 1992), 92.

CHAPTER 17—A WOMAN'S GREATER BEAUTY

1. The American Society for Aesthetic Plastic Surgery, "Celebrating 15 Years of Trustworthy Plastic Surgery Statistics," *Press Center*, March 20, 2012, http://www.surgery.org/media/news-releases/celebrating-15-years-of-trustworthy-plastic-surgery-statistics (accessed March 7, 2016).
2. Greg Wilson, "Heidi Montag: Plastic Surgery Made Me 'Edward Scissorhands,'" *NBC LA*, December 21, 2010, http://www.nbclosangeles.com/entertainment/celebrity/Heidi-Montag-Plastic-Surgery-Made-Me-Edward-Scissorhands-112241089.html. (accessed March 7, 2016).
3. Jack Cafferty, "$10 billion spent on cosmetic procedures despite recession," *Cafferty File*, March 10, 2010, http://caffertyfile.blogs.cnn.com/2010/03/10/10-billion-spent-on-cosmetic-procedures-despite-recession/ (accessed March 7, 2016).
4. J.R. Miller, *The Home Beautiful* (Grand Rapids, MI: Zondervan, 1912), 57.

CHAPTER 18—THE BIBLE'S "PERFECT" WIFE

1. R.C.H. Lenski, *The Interpretation of the Epistle to the Hebrews and the Epistle of James* (Minneapolis, MN: Augsburg, 1966), 87.

CHAPTER 19—A HUSBAND TREATS HIS WIFE WELL BY...

1. A.E. Miller, J.D. MacDougall, M.A. Tarnopolsky, D.G. Sale, "Gender differences in strength and muscle fiber characteristics," *European Journal of Applied Physiology and Occupational Physiology*, March 1993, 66 (3): 254-62.

2. One example of both the disparity between men's and women's strength and the failure of men to use their strength as God intended occurs in athletics. We don't see transgender females trying to compete in men's sports. Rather, we seeing transgender males competing in women's sports. Biological male Gavin Hubbard set the New Zealand junior weightlifting records in 1998. "New Zealand Interschool's Weightlifting Championship 2014 - Round 6" (PDF), *Sporty.co.nz*, https://www.sporty.co.nz/asset/downloadasset?id=58b9b97e-f4ab-4e94-a2fe-507c024cb178 (accessed May 24, 2020).

In 2012 he became a transgender, changed his name to Laurel, and competed in the 2017 Australian International and Australian Open weightlifting competition, where he won the gold medal—all because he had biological advantages over the female competitors. Matt Windley, "Laurel Hubbard wins female 90kg+ division at weightlifting's Australian International," *Herald Sun*, March 19, 2017, https://www.heraldsun.com.au/sport/more-sports/laurel-hubbard-wins-female-90kg-division-at-weightliftings-australian-international/news-story/cd4a5fa012eb9a5ceb0281faceea5c7a (accessed May 24, 2020). Transgender men, who have no business competing in women's sports, typically win because God created the genders with physical differences.

3. "G1581—ekkoptō *Strong's Greek Lexicon* (KJV)," *Blue Letter Bible*, https://www.blueletterbible.org/lang/Lexicon/Lexicon.cfm?strongs=G1581&t=KJV (accessed September 9, 2019).

4. C.H. Spurgeon, *Sermons of the Rev. C.H. Spurgeon, of London*, vol. 20 (New York: Sheldon, Blakeman, 1875), 506.

CHAPTER 20—THE CASE FOR INTIMACY

1. Indirectly, these verses imply that whatever we do with our body should have our spouse's approval. For example, if a man wants to have a beard, he should take into consideration whether his wife wants him to have one. If a woman wants to wear her hair a certain way, she should take into consideration her husband's thoughts.

We should make reasonable efforts to stay healthy. We want to be a blessing to our spouse, be around for many years, and be available to take care of our spouse if he or she becomes sick.

2. Because we are sinners, we have the potential to ruin even the blessings God gives us. We can turn any good thing into a god thing or idol (you'll see what I mean by "a god thing" in a moment). One such example took place with the bronze serpent Moses made in Numbers 21. Israel complained, and as a judgment, God sent poisonous serpents into the camp:

> The people came to Moses, and said, "We have sinned, for we have spoken against the LORD and against you; pray to the LORD that He take away the serpents from us." So Moses prayed for the people.

> Then the LORD said to Moses, "Make a fiery serpent, and set it on a pole; and it shall be that everyone who is bitten, when he looks at it, shall live." So Moses made a bronze serpent, and put it on a pole; and so it was, if a serpent had bitten anyone, when he looked at the bronze serpent, he lived" (Numbers 21:7-9).

Tragically, over time, people began to worship the bronze serpent. When Hezekiah reformed the nation and destroyed the idolatry, he had to include the bronze serpent, which by then had developed its own name:

> [Hezekiah] removed the high places and broke the sacred pillars, cut down the wooden image and broke in pieces the bronze serpent that Moses had made; for until those days the children of Israel burned incense to it, and called it Nehushtan" (2 Kings 18:4).

The object that brought miraculous healing had become an idol. Nehushtan is a reminder that we must be on guard against taking any of God's blessings—such as sex, marriage, children, homes, relationships, money, or jobs—and letting our relationships to them become sinful. Scripture doesn't forbid any of these blessings, but we are forbidden from making them idols. Sex within marriage is no more sinful than the bronze serpent; however, when we become preoccupied with or worship sex, it becomes Nehushtan.

CHAPTER 21—BUILDING ON CHRIST

1. For example:

   - Romans 11:25—"I do not desire, brethren, that you should be ignorant of this mystery." Then Paul explained the mystery to them.

   - 1 Corinthians 12:1—"Concerning spiritual gifts, brethren, I do not want you to be ignorant." Then Paul taught them about spiritual gifts.

   - 2 Corinthians 1:8—"We do not want you to be ignorant, brethren, of our trouble which came to us in Asia." Then Paul explained their trouble.

   - 1 Thessalonians 4:13—"I do not want you to be ignorant, brethren, concerning those who have fallen asleep." Then Paul explained what had happened to those who fell asleep.

About the Author

Scott is the senior pastor of Woodland Christian Church in Woodland, Washington, and a conference speaker. He holds an MA in Biblical Studies from Liberty University. Scott and his wife, Katie, grew up together in northern California, and God has blessed them with nine children. You can contact Pastor Scott or learn more about him at the following:

- Website: www.scottlapierre.org
- Facebook: @ScottLaPierreMinistries
- YouTube: @ScottLaPierre
- Twitter: @PastorWCC
- Instagram: @PastorWCC

Subscribe to Pastor Scott's newsletter (www.scottlapierre.org/subscribe) and receive:

- Free gifts and resources such as videos of his conference messages and guest preaching
- Updates on his ministry, including his upcoming books, and invitations to the book launch teams
- Insights into his life and family

Would you like to invite Scott to a speaking event?

Pastor Scott is a frequent speaker at churches, conferences, and retreat centers. He speaks on a variety of topics that build up believers and serve as an outreach to share Christ with your community.

For more information, including sample messages and endorsements, please visit: www.scottlapierre.org/conferences-and-speaking.

If you would like to contact Scott for a speaking engagement, please do so here: www.scottlapierre.org/contact/.